THE COMING REVOLUTION IN YOUTH MINISTRY
MARK H. SENTER III

VICTOR BOOKS ®

A DIVISION OF SCRIPTURE PRESS PUBLICATIONS INC.
USA CANADA ENGLAND

Scripture quotations, unless otherwise indicated, are from the *Holy Bible, New International Version,* © 1973, 1978, 1984, International Bible Society. Used by permission of Zondervan Bible Publishers.

Copyediting: Noel Calhoun
Cover Design: Joe DeLeon
Cover Photo: Comstock

Library of Congress Cataloging-in-Publication Data

Senter, Mark.
    The coming revolution in youth ministry / Mark H. Senter III.
        p.   cm.
    Includes bibliographical references.
    ISBN 0-89693-917-0
    1. Church work with teenagers. I. Title.
    BV4447.S44   1992
    259'.23 — dc20   91-36931
                                                                              CIP

---

4 5 6 7 8 9 10 Printing/Year 96 95

CONTENTS

ACKNOWLEDGMENTS

I always thought acknowledgment pages were a bit hokey until I stopped to think about all the people who contributed to make this book possible. There were a lot of people who helped me in specific ways and so hokey or not I am going to mention a few.

I could start with my father, who was my first Bible teacher and "youth director." It was after his communication style I modeled much of my public ministry. Or I could mention Ed and Nancy Wilcoxson who were my first youth group sponsors and who encouraged me as I changed from a rowdy kid into a purposeful high schooler. But if I do, it may sound too much like an Academy Awards ceremony, so forget that I mentioned them.

The people who contributed directly to this book do need to be mentioned, however. Rev. Michael Perko, S.J. was of great help as he encouraged me and coached my efforts during my doctoral research at Loyola University of Chicago. Robert Schuster and his staff at the Billy Graham Center Archives, as well as Fern Wymer and the Billy Graham Center Library, made documents and rare resources available while providing a study room in which much of my writing was done.

Reverend Dick Wynn, then president of Youth for Christ, USA and his secretary, June Thompson, as well as Doug Burleigh, president of Young Life and his secretary, Suzie Coddington, provided unconditional access and willing support in locating and using the historical materials of their respective organizations. Dr. Dann Spader of Sonlife Ministries, Wayne Rice of Youth Specialties, Neil Graham of Inter-School Christian Fellowship, Richard F. Abel of Fellowship of Christian Athletes, and Evelyn M. McClusky (101 years of age as of this writing) of the Miracle Book Club similarly furnished information about their organizations.

Additional appreciation must be expressed to Jay Kesler, Doug Burleigh, Wayne Rice, Jack Wyrtzen, Thom Schultz, and Dann Spader for their careful readings and helpful critiques of the first draft of the book. These insights enabled me to be much more accurate and focused in my conclusions. My prayer is that the inferences drawn will be helpful to their ministries.

Funding for the research and writing were provided in part by a grant from the Youth Ministry and Theological Schools Project, Union Theological Seminary, funded by the Lilly Endowment Center and a sabbatical from teaching responsibilities provided by the Trinity Evangelical Divinity School.

Of course my most personal gratitude must be expressed to my wife, Ruth, and two children, Jori and Nick, as they stood by, encouraged, and affirmed me in this project which seemed to stretch on forever.

Mark H. Senter III
Wheaton, Illinois
July 2, 1991

FOREWORD

I have followed the development of this book by Mark Senter with great interest. First, because I am convinced that he has grasped many of the pieces of our fragmented society that will constitute the areas of greatest need of youth in the next decades. His predictions and agenda may not all come to pass, for who of us can really predict all of the environmental forces which will appear in the future? Much of our activity is of necessity reactive to world events, unpredictable and sometimes catacylsmic in nature. For instance who, writing in the midst of the Great Depression, could have predicted the effect that World War II would have on youth in the '50s?

This book attempts to deal with the historical antecedents of modern youth work and to help us see clearly into the future. Because my life has been devoted to youth and their spiritual and intellectual development, I welcome this serious effort. I further welcome it because Mark Senter is a practitioner. He is not wholly a researcher or analyst. His heart is with the people he critiques even when, at times, he must be critical.

I, for instance, have been identified with the parachurch and have seen the work of interdenominational evangelism with nonchurch youth to be something quite distinct from the task of the gathered church in the local congregations. These are not, in my mind, bad and good—they are simply different and both necessary. Whenever I speak of the *church* I speak of the universal body of Christ, including all local and parachurch activity. Some define church in local terms and insist that all not under their particular denominational banner must justify their existence to this established pattern. Sometimes folks forget that when John Knox, John Wesley, John Calvin, Martin Luther, A.B. Simpson, or, for that matter, Bill Hybels, first began their ministries for which they are noted, they were all met by resistance from the respective religious establishments.

It has been my contention that protestantism, especially in America, must come to terms with its parachurch in the same way that our Roman Catholic brethren have come to terms with theirs. Jesuits, Franciscans, and the Little Sisters of the Poor all came into existence to meet specific needs of the church universal. We who have served both in the parachurch and the local church understand these differences and mutualities within the communion. This book helps us to understand these connections and tensions.

Secondly, I am interested in this book and its effect on modern youth ministry because the Youth for Christ movement, to which I owe my soul, is discussed at some depth in this volume. I do not agree with all of the analysis and am mildly wounded by some of the observations; however, I am convinced of the honesty and good will of the author and also readily acknowledge a certain blindness, defensiveness, and lack of objectivity on my part where Youth for Christ is mentioned. I am grateful, however, that in the several years now that have elapsed since I left the presidency of YFC, I have had many of my biases adjusted and have become less myopic in my understandings. My skin is also a little thicker. My experience, though quite long by youth work standards, is still encapsulated in one short lifetime, not yet expended.

God's interest in youth is eternal, global, and devoid of selectivity. It is my prayer that all serious youth workers will find this book a helpful bringing together of much oral history, opinion, and isolated effort into a set of understandable principals and methodologies that will greatly increase the impact of the Gospel on today's youth.

Though it is often difficult to convince the establishment at any level—inside or outside the church—of the imperative of devoting real energy to youth, it still remains my stubborn conviction that the future will not be decided by adults after they have grown out of their adolescence, but that the truly important decisions will be irrevocably established in their early childhood and adolescence. Youth have little real sway over political and economic life and therefore are largely left out of pragmatic considerations of national policy. They do not pay taxes or buy church bonds, but they will own the future. One can only speculate on what a world will look like when the insecurities, anger, and distress created by the current disjuncture in families is played out in adult decisions.

It remains the task of those truly interested in youth in church, parachurch, and education to attempt to understand the nature of youth culture, the demands of the Gospel, the developmental possibilities of youth, and mobilize for what Mark Senter calls, "The Coming Revolution in Youth Ministry."

Jay Kesler

PREFACE

People in authority must develop the vision and authority to call the shots. There are always risks in taking initiatives, but there are greater risks now in waiting for sure things, especially since there are very few sure things in the current volatile climate. At the same time, the people have to admit their need for leadership, for vision, for dreams.

People in authority must do more than tinker with machinery and flex their muscles. They must have an entrepreneurial vision, a sense of perspective, along with the time and inclination to raise the fundamental questions and identify the forces that are at work on both specific organizations and society in general. Such tasks require not only imagination but a real sense of continuity so that, to paraphrase Shelley, one can see the present in the past and the future in the present, clarify problems rather than exploit them, and define issues, not exacerbate them. In this way, one can elevate problems, questions, and issues into comprehensible choices for one's constituents.

Warren Bennis
in *Why Leaders Can't Lead*
(San Francisco: Gossey-Bass Publishers, 1989)

INTRODUCTION:
WHAT IS A REVOLUTION?

"When dizzying changes sweep the world, foreign-policy experts often turn to history to find precedents for the headlines." (*Time* 25 December 1989, 80)

I stared transfixed at the television set. The images seemed surrealistic. A party was taking place atop the same Berlin wall which for years had symbolized the isolation of the Communist bloc countries from the capitalist nations of the West.

The flickering images signified the end of an era. A revolution was taking place. Even if reactionary forces should regain control at some later date, the world would never be the same.

Historians looking at the worldwide events of 1989 made comparisons with the "Springtime of Nations" in the Europe of 1948 and the American and French revolutions of the late eighteenth century. The collapse of the iron curtain, the rise of freely elected governments in eastern Europe, steps toward racial equality in South Africa, even the brutal treatment of student protestors in Beijing's Tiananmen Square, have many parallels in history, and scholars expressed concern that this generation avoid, if possible, the mistakes of the past while affirming the lessons of previous democratic experiments.

Yet, the initial euphoria over the events of 1989 may in the end turn into attitudes more resistant to change on the part of the American people. Daniel J. Boorstin, the Librarian of Congress Emeritus, suggested such resistance is an observable part of the "anatomy" of a revolution. Illustrating from the French and Russian revolutions he warned that the future may once again present the American public with a set of difficult decisions about commitments and loyalties.[1] When the financial realities and social dynamics of the new world order become apparent, the initial euphoria over "freedom" and the demise of world communism may give rise to a new set of tensions.

Revolutions are difficult to evaluate and their significance more difficult to understand. Seldom are they exactly what they appear to be or, under the influence of modern technology, what the media portrays them to be. One safe conclusion can be drawn: radical change has taken place. The future will be different from the past.

Unlike historians and political scientists, youth ministers have spent very little time either documenting the development of their movements or seeking to discover lessons from their predecessors. When a "revolution" in youth ministry occurs, its current practitioners view their methodologies as innovations without precedent. Jay Kesler, former president of Youth for Christ/USA, provides an example. He was quoted in *Group* magazine as claiming, "There are very few things done in youth work that were not pioneered in Youth for Christ or Young Life—be it in Christian camping, various small group activities or music."[2]

Sociologist Tony Campolo took another approach to the history of youth ministry. When confronted with the absence of a credible narration of the progress of youth ministry through the years, he created a chronology based upon sociological theory. In his article in *Youthworker*, "The Professionalization of Youth Ministry," he described Young Life's relational strategy as having emerged from the Youth for Christ program. The fact is Young Life's campus strategy preceded that of YFC by nearly ten years.[3]

History of Evangelical Youth Ministry?
Neither Kesler nor Campolo is at fault. There simply has not been a carefully written record of the many facets of the ways in which evangelical adults have attempted to minister to young people. A careful search of the relevant literature suggests that Frank Otis Erb's book, *The Development of the Young People's Movement*, published in 1917 was the last comprehensive effort on the subject.[4]

When Warren Benson and I were editing our book, *The Complete Book of Youth Ministry*, we ran into a problem with the chapter on the history of youth ministry.[5] Most of what we found in print was no more than a chronology of organizations, when they came into being, how they grew, and what types of ministries they had. Very little space had been given to understanding the cultural context or the historical climate. Even less had been written about the impact that organizations had upon each other or the manner in which individuals influenced each other.

About that time, I decided upon my research topic for doctoral work at Loyola University, Chicago. After 11 years as a youth pastor in two churches and 7 years as a minister of Christian education in another church, I had left youth ministry. It was not that I did not enjoy working with youth. I had simply run out of energy. It was no longer fun being the first person up the mountain.

My opportunity for research allowed me to make a choice. I could have studied any historical figure or agency in the field of Christian education. But my love was still youth ministry. So I committed myself to studying evangelical youth movements and their contributions to local church youth ministry.

There are two schools of thought about historical research. One suggests that the researcher should never choose to study a subject in which he is interested lest he bias his work and invalidate his conclusions. The other insists the scholar must be interested, even passionate about his subject, lest his project die of boredom.

Despite the problems involved, I chose the latter approach to writing this book. While trying to protect against prejudicing myself in favor of specific youth movements, I have a growing respect and admiration for the people who ministered to teenagers over the past 200 years. They were not without fault, but their strengths far outweighed the weaknesses I found.

At times when I held in my hands the original letters or reports written by leaders of the movement, there was a certain magic present. It was almost as if I were holding a sacred tablet. It was obvious that many of these people believed God was doing something new. They felt they were part of a revolution.

A Revolution?

What is a revolution? The word is used in two primary ways. The first describes a complete cycle just as the moon makes a complete revolution around the earth. The other describes a radical departure from what previously existed, such as the American, French, or Communist revolutions.

Both definitions apply to the future of youth ministry. We stand at the end of a cycle. The innovations inspired by the parachurch agencies, which primarily focused on high school students during the Depression years of the 1930s and the war years of the 1940s, have now run their course. In this regard, both Youth for Christ USA and Young Life have become static. Though a majority of church youth ministries have benefited from the methodological innovations of the parachurch agencies, these movements have become stagnant.

A study of history suggests we are about to see a fundamental departure from what we have understood to be youth ministry during the closing decades of the twentieth century. Though most parachurch agencies and denominational programs will continue to exist and make contributions as the church attempts to reach and disciple new generations, their strategies have become flawed. There is no way in which the tactics currently being used will stem the tidal wave of spiritual, moral, and psychosocial problems faced by the current and coming generations of adolescents. A new movement is about to appear and may already be emerging.

In chapter 1 we will look at what is happening in youth ministry today. The next four chapters will build a case for expecting the revolution as evidenced by the past 200 years of ministry to youth. Chapters 6 through 10 will chronicle the weave of two centuries of youth ministry fabric, and lead to a projection as to what the coming revolution in youth ministry will look like in chapters 11 through 13. The book concludes with a series of questions which existing agencies will need to ask of themselves in order to be an effective part of the revolution.

One additional word of explanation should be provided for the serious historian of youth ministry. I have not attempted to provide extensive documentation to the reader. My citations are drawn from sources which are readily available to the reader. For those wishing to dig more deeply into the historical development of evangelical youth ministry, I would suggest they obtain my dissertation entitled "The Youth for Christ Movement as an Educational Agency and Its Impact Upon Protestant Churches: 1931–1979" (Ann Arbor: University Microfilms International, 1990).

Mark H. Senter III
Wheaton, Illinois
July 2, 1991

---

1. Daniel J. Boorstin, "A Timetable for Revolution-Watching," *U.S. News & World Report* (5 February 1990), 47.

2. Thom Schultz, "What's Happened to Young Life and Campus Life?" *Group* (May 1985), 22.

3. Tony Campolo, "Success Can Be Dangerous: The Professionalizing of Youth Ministry," *Youthworker* (Winter 1986), 16-20.

4. Frank Otis Erb, *The Development of the Young People's Movement* (Chicago: The University of Chicago Press, 1917).

5. Warren S. Benson and Mark H. Senter III, eds., *The Complete Book of Youth Ministry* (Chicago: Moody Press, 1987).

CHAPTER 1

The Current Status of Youth Ministry

The day of the "broadcast" is over. "Narrowcasting" has become essential for radio and television stations to survive.

No longer do television stations expect to capture the large market share they did in the 1960s, even with the most creative of programming. There is too much competition.

First came the UHF stations which allowed local stations to compete with the network affiliates. Then came cable television and the advent of specialty stations. Sports, weather, news, movies, shopping, travel and leisure, children's programming, ethnic telecasts and even community-produced shows became available as home entertainment 24 hours a day.

The video recorders and players further changed the way in which television sets are used. Time-shifting became a fact of life since VCRs can be programmed to tape shows which the viewer can watch at any time she chooses.

Rental videos further complicated the lives of network executives. No longer is the viewing audience at the mercy of a small group of people who make programming choices for the nation. At just about any time, day or night, the best (and worst) of video tapes can be rented for $3.00 or less. The consumer is in charge of his entertainment agenda.

The television viewing audience has a bewildering number of choices and the remote control switching device may be the symbol of the day. Change is constant. Loyalty to a channel or even a program is rare. The remote control changer gives young people a bewildering plurality of choices. It is not uncommon for a high schooler to rapidly switch back and forth among two or three programs or athletic events and remain fully aware of what is happening in each.

Pluralism and the High School Campus

The day of youth ministry "broadcasting" is over as well.

Statistics for 1987 identify 13,367,000 high school students in the United States, 12,138,000 of whom were attending 21,406 public high schools. The other 1,229,000 high schoolers were enrolled in the estimated 2,438 private secondary schools. A 1986 analysis of the racial or ethnic composition of public schools (K–12), shows a growing diversity. Seventy percent of the students were white, sixteen percent were black, ten percent were Hispanic, three percent were Asian or Pacific Islanders, and one percent was described as American Indian or Alaskan Native.[1]

Already almost one out of three students is nonwhite. The high school campus has changed. No longer can people concerned with reaching youth for Jesus Christ expect to have a single program or strategy which is attractive to all of the high school population. The ethnic factor alone has made it impossible. Nor can program ideas gathered from national conferences dominated by white middle-class youth workers or traditional educational institutions serve as the basis for attracting and holding high school students in local communities unless those settings compare favorably to the circumstances from which the trainers came.

"What will the U.S. be like when whites are no longer the majority?" asks the cover story of *Time* magazine as the final decade of the twentieth century began.[2] Already one-fourth of Americans define themselves as Hispanic or nonwhite. As early as 1986, school systems in California, Louisiana, Mississippi, New Mexico, South Carolina, and Texas were but a few percentage points from having white children as a minority of their students.[3]

Major cities have long been the habitat of minority groups, but with the growth of world class cities within the borders of the United States and the inevitable migration of upwardly mobile ethnic peoples toward the suburbs, America is in fact changing colors. If immigration patterns and birth rates continue as expected, youth ministry will behold an entirely new face by the end of the century.

Educational entitlement programs created a new climate on campus. "Equal access" has become a way of life. No longer can a few talented or popular people dominate the life of a high school. Athletics are no longer the exclusive domain of a few well-coordinated male seniors. Women's sports have come into their own and in some schools have surpassed the popularity of traditional male sports. Complete competition schedules for freshmen and sophomores in both major and minor sports have brought about a greater breadth of participation.

Money invested by school boards and booster clubs into music, drama, cheerleading, pom-pom squads, speech teams, and other extracurricular activities have altered the perception of what is significant in the lives of high schoolers. Regional, state, and national competitions, as well as summer camps for just about every specialty, have given activities once perceived as the domain of "losers" school-wide status.

Music is another expression of the pluralistic high school society. Instead of attempting to "blast" everyone else with one's preferred music, today's student is most likely to be found wearing head phones listening to the FM station of choice or a favorite musical group or musical style on tape or disc. No longer is there a tyranny of one particular musical style. Individual choice is the fashion of the day.

After-school jobs have produced another type of pluralism in the high school society. A majority of suburban high school students now have a steady source of income which lessens their dependence on parents or community and church agencies for entertainment. Young people have discovered the financial freedom to be selective in the way they use their time. Yet because of work schedules, they do not have as much free time to use.

The new pluralism has had a profound effect on youth ministry in North America. In some places the impact has been coming for a long time. In others, its arrival has been a shock.

Inter-School Christian Fellowship

Canada's Inter-School Christian Fellowship has experienced the need for change for a long time. Only 15 years after the first parachurch high school club program was established in North America, the high school branch of Canadian Inter-Varsity Christian Fellowship faced a strategic decision. Already the general secretary was calling for a total revision of the movement's approach to high school ministry.

In a report to Inter-Varsity Christian Fellowship board in 1946, C.

Stacey Woods observed, "During the Fall months there has been a growing feeling that the work of Inter-School Christian Fellowship, though unquestionably being blessed of God, needed a thorough overhaul and revision from the point of view of method and program." Canada was well ahead of the United States in feeling the effects of a secularized society and the pluralism which often accompanies societies which do not have a central core of moral values.

The idea of a high school ministry based in the public schools was brought to Canada by Howard Guinness in late 1930 after he had been instrumental in bringing a similar movement to life in New Zealand. The original name, Crusader Unions, was appropriated without permission from England's Scripture Union but was quickly changed to Inter-School Christian Fellowship. Later C. Stacey Woods brought the Crusader name to Chicago where he would influence the Teachers' Christian Fellowship to call their ministry to teenagers High School Crusaders, better known as Hi-C.

The strategy, which was modeled after Inter-Varsity's university ministry, was being questioned because high school students simply were not as effective at carrying the load of leadership on their high school campuses as were their university counterparts. Yet no action was taken.

In fact 44 years later still no action had been taken. It was not until Don Posterski, Neil Graham and David Knight convened the ISCF field staff from across Canada during the fall of 1989 that specific steps were taken to bring about significant changes in the ministry.

Forty-four years. That is a long time to ignore the need for much needed changes. Yet the pattern is not limited to Canadian high school ministry.

Youth for Christ and Young Life

"I believe we're in a crisis of youth ministry," stated Mike Yaconelli co-founder of Youth Specialties and resident gadfly of the profession. "Most of our models of parachurch youth ministries were developed in the 1940s, 1950s, and 1960s and are out of touch. When I talk to their staffs they get angry and defensive. I'm sorry. I wish I could say it's a golden age and everything's going great—but it's not. We must focus on how kids really are today—not dwell on what we were or did in the past."[4]

Whether Yaconelli's words are appreciated or not, people within parachurch agencies are expressing similar concerns. When Bill Muir returned to Youth for Christ USA to become the Vice President of the Ministries Division in the Spring of 1989, he discovered the once dynamic organization to be "only two or three bricks from becoming a monument." The national staff was holding onto ministry models formulated in the mid-1960s, but without the creative minds at the grassroots level which would enable the organization to constantly renew itself.

The yearly comparison of statistics compiled by the organization suggests stagnation has beset the once dynamic movement. In 1975-76 reports showed 1,021 clubs in the United States. The number grew gradually to 1,209 in 1983-84 and then declined to the 1,001 mark in 1987-88 which was the last year for which statistics are available.

The number of field staff for Youth for Christ USA similarly shows a decline. From a high of 821 during the 1979-80 school year, the organization reported the equivalent of 549 club workers when two part-time staff members were counted as one full-time person. Some of the decline, however, might reflect the natural attrition which takes place when a new leadership team is put in place by an organization. Rev. Dick Wynn followed Jay Kesler as president in 1985 and served six years until a financial crisis and other organizational factors caused him to decline the possibility of another term in the office. With this second change within a decade more staff erosion might be expected.

Youth Guidance ministries of YFC have evolved over the years. Now referred to as Neighborhood Ministries, the target audience has constantly been young people outside the mainstream of the high school society. Though the number of young people with whom the staff has contact on a weekly basis has doubled from 1980-81 to 1987-88 (4,900 to 10,014), the number of staff members has decreased in the last five years (148 to 133), while the number of Youth Guidance programs has increased only slightly (80 to 88).

One encouraging sign amid the indications of a decreasing number of high school clubs and staff members is the constant of about 10,000 decisions being made for Christ each year from the 1975-76 school year (9,197) until the most recent report at the end of the 1987-88 year (11,395). The highest year for the Campus Life or high school club ministry, however, was 1979-80 when 13,129 students professed faith in Christ. Youth Guidance, similarly, has seen an increase in the number of professions of faith recorded in recent years.

To what can we attribute this decline in Youth for Christ? In all likelihood, it is the ministry's success. Over the past 45 years the organization has given birth to mission organizations (Greater Europe Mission, Overseas Crusades, Trans World Radio), relief agencies (World Vision), publishing houses (Success With Youth, Youth Specialties, Campus Life Books) and magazines (*Campus Life, Wittenburg Door, Youthworker*), movie production houses (Gospel Films), radio programs hosted by former Youth for Christ personnel (David Mains of Chapel of the Air, Jay Kesler of Family Forum), and a host of evangelists of whom Billy Graham is the best known. All of this success in generating ministry agencies has severely limited the directions in which the organization can go at this stage of its development.

To make matters worse for YFC (but better for the kingdom of God), churches have flattered the movement by imitating its strategies and methods. At the same time, they have recruited youth ministers from the same resource pool as YFC previously did, the Christian colleges and Bible institutes. Since churches paid salaries and YFC required staffers to raise support, churches were able to attract and hold an increasingly large number of the more creative youth workers. In many ways, Youth for Christ has done its job so well that its niche in the ecology of youth ministry has been taken over by the very people it spawned.

Young Life's niche in reaching young people for Christ is a bit more secure primarily due to their youth ministry resorts, yet the mission appears to have reached a plateau. Statistics alone do not tell a story, but the annual reports of Young Life over the decade from 1978 to 1987 demonstrate a lack of momentum. The organization has remained relatively stable in three areas: professional staff (479 vs. 476), volunteer staff (6,368 vs. 6,076) and the number of clubs (1,003 vs. 1,042). The only areas of fluctuation were in camp attendance which was up (16,729 to 19,269) and average club attendance which was down slightly (53 to 49).

Factors such as these prompted one veteran regional director to suggest that the movement suspend all ministries during its fiftieth anniversary year and rethink its entire mission. Though the plea was ignored, the suggestion had made its point.

Changes are being made. Young Life, like Youth for Christ, had a change in personnel during the decade as Doug Burleigh assumed the mantle of leadership and began putting in place a new staff at the headquarters in Colorado Springs. Verley Sangster, the first black person to be named national director of a major evangelical parachurch youth ministry organization, has brought fresh ideas at the national level. Clubs ("proclamation units" as Burleigh likes to call them) increased in 1989-1990 to 1,343, field staff in the United States grew to 556, and summer camp attendance reached 28,681. Still the changes made to date have not brought about a sudden surge in the movement's effort to reach more students for the cause of Christ. The average club meeting was attended by slightly over 40 students, which was not only down from the 1987 figures (49 vs. 40), but was a 42 percent drop from the movement's highest average attendance (70) recorded in 1973.

What will happen to these two pioneer youth ministry agencies? If history is any indicator, both organizations will be around 50 years from now and will have a ministry to a specific clientele. The main steam of youth ministry, however, will be flowing through different channels.

Local Church Youth Ministries

Perhaps the best known and most widely imitated church youth group in the nation during the 1980s was Son City (later called Student Impact), based in the Willow Creek Community Church. Each Tuesday evening 700-800 high school students made their way to the church located in South Barrington, Illinois, for competition, team activities and a powerful program which culminated in an evangelistic or pre-evangelistic message by Dan Webster, the church's minister to youth.

Webster, complemented by an outstanding team of volunteer youth workers and paid interns, targeted over 20 high school campuses in Chicago's northwest suburbs. Music, media, and drama blended with a variety of competitive activities attracted a cross section of mainstream high school students. Though many came only once or twice, the ministry was one of the most successful church-based efforts to evangelize young people.

Yet even Son City plateaued. Within two years after the concept was developed by Dave Holmbo and Bill Hybels in April 1972 at South Park Church in Park Ridge, Illinois, the youth group was reported by *Moody Monthly* magazine to have been attended by 500-800 people.[5] By May 1975 attendance reached 1,000 each week as the group was split and held on two nights. Two decades later, the ministry consistently attracted a similar number of high schoolers each week.

As the Willow Creek ministry entered the last decade of the century, Webster made some strategic adjustments to the ministry and increased the number of paid interns and staff members. This gave more ministry power on high school campuses and as a result attendance jumped from 800 to the 1,400 mark. But even this, which was by far the largest church-based youth ministry in North America, was not that far ahead of attendance numbers from the early 1970s.

The year 1979 may have been the time when the torch was passed from parachurch agencies to local church ministries. In that year two associations of local church youth workers came into being. In Colorado the National Network of Youth Ministry was begun as two dozen youth pastors gathered to compare notes and provide support for each other, while in Chicago Dann Spader began a training organization which he called Sonlife Ministries (not to be confused with Son City).

Though the National Network was initially conceived of as an unstructured meeting place for youth workers to gather and fellowship, leaders such as Barry St. Clair, Dennis Miller, and Paul Fleischmann soon saw a need for structure and focus. Influenced by their concern for world evangelism and continued contacts with Campus Crusade for Christ, Fleischmann and St. Clair attempted to mobilize local networks of church-based youth workers into evangelistic units.

The results have been less than spectacular. Occasionally, local clusters of youth ministers succeeded in promoting area-wide evangelistic efforts, but for the most part such efforts were but a side show in the passing carnival of youth ministries. Prayer support and the networking of ideas were also important within the loosely knit organization just as had been true of the Youth for Christ structure in the early 1950s.

A cooperative evangelistic effort in Wheaton, Illinois, during the winter of 1988 illustrates the passing of leadership from parachurch agencies to church-based youth ministries. Even though the headquarters for Youth for Christ USA was located in neighboring Carol Stream, a local group of youth ministers from over 20 churches went together to sponsor a three-day evangelistic extravaganza, but only invited one YFC staff member to serve on the leadership committee, and his responsibilities were only advisory.

Though not officially linked with the National Network, the local group exemplified one of the purposes of the Network — cooperative evangelism. They invited Gary Zeleski and his Allies to hold three nights of meetings at Wheaton Bible Church, which was packed with over 1,500 young people each night. Music was loud and contemporary. Drama and celebrity testimonies were also used, followed by messages given which related to aspects of the student's world. Hundreds responded to the invitations.

Yet when Zeleski and the Allies left town, local youth workers settled back into their patterns of ministry and very little long-term impact was felt. The feelings privately expressed among the local youth workers was that they were glad they had made the effort, but that they had not yet found a method for doing cooperative evangelism.

Sonlife Ministries, founded by Dann Spader in 1979, had a similar vision for promoting a biblical youth ministry which would result in discipling and evangelizing students through church youth groups. With the dream of assisting 10,000 youth groups to adopt the strategy and model ministries in 1,000 communities, with 500 active resource people servicing them, Spader forged a relationship with Moody Bible Institute's extension department and began providing training seminars across the nation.[6]

In a ten-year evaluation, Spader reported that 10,000 leaders went through some aspect of their training in 1989 alone. For the most part these were church people who were either getting into youth ministry (lay and professional) or who were receiving advanced training within the Sonlife system. To complement this training of adults, Spader's team sponsored Sonlife Evangelism and Missions Conference which directly trained 420 high school students to share their faith on the streets of Chicago in 1989.

By the end of the 1980s, 11 evangelical denominations had affirmed the Sonlife training system and had established a working relationship with Spader's organization. The idea of training youth workers within a church-based structure, rather than providing program materials as denominations have historically done, or creating a new parachurch agency which worked directly with young people as Youth for Christ and Young Life had done, was at the heart of what the ministry was all about.[7]

Yet a closer look at the products of the Sonlife system may give youth workers another perspective. A survey was taken in 1986 of 50 people who had taken the Sonlife Advanced Training. Their churches averaged 577 in attendance on Sunday morning. Though the youth workers reported an average of 11 volunteers working with them, they averaged only seven conversions to Christ per church per year. Admittedly better than most youth groups in the nation, but by no means a tidal wave of response.

A similar Sonlife survey conducted in 1989 received 89 responses. Though church attendance was slightly higher and the average number of volunteer workers was lower, the average number of conversions per church per year was only up to nine. These conversion figures were slightly lower than the numbers reported by Youth for Christ for the same periods—8 conversions per club in 1985-86 and 12 per club in 1987-88.

Admittedly, there is a problem with evaluating the significance of conversion growth within a church youth group or parachurch ministry. Basing his calculations on what Sonlife calls "growth level" students, Spader suggests that the annual conversion growth rate for fully developed Sonlife ministries approaches a very healthy 21 percent. But basing growth rate on "growth level" students is like plotting church growth statistics on the basis of only those adults who attend both worship service and Sunday School 80 percent of the time. It does not take into account the entire constituency.

Perhaps a better basis for evaluation would be to start from an average figure derived from lists of high school students enrolled in Sunday School and youth group, and of all the high school children of people living locally who are included on the church roll or active mailing list. The average of these three groups would force the calculation to include students who have dropped out of active involvement in the church but who could still be considered parishioners.

While Sonlife Ministries has been very successful in equipping local church youth workers and their students to gain a "Great Commission mind-set," the work can by no means be described as filling the gap created by declining parachurch agencies. In fact, when asked how many fully developed Sonlife ministries existed at the end of the 1980s, Spader estimated about 100. If those 100 provide the springboard for achieving Spader's 1,000 projected functioning ministries using the Sonlife strategy by the end of the century, these church youth groups may provide the catalyst for spiritual renewal. Sonlife Ministries may become a key player in assisting churches to buck the trend.

As with many ministries, Sonlife tends to judge success based on what it is doing rather than on what is getting done. If it evaluates its ministry based on persons attending training seminars or youth pastors who implement the strategy, it is in danger of becoming part of the passing cycle of youth ministry. If, no matter how difficult it is, Sonlife critiques itself primarily on the basis of high school students who, in conjunction with adults, demonstrate a "Great Commission mind-set" by reaching and discipling peers into the church, then it may play a key role in the coming revolution in youth ministry. But to this point, the progress, though encouraging, seems less than spectacular.

Bucking the Trend

Two ministries to young people appear to have bucked the trend toward stagnation during the decade of the 1980s. Though extremely different in nature, the two organizations appear to have one factor in common—a well-focused target audience. Neither is attempting to be a full-service youth ministry.

Fellowship of Christian Athletes, founded in 1954, has quietly grown to be the most widespread evangelical presence on high school campuses in the United States. At the end of the decade of the 1980s, FCA had regular contact with students on more campuses than the next three largest parachurch youth ministries combined (Student Venture—the high school division of Campus Crusade for Christ, Young Life, and Youth for Christ). In the annual report of the end of the decade, FCA reported 4,134 huddle groups scattered across 18 percent of the secondary schools in the United States.

The strength of the organization is a dedicated core of volunteer huddle group leaders who invest their spare time in the lives of student athletes. The linkage is a natural one. Coaches or people connected with high school athletic programs invite male and female athletes to participate in a group meeting where the language of sports is mixed with the Word of God. Though one need not be a member of a team to participate, the language of conversation must be understood.

Like Youth for Christ and Young Life, Fellowship of Christian Athletes had a change of leadership during the 1980s. Richard F. Abel assumed the reins of leadership from John Erickson in 1988 and proclaimed FCA to be the best-kept secret in America. The key to this secret was lay volunteers. The organization did not need to be highly visible in order to pay staff members to work on a particular campus because a willing worker was already in place. The natural relationship between huddle group leader and student, most frequently established on the playing field, enabled the adult leader to be aware of the issues which needed to be addressed. Huddle group talks reflected these insights.

Weaknesses do exist, however. Quality control may be the most pressing. There has been little contact between volunteers and the local or regional professional staff. In 1988 the 3,961 huddle groups were supervised by 191 field staff, a ratio of 21 groups per staff member. A majority of the field staff member's time went into area or regional activities rather than the development of lay leaders. The result was an uneven quality of huddle groups. Christian concepts may have been swallowed up in cultural interpretations of Christian living. In some places the gospel of success may have functionally replaced the concept of salvation by faith in Christ. Records of conversions are not readily available. Thus, the question of ministry effectiveness on the huddle group level must be evaluated more carefully.

The second youth ministry which continued to be strong at the end of the 1980s was Youth With a Mission. Founded by Loren Cunningham in 1960, Y-WAM began with 5,000 short-term (less than a year abroad) missionaries and 887 North American full-time personnel overseas operating out of 90 centers established as separate corporations. By the conclusion of the decade there were over 300 study centers around the world servicing 13,954 short-term missionaries and 2,506 career personnel. That is a 179 percent increase in short-term missionaries in the third decade of the movement's existence. Young people are not the target of this mission, they are the evangelists. Americans are not the exclusive source of workers, for Y-WAM draws from all nations and sends to all nations.[8]

Like FCA, the key to the ministry's continued growth was focus. The image of waves of young people going overseas to do evangelistic work remained a constant vision. Training centers located around the world merely became a method for accomplishing that dream. The ship, Anastasis, which set sail in 1982, enabled the movement to further fulfill its goal. Other strategies include drama, music, relief work, mobile teams on bikes, and a host of efforts to reach people in the urban centers of the world as well as the unreached peoples.

Evangelism was at the heart of Y-WAM, and though the age of an average participant in missionary trips is beyond the high school age group, there are still a large number of high school students who participate on the short-term events.

Current Status

The decade of the 1980s has drawn to a close and the health of ministries to high school students in the United States is less than exciting. For the most part ministries which employ youth specialists are locked within the white middle class as church boards urged by parents attempt to insure the passing of Christian values from one generation to the next.

The predominance of middle class people in youth ministry in the 1990s is a reflection of the dominance of the middle class in America. Third World countries and nations formerly part of the Communist bloc have no significant middle class. Consequently, they have not benefited from the rise of indigenous youth movements or professional youth pastors. Nor have they become captives of an institutionalized form of youth work.

Parachurch agencies which attempt to reach the entire student population with a single strategy have ceased to grow. Statistics suggest that each agency has carved out a niche for ministry and has settled within the safety of that stratum in the ecology of the youth culture.

Though the church has increased its participation in responsible evangelization of adolescents, the evangelistic inroads to the current generation has produced a negative growth factor. Even where the combination of church and parachurch agencies has been able to keep up with the once again increasing population of the public high school, the conversions have remained primarily within a homogeneous grouping compatible with the values of the evangelical church. Urban dwellers and minorities have been overlooked, as have the students on the fringes of the high school society in suburban and rural communities.

The time has come for revolution—a total restructuring of youth ministry. Continued modifications of the current system simply will not keep up with the changes in the world in which we live. Youth ministry has grown old. Leaders have become conservators of treasured memories. Ownership of property, advanced degrees, and successful youth ministry business ventures have minimized risk-taking and cultivated a desire for respectability.

The problem which must be faced is, who will lead the revolution and what will the resulting forms of youth ministry look like? In order to answer these questions we must look at the history of youth ministry, for in a rather uncanny manner it would appear that concerned Christians have come to this point, not once, but twice before in the short annals of ministry focused on youth.

---

1. *Digest of Education Statistics 1989,* Twenty-fifth Edition (Washington: National Center for Educational Statistics, 1989), 9, 12, 56.

2. "Beyond the Melting Pot," *Time* (9 April 1990): 28-35.

3. *Digest of Education Statistics 1989,* 56.

4. Mike Yaconelli, "Where's Your Passion? (Part I)," *Journal of Christian Camping* 22 (March-April): 6.

5. Steve Smith, "Son City—Where the Action Is," *Moody Monthly,* 75 (December 1975): 100.

6. The connection with Moody Bible Institute ended in 1990 when the ministry became an independent organization based in Wheaton, Illinois.

7. The denominations include: The Evangelical Free Church of America, Fellowship Baptist of Canada, United Brethren in Christ, the Associated Gospel Churches of Canada, the Christian and Missionary Alliance of Canada, Fellowship of Atlantic Baptist in Canada, Grace Brethren, Evangelical Presbyterian, Conservative Baptist, Christian and Missionary Alliance of the United States, and the Free Methodist Church.

8. Compare *Missions Handbook: North American Protestant Ministries Overseas* 12th Edition (Monrovia, CA: MARC, 1979): 32, 508; with *Missions Handbook: USA/Canadian Protestant Ministries Overseas* 14th Edition (Grand Rapids: Regency Reference Library, 1989): 56, 248.

PART ONE

Understanding the Revolution

C alling for a revolution and criticizing ministries which have been used by God to reach thousands of young people for Christ puts a person in a vulnerable position. On one hand, the crier may be viewed as an angry or frustrated person bent on retaliation toward a system from which he was alienated. On the other hand, the advocate of revolution may be expected to be living a revolutionary life-style, supposedly the style for which he calls.

Neither of these scenarios fit me comfortably. My life has been spent as a participant in youth ministry. Admittedly, my entrance into the field was an accident, but the success that followed gave me 11 marvelous years in primary youth ministry, seven more years supervising youth workers and nine years training youth ministers at Trinity Evangelical Divinity School.

Nor am I a revolutionary. To be sure, there was a revolutionary period of my life when I took on the appearance of a radical, selling my "extra" clothing and living on 40 percent of my income in order to give every cent I could for the extension of the Christian Gospel. But through the years I have mellowed. Currently, I live the rather normal life of an academic studying the development of youth ministry while speaking frequently.

Yet it is my conclusion that youth ministry is on the verge of a radical transformation. I call it a revolution for it is both a complete change and the end of a cycle. Within this decade new leadership, new ministry systems, and new agencies must and will emerge.

People in academic situations sometimes ask very odd questions.

Some are so profound that only a three year-old could answer them. Take, for example, the inquiry, "Why should a fish never be asked what it feels like to be wet?"

The preschooler would give the most sensible answer by responding that fish do not talk. But the question is much deeper than a youngster is able to grasp. A more insightful answer might be that the fish does not know what it feels like to be wet for he has never been anything but wet. Until that fish is able to get outside the "wetness" of his world, he has no perspective from which to evaluate his existence.

For over 20 years youth ministry had been my "wetness," my environment. It was hard for me to gain an adequate perspective either on what I was doing or on what others were doing who shared my assumptions about the dynamics of youth work. I had no thoughts of a revolution in youth ministry. My only desire was to make what we were doing more effective. After all, is that not what a training institution like Trinity is all about?

The answer, in good old seminary double talk, is "yes and no." Yes, the professors do need to ask the question, "How can you become effective in doing God's work?" But they must also ask the question "Why should we be training you in this manner, at this time and location?"

As I began to ask the "Why?" question I stumbled onto the coming revolution in youth ministry. The question is handled in different ways by the various disciplines. Theologians approach the issue by attempting to discover God's perspective from the pages of Holy Scripture. Sociologists look for social process, psychologists analyze inner motivations, and historians seek lessons from the past which inform actions today. I chose the historical approach but attempted to integrate the other disciplines into my work.

During my doctoral work at Loyola University, Chicago, I took several classes with Father Michael Perko, a Jesuit priest. One of his primary interests was the relationship of education to religion. The more we talked, the more he drew from me an interest in the non-formal educational process which we have come to call youth ministry. I found Father Perko to be a marvelous resource in studying that aspect of evangelicalism.

What I wanted to discover were the roots or sources from which the current expressions of youth ministry had grown. The task was frustratingly slow. To understand the current expressions of youth work I needed to identify what had taken place before the current generation of youth ministers came upon the scene. The issue was not so much, "Was there life before Young Life?" and "Did people reach youth for Christ before Youth for Christ?" but "What did youth ministry look like before these two parachurch agencies came upon the scene?"

The frustrating part about such a study is that people who did work with adolescents seldom took the time to record or carefully document what they were doing. Most just did the work. Then, because of changes of personnel and switches in office locations, old records were discarded and I found myself left with little but the fading memories of aging youth workers.

My desire to glimpse the big picture was made more difficult by the fact that most of the historical pieces available were house histories, that is, they were written by people sympathetic with the particular agency being chronicled but who had little perspective on what had happened earlier or was happening elsewhere. In fact the most recent comprehensive work which had been produced was dated 1917, long before the current expressions of youth ministry existed.[1]

Hours were spent in the Archives of the Billy Graham Center reading through the materials related to the subject. Trips were taken to Colorado Springs and Minneapolis. Transcripts were made from interviews documenting the impressions retained by key figures over the years. Volumes of magazines were read in search of historical documentation.

I know, it all sounds very boring, but the opposite is true. There was something magical about holding a letter, journal entry or even committee report in my hands while sensing the passion with which the words were crafted. These men and women obviously felt that they were part of something special that God was doing. Repeatedly it was described as revival and at times this historian felt like he was eavesdropping on what they were convinced was a mighty work of God.

Still, I could not pull all the scattered pieces together. Then, as so many times happens in this type of inquiry, a phone call to Columbus, Ohio, provided a breakthrough. While attempting to get information about the International Society of Christian Endeavor, I was told of a researcher who was in their archives as we spoke. A few days later that researcher, Judith Bowen Erickson, a sociologist from the University of Minnesota, directed me to some resources that brought the coming revolution in youth ministry into focus.

Quickly the pieces fell into place. Not so quickly, I wrote about them. The more I wrote, the more I became convinced that God was about to do something comparable to the early days of the Sunday School movement, or to the beginning of the Society for Christian Endeavor and/or to the excitement of the early Youth for Christ movement.

My task was simply to reconstruct, as faithfully as possible, what had happened as evangelicals attempted to bring about spiritual changes in the lives of young people. Then I could suggest what might happen in the days ahead. The coming revolution in youth ministry was beginning to come into focus.

In this first section of the book, the nature of the revolution which is coming is explained. Chapter 2 will start with a verification of the idea of cycles in two disciplines other than Christian education or history.

One of the most interesting aspects of the idea of a coming revolution is the predictable pattern and the movements in society which enable the revolution to happen. Chapter 3 looks at the context in which youth movements arose while the following chapter will focus on the cycle from beginning to end. Part I will conclude in chapter 5 with a look inside the first three revolutions to discover the essential elements of those movements to discover how they began and spread.

---

1. Frank Otis Erb, *The Development of the Young People's Movement* (Chicago: The University of Chicago Press, 1917).

CHAPTER 2

Whatever Goes Around Comes Around: The Concept of Cycles in History

There are times when a person does not trust himself. This was one of those moments. As I sat surrounded by my file folder and photocopied articles in the room which I used as an office in my Carol Stream (Illinois) home, the answer seemed much too obvious. There had to be a cycle, a predictable way in which youth movements in the church happen. The evidence was piling up. The circumstances which accompanied the emergence of the Society for Christian Endeavor seemed to parallel the situation from which the Youth for Christ movement originated. Now it was becoming apparent that the Sunday School and YMCA movements in America during the early and mid-nineteenth century had similar characteristics. It just seemed too obvious to include in my doctoral dissertation.

Education had taught me to distrust my first impressions, not because they were poorly reasoned but because my obvious answer might be apparent to only one person—me. Reading and writing came to me with difficulty. When it came to committing myself to an idea in the academic community based on materials that I had read, I always felt a bit insecure. There seemed to be a nagging voice in the back of my mind suggesting that I had not read widely enough and therefore should not be drawing conclusions.

The same voice was bringing my research to a grinding halt. The progress on my dissertation was lagging way behind where I felt I should be. I wished for one or two credible sources on the idea of cycles in history and then I might be off and running. The verification came from an unexpected source.

Discovery on a Cruise

One of the unexpected joys of Christian ministry is receiving an unanticipated benefit. It had happened once before when the parents of youth group members in a church I served had shocked me with a surprise party and given my wife and me a "get-away" weekend. Though honored I did not know how to respond to it. I felt guilty for the resulting relaxation. It happened again one fall afternoon in 1986. Ruth called me from her office at *Partnership* magazine.

"Guess what Harold Myra just gave us?" she asked. (Harold was the publisher of the marketing ventures at CTi.) "A cruise in the Caribbean! It's a gift of appreciation from one of our advertisers."

"That's great!" I said with all the enthusiasm I could muster. "Sounds like fun!"

My conflicting emotions were not fun, however. Inside was a strong feeling of dissidence, a conflict between law and grace. Harsh voices from my past called for sacrifice and discipline of material possessions while gentler sounds rejoiced in God's goodness.

Sometimes I wonder how my evangelical heritage may have stifled my ability to celebrate the gifts of life. Yet, on this occasion, it did not take too much work to accept this present. A month and a half later we were aboard the *Carebe II* sailing out of the Port of Miami.

Yet to salve my nagging work ethic, I had tucked Peter Drucker's *Innovation and Entrepreneurship* into my luggage for a little "light" reading as we soaked up the late fall sunshine and steamed toward the Dominican Republic, Puerto Rico, St. John's, and St. Thomas. Management theory had long been an interest of mine and so as Ruth and I relaxed in lounge chairs on the upper deck, Mr. Drucker became an additional companion.

The second day out of port we sat on deck watching the sea gulls frolic off the port stern. For the first time in months we were beginning to relax. I dozed a bit, watched the cloud formations, and then reached for Mr. Drucker's book. Ruth had nestled down behind a pair of sunglasses and was already absorbed in reading Annie Dillard's *Pilgrim at Tinker Creek*. This was the ultimate way in which to relax.

Within four pages of *Innovation and Entrepreneurship* I was working on my dissertation again. Unexpectedly, I had come across a description of the cycles I had been finding in youth ministry, except Drucker was portraying economic cycles. I became excited. This was a new type of relaxation. Energy began to build inside me. I wanted to interrupt Ruth's wanderings through *Tinker Creek* but refrained myself. She thought I was crazy to bring a management book along in the first place. I read on.

Drucker's ideas of growth in the entrepreneurial sector of the United States' economy was based on a model created by a Russian economist named Nikoli Kondratieff who was executed in the mid-1930s on Stalin's orders because his model predicted the failure of the collectivized Russian agricultural policies. Drucker called it the "fifty-year Kondratieff cycle." I could only hope that my colleagues in the church would be kinder to me than Stalin had been to Kondratieff when I projected a collapse in the area of youth ministry.

Simply stated, the theory was this: Every 50 years a long technological wave crests. For the last 20 years of each cycle the growth industries of the previous technological advance appear to be doing exceptionally well but what they really are doing is using up capitol which is no longer needed to grow. The situation never lasts more than 20 years. Then there is a sudden crisis followed by 20 years of stagnation before which new and emerging technologies can overcome the sluggishness of the economy.[1]

That was it! Fifty-year cycles broken down into stagnation and transition periods that I had begun to discover. For the first 20-30 years of a youth movement there was an excitement and constant innovation which drove it forward in attempts to reach young people for Christ. Then around year 30 something happened. Stagnation began to characterize the movement and increasingly did so for the next 20 years while the movement's earlier momentum and good reputation carried it along. Finally, a crisis happened and there was no longer a way to disguise the fact that the movement was bankrupt. For an additional 20 years youth work would struggle before entreprenuerial innovations in working with young people could set in motion a new cycle of youth ministry.

Home from the cruise I had new energy. Not only was I tanned and relaxed, but my research was in motion again. My next step would be to check out my "cycle theory" with some fields of study a bit closer to the theological disciplines than Drucker and economics.

Biblical Cycles

I am uncomfortable with proof texts drawn from the Bible. By "proof text" I am referring to isolated verses which are used to support an argument. Though it is sometimes adequate to base a theological conclusion on one or two such texts in the Bible, more often than not this approach to biblical interpretation leaves the reader with more of the author's bias than that of the biblical intent.

During my early days in youth ministry I was being trained in principles of coping with the predictable conflicts that would arise in the course of dealing with young people. The instructor asked us to look at the passage in Matthew where a centurion in the Roman army asks the Lord to heal a highly valued servant. When Jesus complied and was about to enter the soldier's home the military man sent a message saying, "Lord, don't trouble yourself, for I do not deserve to have you come under my roof.... But say the word and my servant will be healed. For I myself am a man under authority, with soldiers under me. I tell this one, 'Go' and he goes; and that one 'Come' and he comes."

To these words, our instructor pointed out, Jesus responded with amazement, "I tell you, I have not found such great faith even in Israel" (Luke 7:9). Then he asked us, "Why do you suppose Jesus commended this centurion in this manner?"

The discussion went on for several minutes until it became obvious that none of us was even close to the answer the instructor wanted. Finally, the teacher let us in on his "proof text" secret. "Jesus affirmed the centurion's response because he understood God's chain-of-command." From this passage he went on to explain how God's chain-of-command operated in family settings and why children need to obey their parents' instructions.

That type of biblical interpretation has scared me ever since. As I approached the issue of cycles in Scripture I wanted to make sure that I was not making God's Word say something which the Holy Spirit never intended for it to say.

Another idea concerned me as well. The God of Scripture is too great to be trapped into mechanistic patterns of sociology. In all likelihood God would not work in fifty-year cycles or any other type of predictable paradigm. He operates strictly in accord with His own sovereign wisdom.

Yet as I studied through the Scriptures, the concept of recurring cycles began to appear. It was hard to detect in the New Testament which was stretched over little more than one fifty-year period. Still, the dynamic spiritual movement which began on Pentecost was critiqued by the angel to the church in Ephesus in the book of the Revelation as having left its first love (Rev. 2:4). The angel of the church at Laodicea was even more critical. "You are neither cold nor hot—I wish you were either one or the other! So, because you are lukewarm—neither hot nor cold—I am about to spit you out of my mouth" (Rev. 3:15-16). Both of these passages sound like churches which have stagnated, which had come to the end of a cycle. Perhaps the cycle idea was at least not in conflict with God's revelation of Himself in Scripture.

The Old Testament, which spread over more than 1,000 years, presented a clearer picture of the cyclical nature of God's work in history. Though not clear 50-year sequences, the general pattern can be seen both in the book of the Judges and among the Kings of Judah in the divided kingdom. In both cases God worked through a person to bring about a spiritual awakening followed by a gradual period of stagnation ending in divine wrath before God raised up another person and a spiritual awakening followed.

Though the Bible does not clearly specify a recurring pattern of revival which could be considered normative for the church today, the idea is by no means in violation of either God's character or God's Word. Such confidence is always reassuring for a person who teaches in a theological seminary.

The next step would be to look at my cycles from the standpoint of sociology. Just how would people who spend their lives studying the predictable living patterns of groups of people view the idea of cycles? From my study in seminary, years before, I had an idea of what the answer might be.

Sociological Cycles

One of the most stimulating parts of my seminary experience was the discussions we had outside the classroom setting. One such conversation took place on a February evening in 1969 when Ruth and I invited a group of fellow Trinity students to spend an evening discussing the future of the church. The 1960s had been a turbulent time. Most traditional structures like the church were under fire from my generation. So when I questioned the direction in which the church of the future should move in order to advance the kingdom of God, I was surprised by the answer given by one of my colleagues.

Duane had taken a religious sociology course and had been exposed to the writings of the German theorists Ernst Troeltsch and H. Richard Niebuhr as well as the American student of religious sociology, David O. Moberg. So, when Duane began describing a cycle through which churches moved over a period of years, I was fascinated.[2]

The first stage he described using the word from sociology, *cult.* The phase was characterized by a visionary and authoritarian leader, tight and somewhat arbitrary rules and an antagonism for anyone who did not understand God in the exact way in which he did. After the original leader passed from the scene, the group became a *sect* with a plurality of leaders, a more systematic set of rules and an increasing tolerance for other groups who shared essential convictions.

The third stage Duane described as an *organized church.* In this phase the church had broadened its leadership base to include a cross section of the church democratically chosen, rules had been softened to be understood as principles, and cooperation with other churches of like mind was normative. Stage four he characterized as a *denomination* with a wide range of tolerance for everything from leadership styles to doctrinal issues. Though the church had gained more credibility and power, by this time it was beginning to decline. This stage was inevitably followed by *disintegration* during which time people tended to leave the church, either for a church earlier in the cycle or for nothing at all.

The discussion of the evening was heated as each person reflected on his religious heritage. Most of us had come out of a church experience which the sociologists would describe as being a sect and were somewhat uncomfortable with the remaining legalism we were experiencing. Yet we were not willing to risk our doctrinal convictions as the cycle theory suggested would happen.

The evening had been rather disconcerting to me. I felt as if I was locked into a pattern which would inevitably lead to destruction. I did not want to be trapped aboard a sinking ship. I wanted to have an impact in my generation for God.

Vigorously I began reading religious sociology and discussing these ideas with others. In time I came to two conclusions. The first was that there were patterns of development through which organizations, including churches and parachurch agencies, move. These cycles were not as rigid as my friend had described or that Troeltsch and Niebuhr had theorized but they did, in fact, exist. The second conclusion was that people were not locked into the cycle. Individually, or in groups, they had the freedom to escape at any time and in effect start new cycles.

This is exactly what youth workers needed to realize. Though there is a ministry cycle which over time will lead from effective to ineffective activities, there is still hope. Though they may have to pay a social price, youth ministry specialists can still break with the old ways and become part of a revolution.

Upward Mobility

Upon my return from our cruise, I once again began studying religious sociology and discovered two factors which seemed to have an impact on the coming revolution in youth ministry. The first is that over the years there tends to be an *upward mobility* in religious movements. The most powerful spiritual movements have drawn their broadest base of followers from the lower classes of society and in time, as those people gave up their social vices due to their newly found religious convictions and redirected their energies into productive endeavors, God blessed them with material possessions.[3]

This idea was reinforced by Jay Kesler, former president of Youth for Christ. Describing the upward mobility of staff members he had observed in the early days of Youth for Christ, Kesler commented, "For most of us YFC seemed like an upward step from a cultural and professional viewpoint. Our fathers didn't wear ties, we wear ties. Our fathers didn't go to college, we went to college. For us it represented a window of opportunity that we could never have had any other way, except through this kind of a movement."

Though there were exceptions, Kesler and hundreds of others went into the Youth for Christ movement simply by seeking a way to serve the Lord and in the process found their way into the middle class. It happened as a by-product of their dedication to the ideals of reaching a generation of young people with the Christian Gospel. They learned to communicate both interpersonally and in public. Skills in management became essential tools of their craft. An understanding of culture as well as theology prepared them to use the radio effectively and later to write articles and books. They were looked to as leaders in the evangelical community. They had become leaders and solid members of the middle class.

While there may not be a necessary link between a person's position in the middle class and the lessening of evangelistic zeal, there generally seems to be a relationship. Somehow, the second generation evangelical young person who was also a part of the middle class tended to be more concerned with a comfortable lifestyle than did his parents. Progress through the cycle appears to put a damper on the spiritual fervor of people.

Institutionalization

The second factor which I discovered as I further pursued the concept of cycles was Max Weber's idea of *institutionalization*. The father of sociology described the process simply as the "routinization of charisma." By that Weber meant that movements which start out with highly charismatic leaders and a loose association of followers go through a predictable process (a cycle, if you will) through which they move from highly focused activities to diffused endeavors which become self-maintaining. The work rather than the desired outcome becomes the end product.[4]

According to Weber, institutionalization is characterized by four processes. The first, called *formalization*, is the very useful procedure through which newcomers to the movement are helped to avoid the blunders through which people previously in the movement had gone. Program manuals, training schools, and more subtle procedures of reporting results become means for formalizing the activities of the movement. The problem is that people soon began to think of those procedures as being the essence of the movement rather than a flexible means to an end.

The Saturday night rally in the Youth for Christ movement is a classic illustration of formalization. In the closing days of World War II and the next few years the nation desperately needed an opportunity to come together and celebrate. Ten years of depression followed by six years of wartime austerity left the nation in a mood starved for an opportunity for public gatherings. So when Saturday night rallies became known as the "hottest act in town," formalization began to happen. Rather than continually asking, "How can we more effectively reach youth for Christ?" the leaders of the local organizations queried, "How can we make the rallies more effective?"

The rally died a slow death. By the mid-sixties few weekly YFC rallies existed. For those which survived, their target audience changed. The Youth for Christ rallies which took place at the end of the 1980s in Chicago and Kansas City were primarily aimed at Christian teenagers from church youth groups. Their ministry was to reinforce Christian values in believing young people who were being assaulted with anti-Christian philosophies every day of their lives. Only the function of the rally remained the same. The highly publicized meetings provided visibility and financial support for the local Youth for Christ organization.

The second part of the institutionalization cycle is what Weber called *self-maintenance and conservatism*. Most movements would end up in bankruptcy court if the second generation of leadership within an organization continued to spend money the way the original visionary had done. The problem arises when this conservative instinct inhibits the type of creative activity which made the movement what it was in the first place.

In the early days of Young Life and Youth for Christ the entrepreneurial leadership of people like Jim Rayburn and Torrey Johnson took financial risks in order to bring their dreams to reality. In 1945, while Young Life was having great difficulties paying staff salaries, Jim Rayburn and his benefactor, Herbert J. Taylor, did an end run around the vote of the organization's board of directors against buying a camping facility in Colorado, and Taylor invested $50,000 into Rayburn's dream by purchasing Star Ranch and leasing it to Young Life for one dollar per year. The action, as unorthodox as it was, committed the movement to a direction which has paid handsome ministry dividends over the years.

Torrey Johnson was a risk-taker in the early days of Youth for Christ in Chicago. When confronted with the opportunity to lease Chicago's 3,000 seat Orchestra Hall for 21 weeks of Saturday night rallies during the spring of 1944, the young pastor cleaned out his own bank account for the $2,500 down payment. From these meetings and hundreds of other similarily funded rallies across the nation came the organization known today as Youth for Christ USA.

Despite the glamour there is to such stories as these, both organizations came close to collapsing under such leadership styles. The people who suffered most were the staff members who often had paychecks delayed and in some cases who were not paid at all. At times the young men and women who shared the dream of seeing the lives of young people changed in a positive direction had to spend a third of their time and energy raising funds. Something had to change.

With the advent of new leadership—Bill Starr at Young Life and Ted Engstrom at Youth for Christ—procedures changed. The organizations began to move toward a greater organizational sophistication. Principles of management were employed in order to enable the staff to become more efficient and hopefully more effective.

With the changes came a conservatism. Instead of living constantly on the "ragged edge" the organizations stepped up their efforts to insure the continuation of their respective missions. More efforts were spent on maintaining accurate records, clarifying policies and procedures, and writing manuals in order to standardize the way in which the ministries were handled across the nation. With all these changes came the need for more staff at headquarters and that meant more money had to be raised. The result tended to be a greater conservatism of methodology.

This aspect of the process of institutionalization is impossible to avoid if the mission is to survive. Yet two questions should have been asked by each mission. "Should the movement continue if an increased conservatism in methodology is essential for survival?" If not, the second question then follows, "How do we dispose of the assets in such a way as to stimulate a new movement?" If the answer to the first question is affirmative then the follow-up question is, "How do we organize ourselves in a fashion that frees the front-line youth worker to innovate and grow a ministry without burdening him with the responsibility of fund-raising and the paperwork so often used to facilitate such activities?"

Weber's third indicator of the institutionalization process is what he called *infusion of values.* By this the sociologist meant that individuals within the movement became so closely identified with the activities or facilities of the movement that they had difficulty separating themselves from specific methods even when such methods ceased to be as effective as they had been at an earlier date.

Evelyn M. McClusky was the mother of the parachurch club ministry concept in the United States. In 1933 she gave birth to the Miracle Book Club in Portland, Oregon, primarily based upon her finely crafted skill of story-telling and Bible exposition which was published in a series of books during the late 1930s. For her personality the materials and style were perfect. Many women across the country found the strategy of youth work similarly well suited.

But as the movement grew and began attracting such highly talented people as Young Life's Jim Rayburn and Kansas City Youth for Christ's Al Metsker (before either of these organizations had been founded), Mrs. McClusky simply could not separate her way of ministering to high school students from the methods employed by young innovators. She had quickly fallen prey to an "infusion of value."

Over the years such youth ministry tools as Bible quizzing, student-lead club programs, inductive Bible studies, denominational programs of music and drama competition, even the concept of a national model for high school ministry, may have all slipped into the category of approaches to youth ministry "infused with value." Adult leaders wedded to these methods have questioned whether effective ministry can be done without employing their particular tools.

The final aspect of the institutionalization process is that of a *distinctive social composition*. People associated with a movement begin to be identified by certain characteristics such as dress, speech, intensity, or style of doing ministry.

During my first year of teaching at Trinity Evangelical Divinity School, I was sitting in a departmental meeting when I noticed with embarrassment that I had put my felt-tipped pen into my pocket with its cap on the wrong end. A large black spot was developing at the base of my shirt pocket. I briefly excused myself from the meeting to see if I could correct the problem before the ink set permanently. My secretary volunteered to work on removing the spot so I returned to the meeting wearing my undershirt. Just before reentering the meeting room, an old youth worker instinct came over me and I retied my tie around my neck with nothing but a V-necked shirt underneath.

My colleagues had a chuckle at my appearance as I sat down and we returned to the business at hand. Moments later the meeting was again interrupted, this time by a late-arriving professor who was accompanied by an editor from a well-known publishing company. After the somewhat dumbfounded editor had been introduced to each of us, the department chairman felt it necessary to explain my appearance by commenting, "Professor Senter teaches youth ministries." Somehow a tie worn without the benefit of a dress shirt gave indication of a "distinctive social composition" of youth workers.

When I was attending Moody Bible Institute the distinctive social composition of ministry groups on campus was common knowledge. Youth for Christ males were the practical jokers and could frequently be found eating pizza at weird hours at Gino's on Rush Street. The Campus Crusade workers were preppie and sprinkled their conversation with words like "exciting" and "shared." The InterVarsity types looked as if they had dressed in the dark and were more intellectual and concerned about philosophical presuppositions, while the Young Life workers were conspicuously absent from Moody altogether because their lifestyles were too liberated.

Such social composition allows individuals to feel comfortable with a movement. It does not take long to begin detecting the clichés used by a particular ministry group. While attending a conference of Sonlife leaders, I continually heard reference to persons being a "high I" or a "high D." The references were based on a particular leadership style test which they had all taken and with which they were quite familiar. As a newcomer I didn't understand the implications of their comments. I felt like an outsider because of their distinctive vocabulary.

This whole process of institutionalization as identified by Max Weber was simply another indication of a pattern to which movements, churches, or businesses are subject. It was a type of cycle through which movements normally pass. I at last began to feel comfortable with my idea of repeating patterns of youth ministry.

But Fifty-Year Cycles?

Finally, I was convinced that the idea of youth ministry going in year cycles was valid. But one question lingered. Would Kondratieff's idea of a fifty-year economic cycle transfer to a sequence of similar length in youth ministry? The history of youth ministry seemed to suggest such a pattern, but I wondered if anyone else had identified the half-century configuration.

John Perkins, the founder of Voice of Calvary Ministries, had envisioned a fifty-year span of effectiveness for his Mississippi-based organization. In commenting on the people who had been developed through his ministry Perkins commented, "I feel good about the black leaders that have emerged in Mendenhall and Jackson. Things will go on in Mendenhall for 50 years. Things will go on in Jackson for 50 years. After 50 years, anything can go wrong."[5]

Though the black leader was not a youth worker, his idea of a span of effective ministry corresponded with the Kondratieff cycle in duration. It suggested a length of time in which the founder and those most closely associated with him could keep a ministry on track, and while the organization might continue beyond that period, effectiveness of efforts would not be as certain.

The most startling confirmation came from the archives of Young Life. As the movement prepared for its fiftieth anniversary in 1990 (celebrated nearly eighteen months shy of the fiftieth anniversary of its incorporation), word circulated that the founder had anticipated that Young Life would only last 50 years. I wrote to Doug Burleigh, president of Young Life and he graciously confirmed the rumor by providing a copy of the original articles of incorporation dated 16 October 1941.

Article IV stated simply, "The term for which it [Young Life] is to exist is fifty years." Whether it was a legal formality of the day or a purposeful statement by Jim Rayburn and the board of directors is not clear. The idea, however, does seem to be consistent with the founder and his concepts of ministry.[6] The idea of a fifty-year cycle in the field of youth ministry appeared to be a concept shared more widely than I had realized.

One question remained. Were the cycles of youth ministry tied to external factors such as the nation's economic and political affairs and the calendar, or were the cycles actually a span-of-effectiveness through which any youth ministry might pass? A close look at the major agencies of youth ministry over the past two centuries supported the idea that effective youth work peaked and began to decline around either the fifty-year mark or at the death of the founder. This would seem to support the span of effectiveness idea.

Yet every 50 years or so one or two major youth ministry agencies, by the grace of God, appeared on the scene and provided such insightful leadership that their very presence became the benchmarks by which that generation of youth work was judged. These major players did seem to be tied to external factors. Their emergence did appear to be predictable.

The Next Step

The file folders which cluttered my Carol Stream office were beginning to seem manageable. The idea of cycles in the history of youth ministry was not as farfetched as I had feared. In fact, the idea seemed extremely plausible. I had gotten past a rather formidable barrier in completing my research on the history of youth ministry. There is comfort in discovering that people share your ideas, especially scholars whose word you trust.

If there were cycles in youth ministry as there appear to be in economics, biblical history, and sociology, then the next question was what would be the component parts of each cycle. In other words, how might a person be able to tell when a cycle had begun, was building toward maximum effectiveness, or was drawing to a close? The next step in discovering the coming revolution in youth ministry required answers to those questions.

---

1. Peter F. Drucker, *Innovation and Entrepreneurship: Practices and Principles* (New York: Harper and Row, 1985.), 4-5.
2. See David O. Moberg, *The Church as a Social Institution,* Second Edition.

(Grand Rapids: Baker Book House, 1984), 73-99.

3. H. Richard Niebuhr, *The Social Sources of Denominations* (New York: The World Publishing Company, 1957).

4. Max Weber, *The Theory of Social and Economic Organization* (New York: Oxford University Press, 1947), 363-373.

5. Randall Balmer, *Mine Eyes Have Seen the Glory* (New York: Oxford University Press, 1989), 149.

6. On 5 December 1977 The Young Life Campaign revised its articles of incorporation and among the changes was Article III, *Existence* which states, "Young Life shall have perpetual existence."

CHAPTER 3

Seed Plots for Youth Ministry:
The Context in Which It Began

If cycles of youth ministry were obvious to me, someone else must have written about them as well. All I wanted to do was to find out what had been said. It would save me hours of work as well as rescue me from duplicating what someone else had written. I could avoid making mistakes in my theory by learning from those who had preceded me.

Some years before, as a 27-year-old youth pastor, this concern for checking my thoughts against the insights of others had not concerned me. Like many youth workers, I was an entrepreneur, a maverick, a lone ranger. Most of the youth work which I had read about or heard described by Christian educators had not taken into account creative professionals such as myself. So, when I came to the point in my seminary education that I had to write a thesis, I was frustrated by the expectations imposed upon me, requiring me to defend my ideas by doing historical and theoretical research.

"This is a waste of time," I told myself, "My ideas about setting up projects for my youth group and then learning Christian truth as a by-product of the process were a product of my own innovations."

I had never heard of anyone doing drama, musicals, media presentations, or tutoring for urban children as their normal youth group activity, as we were doing in my church. Even though a number of churches had formed youth choirs, these usually competed with, rather than contributed to, the youth group activities. They were year-around operations, rather than short-term, yet vital parts of the youth group environment.

Thus, it was with shock that late in the process of writing my thesis I discovered William Heard Kilpatrick had taught virtually the same concepts at Columbia University Teacher's College during the 1920s. Though his ideas were not aimed at the discovery of biblical truth, the strategies he and his students used were virtually the same as my own.

That simple jolt gave me a new perspective on the value of research. I could have saved myself a great deal of time and improved the quality of my thesis had I not resisted the rather difficult work of checking my ideas against the probability that someone else at some period of time had entertained similar ideas.

There are some people who will try nothing new unless they have it clearly outlined in a book or article. I was just the opposite. I avoided published programs like the plague. It was a form of pride, perhaps a type of youth ministry arrogance. My discovery of William Heard Kilpatrick's work humbled me. It caused me to look more actively for the wisdom and insights of others.

Now I wanted to use a computer database search to discover the insights of others but was frustrated by my lack of success. Words like "youth," "young" and "adolescence" produced thousands of articles, while phrases like "Youth for Christ," "Young Life" or even "Christian Endeavor" provided amazingly few articles or books. Then one day, nearly by accident, I located a phrase which unlocked a whole vault of literature. The phrase, simply enough, was "youth movements."

I discovered the phrase through a University of Minnesota sociologist, Judith Erickson. Looking for information about Christian Endeavour, I placed a phone call to St. Paul and netted a much more significant catch of information. Professor Erickson, it turned out, was one of the nation's leading scholars on the subject of American youth organizations and in five seconds gave me the very descriptors for which I had spent months looking. The phrase "youth movements" directed my attention to the information which enabled me to discover the context from which youth movements spring. The discovery process, as strange as it may seem, began to feel like the plot of a Robert Ludlum spy novel.

Types of Youth Movements
I had often wondered why youth groups did such a poor job of reaching their peers for Christ. Though most of the youth workers I knew

encouraged and even trained high school students to carry the Christian Gospel to their friends at school, the actual results of evangelistic efforts by students were minimal. As I began to read about youth movements, an answer to this dilemma became apparent to me. *The primary function of youth movements is that of passing the values of one generation to the next.*[1] That was probably the reason why youth groups were not particularly evangelistic—the parents of youth group members, despite what they claimed, did not particularly value evangelism. What they appeared to hold in highest esteem was having their adolescents survive the teenage years and not become the "black sheep" of their families.

The process of value passing, however, finds three different expressions in youth movements. The first can be described as *spontaneous youth groups* or *student movements*. These arise at the instigation of young people themselves and find leadership and direction from within the peer group. They perform two functions for youth. Either they become a means for alienated youth to reenter the mainstream of society or they allow idealistic youth a socially acceptable outlet for their militancy.

Outside of North America where youth are understood to include everyone who is not married and does not have children, this is the most common type of youth ministry as the twentieth century draws to a close. Usually, such groups are led by young adults in their twenties who are not considered mature enough to accept responsibilities in the church's power structure but are allowed to learn leadership skills in the youth group.

The Jesus Movement of the 1960s, though short in duration, was a classic illustration of a spontaneous student movement. During the Vietnam conflict, a period of extreme social unrest in the United States, young people felt alienated from adult values. The media described it as a "generation gap." Clothing, hair styles, music, and the flaunting of societal taboos symbolized the disaffection felt first by later adolescents, and later by even grade school children. The movement was led primarily by young adults who were uncomfortable with the status quo, especially in the church, or had experimented with counter-culture lifestyles and had found them empty.

The movement died when well-meaning Christian adults began organizing the movement in behalf of youth. Mike Yaconelli correctly wrote the obituary for the Jesus Movement even before Campus Crusade for Christ's Explo '72 hastened its interment.[2] The media-oriented Jesus Festival drew 80,000 students and laymen to Dallas, Texas, for what was suggested to be "the most significant Christian student gathering in history." But after the buses and vans filled with young people left the Cotton Bowl and headed home, the Jesus Movement was dead. Though symbols of the movement lingered on, the heart of the movement had died. It was no longer led by youth.[3]

Rarely is this type of youth movement found on the high school or junior high school level. Early and middle adolescents do not seem to have the social maturity, cognitive development, or leadership skills necessary to sustain such a movement for more than a few weeks. Thus, student movements led by students below the college level are absent from the annals of youth ministry.

The second type of youth movement is that which *utilizes adult leadership* sponsored by church or parachurch agencies to work with young people in *non-formal settings*. By non-formal settings I mean places outside the formal classroom where attendance is required. These adults may be paid for their work with youth, but for the most part they are volunteers who donate 5 to 20 hours each week to help young people reaffirm and strengthen their Christian faith.

Most of the parachurch youth ministries fall into this category. Fellowship of Christian Athletes, Young Life, Youth for Christ USA, and Student Venture are the best-known efforts to minister to high school students outside the context of the church.

Other organizations exist outside the local church but are designed to service club programs within the context of the church. These include interdenominational agencies such as Awana, Pioneer Clubs, Christian Service Brigade, Adventure Clubs, and Word of Life Clubs. Denominational youth organizations also fall into this category.

The highly structured nature of the materials published by these groups make their various systems most attractive to churches which have no paid youth ministry personnel. Area, regional, and sometimes national rallies, social activities, camps, and conferences provide additional opportunities for adults and young people from local churches to spend valuable time together. Lay leaders enjoy the freedom of spending their volunteer hours in face-to-face contact with students, rather than toiling behind the scenes to create programs and hoping their face-to-face experience with youth would be productive.

Youth ministers employed by local churches have adapted many of the ministry strategies developed by parachurch workers and used them within local church youth groups. For the most part these are people highly skilled in interpersonal relationships who can use those abilities to convey Christian truth from one generation to the next.

The third type of youth movement is that of the *graded educational system.* Most youth workers may not consider a system of parochial schools as a method of doing youth ministry, and yet for many years Catholic, Lutheran, and Christian Reformed Church leaders have placed a majority of their time, energy, and financial support of youth work into their school systems. More recently, fundamentalist Protestant churches have followed the same approach to passing their values and view of the world to a new generation.

Though this type of youth movement may lack the spontaneity and voluntary attendance many people associate with youth ministry, the method precedes most of today's approaches. New England's "common school," which was the forerunner of the public school system in America, came into being to achieve the same ends as youth groups do today. Leaders of the colonies wanted to teach young people to live moral and Christian lives and thus required school attendance.

Why Youth Movements Began: Secularization

Youth ministry as it is known today is a late addition to the work of the church. Try as we may, no youth groups can be found in the pages of Scripture. The stories of Martin Luther, John Calvin, Meno Simons, and John Wesley are nearly exclusively the stories of adults.

Not until the late eighteenth century is there a concerted effort to minister to young people within the context of the church. The Sunday School was first. Then came the Young Men's and Young Women's Christian Associations. Throughout the nineteenth century individual churches in a wide variety of denominations provided activities for their youth but it was a visionary pastor named Francis E. Clark who put together the ideas for a youth society in his own church and then successfully promoted the idea to a nation which was waiting. It was an idea whose time had come.

But why did youth societies begin happening in the nineteenth century and not before? Why did they flourish in England and the United States, and long before the idea of a youth movement took root in other nations? Several suggestions might describe the context.

During the 1800s a process of *secularization* began to decrease the influence which church and home had previously exerted over young people. The 1859 publication of Darwin's *On the Origin of Species* symbolized the change. No longer was a Christian understanding of the world the environment in which young people were being raised.

Many people think of secular ideas as being those which have no religious content and this is partially true. More accurately, however, secular thinking divides all of life into categories which can be verified through scientific reasoning. Math, biology, chemistry, physics, sociology, economics, and anthropology are but a few of these categories. To the extent that religion could be "proven" it could then be considered a category. The problem was not with the categories but with the lack of Christian theology both within the categories and to tie all of the categories together.

Parents felt like they were losing control. The formal educational process which shaped the lives of their children had begun to reflect the growing diversity of America. Gradually, religious and moral influences, including the teaching of the Bible, were being excluded from the public schools. The mores of the farm or small community were not the convictions of city dwellers, and young people were migrating to urban areas in search of jobs.

I have never liked the word "secular" very much because of the way in which it was used during my adolescence. Yet my experience illustrates the process of secularization happening even as my parents attempted to escape secular influences.

I attended a Christian college preparatory school just north of Orlando for the last two years of high school. Though it was a great experience for me, there were negative sides. During our daily chapel and vesper periods (it was like Sunday every day), we were constantly beseeched to avoid secular music, worldly (i.e. secular) styles of dress, and secular forms of entertainment. The indoctrination was so complete that classical music (which must not have been "secular" for some reason) was the most popular form of diversion in my dormitory.

The irony of such teaching was that it brought about a process of secularization rather than preventing it. Instead of discovering the world as a place sovereignly administered by an all-wise God, creation had been broken into fragments with God in control of only the smallest and least attractive parts. Rather than learning to make decisions and thus discover the world from God's perspective, I was left with a set of rules for becoming spiritual, and by mistake I left

God out of the rest of the world. I had become secular through the back door.

The very existence of the school was an evidence of the third type of youth movement—a graded educational system. The parents of my classmates read like a who's who of evangelicalism. Names like Zondervan, Graham, Wilson, Wyrtzen, and a host of lesser-known preachers and missionaries were common in the student body. Though Hampden DuBose Academy was a well-known boarding school, the reason why we were enrolled in this small school amidst the orange groves in Florida had more to do with our parents' desire for us to escape the secular influence of the public schools around the nation than to receive a quality education. Only a few parents were wealthy. Most had to make significant personal sacrifices in order to provide their children with an education which would pass Christian values from one generation to the next.

The same dynamics were present in the other two types of youth generation movements as well. Local young people's societies provided young people a place to socialize where Christian values would be honored. A formal Spring banquet was provided so that Christian young people would not be tempted to attend the school-sponsored prom. The card game Rook was substituted for playing cards which were often associated with gambling. Parachurch clubs became a Christian alternative to Demolay and other nationally sponsored social or fraternal clubs on the high school campus.

The common denominator for much of this concern over the passing of values from one generation to the next was the presence of a middle class in society. The presence of a middle class in North America and its absence in other areas of the world has greatly influenced the development of youth movements.

When Youth Movements Began: Times of Social Unrest

Youth for Christ leaders always had a sense of the dramatic, so kneeling in prayer on airport runways was no big deal. After all, if youth evangelists Billy Graham, Torrey Johnson, Charles Templeton, and Strat Shufelt were to carry the Good News of Jesus Christ to a war-hardened Europe, the whole effort had to be bathed in prayer. So as cameras snapped their pictures, the team bowed in prayer before boarding a plane at Chicago's Midway Field.

It was March of 1946. Saturday night Youth for Christ rallies had drawn thousands of young people to hear fiery speakers with a flair for the dramatic. Now the first of many Youth for Christ teams was headed for England, Ireland, Scotland, Sweden, and Norway with the express purpose of sharing their youth evangelism "know how" with the religious leaders in Europe. The sad irony of the trip was that it was a journey to the home of youth ministry, an expedition made necessary by the absence of European Christian youth movements during the 1940s.

Youth ministry began in England during the Industrial Revolution in the late eighteenth and early nineteenth centuries. This dramatic period of economic and technical change began on the continent and in England well before it happened in the United States. Factories replaced family-owned shops. Mass production became the normal process for making everything from clothing to buggies. With this change in the manner of production came the need for a new labor force. Children were employed in factories. Young people moved to the cities to obtain jobs which were no longer available in rural areas.

Concerned over the ragamuffins who worked 12- to 14-hour days, six days a week, Robert Raikes popularized a ministry to children in Gloucester which came to be known as Sunday School. Its purpose was to teach children to read and behave properly using the Bible as a textbook. Within five years the idea had spread to Virginia and by 1790, Boston, New York, Philadelphia, and a host of other cities were imitating Raikes' ideas.[4]

As the Industrial Revolution continued, concern was expressed for young adults who had left their families for the jobs amid the worldly influences of the cities. Few places in the growing urban centers were friendly to young adults who wished to retain their Christian values. Housing was awful. Sexual temptation was everywhere. Crime and violence was nearly unavoidable. Something needed to be done to redeem the youth of England.

George Williams was a prime mover in responding to this need. As a dry goods merchant he began a Bible study for apprentices, clerks, and young male assistants in the dry goods industry. From this modest beginning in 1841 came the founding of the Young Men's Christian Association on 6 June 1844, in London. Like the Sunday School before it, the YMCA quickly found its way to North America and by 1851 the ministry had established roots in Montreal and Boston.[5]

Though the YMCA of the late twentieth century is thought of primarily as an athletic facility with camps and educational services also provided, its original objectives were distinctly Christian. Bible studies and prayer meetings, training classes for Sunday School teachers, even athletic competition were seen as ways in which to reinforce Christian beliefs and values.

Before the Industrial Revolution such activities were not necessary. The extended family and the church combined to do all the teaching most people felt was necessary. Though a strong case can be made demonstrating the ineffectiveness of the traditional delivery systems for instruction in Christian truth and values, Christian people of the eighteenth century felt little need for help. The boundaries of their world were the fields surrounding their villages. Traditional taboos were held in place by the unchanging fabric of the local social system.

By the nineteenth century those feelings of self-sufficiency had begun to evaporate. Even adults responded as college students paved the way for the modern missionary enterprise.[6] Influenced by the organizational structures of the Methodists, as well as the success of the Sunday School and YMCA/YWCA movements, new systems were created for working with young people. A new day had dawned in the concern to bring the light of the Gospel to youth.

There was a third part to the youth ministry equation, however. It was not enough to sense a need for ministry to youth. People had to mobilize to deal with the concerns. Into this vacuum came a rapidly growing segment of the population. They were products of the Industrial Revolution. They were members of an economic middle class.

With Whom Youth Movements Began: The Middle Class

As a part of a team sponsored by the National Association of Directors of Christian Education (now called the Professional Association of Christian Educators), I spent a week teaching youth ministry at Mexico's National Christian Education Conference. It was held in the nation's capital, Mexico City, which is the world's largest city. Hundreds of middle-class Mexican lay people made their way daily via the Metra (subway system) from their homes or the homes of friends to the church where the conference was being held. Even though the conferees were not poor people, few would have been able to afford the conference if it had been held à la Youth Specialties in a hotel.

There were no youth pastors present. The only parachurch ministry people in attendance drew at least part of their support from people outside of Mexico. Consequently their style of youth ministry looked very much like youth societies from the United States during the early part of the twentieth century. Elected officers presided over weekly meetings which sounded like youth-led imitations of the church's worship service. Social activities were an integral part of their monthly cycle. Camping experiences were set in rustic situations.

On Sunday evening I traveled with my interpreter to the outskirts of that great city. The further we traveled away from the grandeur of the central business district, the smaller the houses and shops became. Just before we turned down a tiny street to where stood the half-remodeled boxing gymnasium which served as his father's church, Ricardo stopped his truck and pointed to a sea of huts located on the other side of an arroyo. "That's where the poor people live," was his wistful comment.

I knew, as did Ricardo, there was no youth ministry happening on the other side of the arroyo. It barely existed on our side where an articulate young man in his early twenties could work a normal job during the day and then help his father start a church during the evening hours. The needs were so great in both neighborhoods that any specialized ministry was impractical. More graphically than ever before I saw that youth work was a by-product of the middle-class people of a nation. Its style and strategy were, in part, dictated by the economic conditions of its environment.

Youth ministry in the United States has been able to flourish because of the presence of a growing middle class who are both the leaders and beneficiaries of the movement. Middle-class adults and occasional upper class benefactors have provided leadership for keeping adolescents off the streets and on the straight and narrow. Seldom have people emerged after 10 or 12 hours of filthy, sweaty, exhausting labor in coal mines or textile mills and hustled off to church for a busy night of working with young people. For most lower-class parents, such a scenario was not possible.

It has consistently been people who are relatively secure financially and have been appropriately educated, who have had the time, creativity, and energy to work with young people. Though people like Jim Rayburn, founder of Young Life, and Torrey Johnson, first president of Youth for Christ, were not wealthy people, they benefited by both education and the financial resources of loyal supporters. Jack Wyrtzen, founder of Word of Life Fellowship, and Percy Crawford, originator of the Young People's Church of the Air, attracted middle-class support by means of their radio programs. Francis E. Clark, father of the Society for Christian Endeavor, and Evelyn M. McClusky, mother of the Miracle Book Club, captured the interest of middle-class Christians through articles and books.

Though many youth workers, especially during the early days of a movement, live at or below the poverty line, their status is not measured by personal income. Ability is a far better criteria of their social standing. In fact, when some of these poverty-stricken youth workers leave youth ministry behind, they do exceedingly well in their next chosen field of endeavor, whether in Christian ministry or in the world of business or education, for they have developed entrepreneurial instincts.

More important than the personal status of the leadership of a youth movement is the existence of a significant pool of middle-class young people from whom to draw support. If young people have no time for a youth movement due to their need for food, shelter or safety, a youth movement will not exist. Charles Dickens' story of Oliver Twist describes the slums of London where youth ministry should have been happening. There was an enormous pool of needy children, but the economic necessities of life had left them victims of the likes of Fagin, a master thief, who provided room and board in exchange for stolen goods.

The economic climate of the United States during the past two centuries, by contrast, has provided a virtual reservoir of middle-class youth and it has been these people to whom a majority of church and parachurch activity has been focused. The Society for Christian Endeavor found a stream of middle-class young people in the closing years of the nineteenth century as is evidenced by the fact that 56,425 delegates registered at a 1895 convention in Boston. Poor people do not register for conventions.

Resort-like camps sponsored by Young People's Church of the Air (Pinebrook), Word of Life Fellowship (Island), and Young Life at various sites around the nation are another evidence of the appeal of youth movements to the middle class. Someone had to pay the bills for transportation to and from those camps as well as the higher than normal fees which covered professional staffs and programming costs. The young people who attended each were either children of middle-class parents or received scholarship assistance from middle- or upper-class adults.

It should be noted that youth ministry does exist in countries where the middle class has been systematically repressed. Christian youth movements in Eastern Europe have challenged the faith of the people with whom they have come in contact. But the forms are far different than the models currently in evidence in the United States. They more closely parallel the dynamics of the Jesus Movement and depend on college-age leadership rather than upon adult sponsors or paid youth ministry specialists. These dissimilarities will continue into the post-communism era until a functional middle class develops within the countries of the Eastern bloc.

What About Cycles?

The various types of youth movements and the factors of the secularization, the social unrest, and the rise of the middle class gave me a much better understanding of why youth ministry is such a recent feature in the history of the Christian church. Youth movements as they are known today were not even necessary until the past two centuries.

Still, the question of cycles remained. If, after the age of youth ministry began unfolding, there was a dynamic process which enabled the Christian church to periodically revise its approach to discipling young people, were there predictable parts of these cycles? My continued journey through archival materials suggested there were.

---

1. S.N. Eisenstadt, *From Generation to Generation* (London: The Free Press of Glencoe, 1956).

2. Mike Yaconelli, "Obituary," *The Wittenburg Door* (October 1971): 10.

3. Paul Eshelman, *The Explo Story* (Glendale, CA: Regal Books, 1972). i.

4. Robert W. Lynn and Elliot Wright, *The Big Little School: 200 Years of the Sunday School* (Nashville: Abingdon, 1980).

5. C. Howard Hopkins, *History of the YMCA in North America* (New York: Abingdon Press, 1951).

6. David Morris Howard, *Student Power in World Evangelism* (Downers Grove, IL: InterVarsity Press, 1970).

CHAPTER 4

Same Time Next Generation:
The Predictable Crises of Youth Ministry

T he article I held in my hands read like a master's thesis — precise, logical and dull.

Still, the words were interesting. It was one of those situations where you knew the author had to be right because she agreed with you. It was obvious that Katherine Niles was a very perceptive person.

She had studied 18 youth groups (church and parachurch) in and around Portland, Oregon, and had come to the conclusion that youth ministry was in trouble. Phrases jumped out at me: "confusion and need for readjustment," "a very limited range of influence," "even in large churches . . . attendance at meetings . . . was seldom more than 20 or 30 persons," "the proportion of the sexes was decidedly in favor of the girls," "the members were almost exclusively white Americans . . . middle class," there was a "low ebb of a vital devotional interest among the young people."[1]

Niles' words sounded like a dull version of Mike Yaconelli or Tony Campolo critiquing youth ministry in the 1980s. But the date of the article was June 1929, four months before the stock market crash and all the economic hardship which might have led churches and parachurch agencies to cut back on their support of programs for young people.

What I found even more interesting was the first sentence in the article. It began, "Young People's Societies came into existence nearly fifty years ago [and] for a considerable time these societies were enthusiastically welcomed by young people and championed by forward-looking leaders of the church." In 50 years youth societies had gone from brilliance to boredom.

The idea of a fifty-year cycle had appeared once again. This time it was from a writer within the youth ministry establishment. More than ever I was convinced that the cycle idea was valid but now I needed to discover what a youth ministry cycle might look like. Would there be distinctive characteristics which would help a person plot the stage at which youth work might find itself at a given time, or would people merely have to wait until a movement had run out of steam and then conclude, "That was it"?

It All Begins

For as long as many Hungarians could recall, the only way to get ahead in the world was to join the Communist Youth League at an early age and remain a loyal member of the government-approved youth group. Everything from local theatre groups to after-school discos was run by the league. For 40 years anyone wanting to enter politics, play for the national soccer team, or even volunteer to work with the Red Cross had to belong.

Thus, it was a shock when the league disbanded in April 1988 and attempted to reorganize as the Democratic Youth Organization. Membership in the league, despite its stranglehold on most activities for young people, had dropped from over 800,000 to barely 480,000 and projections were that it would drop below the 100,000 level before long. It was a classic illustration of a youth movement outliving its usefulness and then falling under its own bureaucratic weight.

The Communist Youth League was formed by Hungary's newly installed Marxist government shortly after World War II. Though much more powerful than its counterparts in the West, the youth movement was used by its sponsors as a means of instilling what they felt to be important values into the rising generation. The chaos of the war years along with the economic problems which followed World War II set the stage for the League's rise to prominence. The Communist party recognized that its best route to controlling the future of the country was to capture the loyalty of the youth. For this purpose the League was born.

At times when society's institutions weaken or collapse, and corresponding *rapid social changes* take place in society, the stage is set for the rise of youth movements. The most publicized type of student movements are those which are initiated by college students. During the closing years of the 1980s, young people were in the forefront of the protests for freedom and economic change in the Communist nations. China, East Germany, Czechoslovakia, Hungary, and Rumania, not to mention the Baltic states of the Soviet Union, all saw students in the vanguard of the protests against Communist rule.

Twenty years earlier American youth, angered by television images of bigotry and violence, marched against racial injustice and the inappropriate use of military power in southeast Asia. Their protests contributed to the passage of civil rights legislation and later the defeat of Hubert H. Humphrey in the 1968 election for the presidency in the United States.

About this same time, governments all over the world fell following massive student protests, including: Venezuela, 1958 (Marcos Perez Jimenez); Japan, 1960 (Nobusuke Kishi); South Korea, 1960 (Syngman Rhee); Turkey, 1960 (Adnan Menderes); South Vietnam, 1963 (Ngo Dinh Diem); Bolivia, 1964 (Victor Paz Estenssoro); Sudan, 1964 (Ibrahim Abboud); and Indonesia, 1966 (Sukarno). These were, for the most part, student-led youth movements in which adults served as advisors.[2]

Adult-led youth movements also arise in periods of rapid social change but their purposes are different. Whereas student-led movements attempt to change societal values by introducing a new government, adult-led youth organizations attempt to purify and perpetuate the values of the existing government, church or social group. Hungary's Communist Youth League was a classic example of such an attempt. There were others as well.

In the 1930s Germany was smarting under the twin indignities imposed by the Treaty of Versailles and bleak economic conditions. With Hitler's rise to power came economic prosperity and a casting aside of the restrictions imposed by the victorious powers from the first world war. The German people enjoyed this rapid social change as Hitler solidified his power. One of the means he used was to put in place the brown-shirted Hitler Youth for the purpose of propagating Nazi doctrine. It was a youth movement—a national youth group.

The comparison between Hitler Youth and Christian youth groups was made in Christian publications in the United States, and the call was made for fundamentalist young people to respond with the same kind of loyalty to Jesus Christ. It would not be long before the Young Life Campaign and the Youth for Christ movement would arise out of the societal changes brought about by the Depression and the war years. These movements, both in their publications and in club talks, demonstrated the superiority of Christian values to those of other "isms" (Nazism, Communism, Socialism, Modernism, etc.).

Rapid social change in society is a key clue that a new cycle of youth ministry might be happening in the Christian world. In the past such change has accompanied war, economic recession or depression, major migrations of people, and technological changes. When two or more of these factors converge, then the stage may be set for a new revolution in youth ministry.

Grassroots Movements

"Christian Youth Building a New World" proudly proclaimed the *International Journal of Religious Education* as 1935 got under way. With a flourish of optimism, a new youth ministry organization came into being. The United Youth Program was the product of committee chairmen and department heads. Its programming ideas were hammered out in organizational headquarters and published in well respected journals. Launched by the International Council of Religious Education, the cooperative program was endorsed by the International Society of Christian Endeavor, the National Boards of both the YMCA and YWCA, the Boy Scouts of America, and the Youth Committee of the Department of Evangelism of the Federal Council of Churches. It seemed destined for success.

Yet five years later the same journal would comment, "No matter how impressive the list of activities of the United Christian Youth Movement might be, it is all too true that the Movement has been one of leaders and that the average member of a young people's group has never been conscious of it."[3] It was not a grassroots movement. It was not a student movement. It did not survive.

A sophisticated reading of denominational histories is not required to be impressed with the great ideas for youth programs which have been generated over the years. Slickly published materials supported each new venture. Yet one wonders if anyone but adult leaders had even heard of them, much less used them. Repeatedly, denominational executives have made the "Bull Moose" mistake. In the cartoon strip, "Little Abner," creator Al Capp depicted a corporate tycoon named General Bull Moose boldly proclaiming, "What's good for Bull Moose is good for the nation." These denominational youth ministry specialists have attempted to generate programs from the top down and very seldom has it worked.

Youth movements begin as unconnected responses to the needs of young people. When there is a period of social change adolescents respond in ways that concern adults. Seldom do these godly people wait for someone halfway across the nation to provide a program. They simply begin doing something. Before long they discover that someone else has been ministering to young people in a similar manner and begin sharing insights and comparing notes. Weaker strategies are dropped in favor of more effective methods, and in time a movement takes form.

Though the pattern had been followed twice before, the emergence of grassroots youth ministries at the very time that the United Christian Youth Movement was attempting to get started illustrates the point. In 1942 John Miller began something he called "High Light"—not, as he says, "Miller's High Life." It was a simple Bible study for kids in four Washington, D.C. high schools which he and a friend led. Two years later John heard Jim Rayburn speak, and shortly thereafter joined Rayburn's Young Life Campaign.

About the same time, in northern New Jersey, a young businessman named Brandt Reed was approached by a group of high school students and asked to meet with them to help in their witness for Christ at school and to discuss other problems which they faced. From that simple conversation came an organization known as High School Born-Againers (Hi-B.A.).

In Buffalo, New York, Alan Forbes started a ministry in 25 high schools which he called Youthtime. On the west coast Mike Martin responded to his daughter's comment that "Everything at high school is planned for those who aren't Christians, and nothing for us. I wish someone would do something for the Christian gang!" He left his business and started "King's Teens" and within a relatively short time had clubs in California, Oregon, Washington, and Alaska.

In Chicago it was High School Crusaders (Hi-C), in Kansas City, Youth on the Beam, both of which had been influenced by the Miracle Book Club founded a decade earlier. Linkages among these clubs were minimal. For the most part they were the result of a man or woman who had a vision for reaching young people and was willing to invest time, energy, and money to make the dream a reality.

The strength of a youth movement as a cycle begins is not the national leadership, but an apparent working of God in the lives of individuals scattered across the nation, which moves them to take a risk and see what God might do in response. From these humble and disjointed beginnings a more unified movement results.

An Acknowledged Leader

Though the wooden planks on the back of the benches cut into my back and the sawdust carpet underfoot reminded me of a tent revival meeting in my home state of South Carolina, the atmosphere was charged with the kind of electricity I would have expected at Indiana's famed high school basketball tournament. Billy Sunday Tabernacle in Winona Lake, Indiana, was packed with shouting, stamping, cheering high school students in the midst of the nineteenth annual convention for Youth for Christ International.

My exposure to youth ministry had been far different. Dad had been the first pastor of Southside Baptist Church and as a seventh grader I was elected president of the high school youth group. Each Sunday afternoon we met in a garage, which had been converted into a classroom building, behind our white-framed church. Ed and Nancy Wilcoxen did what they could with the rag-tag assortment of junior and senior high school students which composed the group. Monthly socials, a basketball team, and summer camp in addition to the weekly gatherings stand out as what youth ministry was all about. But it was nothing like what I was seeing at Winona Lake.

The stage was a sea of excitement. Students performed a calibre of music I had never heard before. It surpassed the best high school variety show I could imagine. An a cappella trio used exceptionally close harmony to describe in nearly romantic terms time spent with Jesus Christ in the cool of a summer's evening. A trumpet soloist left the crowd gasping as he flashed from triple-tongued runs to notes which seemed to be octaves above the staff. Sandwiched between other features was music by a massive choir accompanied by a jazz band-quality orchestra. I had never seen anything like it.

Then the shouting began. Bible quiz teams dressed in outfits particular to the area of the country from which they came competed in one of the most dramatic contests I had ever seen. Each of the 20 questions had the intensity of a sudden death overtime, yet the quizmaster was in total control. Every round was introduced when he silenced the thousands of teenagers with the single word, "Question!"

After a pause he began a question based on the biblical book of Hebrews. Seldom did more than three words pass before all 10 quizzers had jumped to their feet, one was acknowledged and in 30 tension-filled seconds both completed the question and gave an answer. When the quizmaster indicated the response was correct, the tabernacle erupted as if a three-point shot had won the game at the buzzer. Cheers, flags, and chants fed the tumult. My youth group had never seen anything like this back home.

The year was 1963 and what I was witnessing, though I did not realize it at the time, was Youth for Christ as the acknowledged leader of the field of youth ministry. Their entire system across the nation built to this event and the moment a few minutes later when a superb youth speaker would present a biblical message which every student would understand as clearly as the rock 'n roll disc jockeys who filled the airwaves.

Across the nation YFC was innovating youth ministry strategies. In Portland, Oregon, high school students made a motion picture in an effort to tell their peers from coast-to-coast about Jesus Christ. A custom car club was the inspiration of Youth for Christ in Fort Wayne, Indiana. Teams of teenage musicians traveled around the world singing and playing the Christian Gospel.

Though Young Life had been incorporated four years before Youth for Christ International and had developed their club methodology and camp philosophy to a greater degree of sophistication, Youth for Christ had emerged as the acknowledged leader in the field of youth ministry. Innovation at the grass roots level and visibility were the keys. Weekly rallies and attractive personalities had caught the attention of both the secular and religious press. Youth for Christ magazine served as a key to dispensing ideas for ministry and featuring creative ministries.

In each cycle of youth ministry, one organization surfaces as the acknowledged leader. During the mid-nineteenth century the leader was the YMCA which was nearly exclusively outside the organizational structures of the church. The International Society for Christian Endeavor was the primary voice of the second cycle and though it was interdenominational in character, it consistently worked within the existing ecclesiastical structures. Youth for Christ was distinctly parachurch in nature. Though started primarily by young pastors and Bible college students, the movement had very little accountability to local churches and less to denominational structures.

It is difficult to place a time frame on the appearance of the acknowledged leader within a cycle. Whereas Christian Endeavor appeared at the very beginning of its cycle, Youth for Christ and the

YMCA materialized some years after their cycles had begun. By contrast, the duration of the acknowledged leader as truly the innovator seems fairly consistent. Twenty to 25 years is the period of maximum influence. By the end of that period the leader's methods have been so widely copied that the effectiveness of the innovator has been defused.

Imitators Appear

If imitation is the highest form of compliment, the Society for Christian Endeavor was highly honored by most of the denominations in America during the final two decades of the nineteenth century. Before its founding by Francis E. Clark in 1881, there had been no national Christian youth societies in America. Once Clark's ideas had been popularized by means of books, articles, programming materials, and word of mouth, 11 denominational youth programs were hastily organized. By 1895 all of the major denominations in the United States had societies which were for all intents and purposes clones of Christian Endeavor.

There was one major change, however. Clark's organization required a "pledge" of all members which was very demanding. It emphasized daily Bible reading, prayer, weekly attendance at the society's meeting, and regular reports on progress in one's Christian endeavor. As denominations adopted the program, the pledge was weakened. Most of the denominations felt the requirements for membership were too pietistic, too strict. So the Society's system was retained but the central core, built around the pledge, which brought about accountability in Christian Endeavor, was lost.

Invariably, imitators take the original methodology and omit the very idea which gave it life in the first place. All that is left is a shell. Like a seashell the methodology may be attractive in and of itself but the original life is gone. Occasionally, a new life form will inhabit the old shell and bring about a different type of existence but seldom is the second-generation inhabitant as well-suited to the shell as was the original life form.

The Christian Endeavor idea was designed to sustain a spiritual awakening among young people. Fulfilling the pledge kept members endeavoring to discover God in what Clark considered historically proven ways. Even risking a type of legalism which could creep into the prescribed disciplines, the founder felt the possible danger was worth the hazard. But soon after denominational societies were formed, new lives inhabited the "shell." The new societies broadened their focus to include teaching denominational loyalty, and leadership development. Though worthy objectives, these life forms used the "shell" in an increasingly different manner.

Unfortunately, imitators tend not to create new movements. They merely rearrange the pieces of the old movement and package them under a slick new name. There is a transition from being goal-oriented to being tradition-oriented. Concern for keeping activities happening for the young people becomes more important than achieving a desired objective either in the lives of the group members or through them in the lives of others. In time programs established by the imitators become comatose, but they seldom die. The agencies which support them, usually churches, perpetuate them through artificial life-support systems.

It is at this point in a cycle that youth ministry is especially susceptible to the trauma of events outside of youth ministry per se. Usually, one or two events sound the death knell for the current cycle of youth ministry even though the existing youth programs may continue for many years to come.

An Outside Event Marks the Conclusion

From the founding of Harvard College in 1636 right up until the middle of the twentieth century, higher education was either a private matter or a responsibility specifically prescribed by the United States Constitution to individual states. Though there had been a couple of congressional acts which granted land to the state for the purpose of education, expansion of colleges and universities had been a rather slow process until the end of World War II. Suddenly something happened that caught the educational establishment by surprise. It was called the G.I. Bill.

In a break with a century-and-a-half precedent, the Congress of the United States voted to underwrite the college expenses of all returning military personnel. In one act of Congress, higher education was changed forever in the United States. No longer was it the exclusive domain of the wealthy. Hundreds of thousands of former servicemen and women who had never dreamed of going to college would now become engineers, lawyers, bankers, and doctors according to their choice and personal abilities.

Higher education in the United States had changed, not because of an internal process but because of an outside event. The same is true of the cycles of youth ministry. The end of the first cycle best illustrates the closure which is brought by an event external to youth ministry. For the majority of the nineteenth century youth ministry had been focused on young men and women in their late adolescence who were living in urban centers of the nation. But in 1875 the Supreme Court of the United States made a ruling which changed the nature of youth ministry.

Prior to the *Stuart vs. School District No. 1* of Kalamazoo decision tax money had not been used to support high school education and consequently only one out of 50 young people were enrolled in high schools. This amounted to about 80,000 young people. Twenty-five years after the Supreme Court's Stuart decision high school enrollment surpassed a half million students and the need to minister to young people still living at home became an essential focus of the church. Suddenly, one cycle of youth ministry had ended and now it was time for another to emerge.

Conclusion

The cycles of youth ministry did have a predictable shape to them. They started amid a period of rapid social change and soon saw grassroots youth ministries springing up under the hand of the Holy Spirit all across the nation. In time, an acknowledged leader emerged in the form of a nationally recognized youth ministry organization, but, though its ministry continued for years, imitators began using the essential strategy without the well-focused purpose. After a period of slow stagnation, an event outside of youth ministry changed the environment and set the stage for the next cycle.

But still another question came to me. "If I were looking to discover a new cycle of youth ministry, were there any patterns from previous cycles which might suggest how it might happen in the future?" To my delight, the parallels among the first three cycles seemed to suggest answers here as well.

1. Katherine Evelyn Niles, "A Survey and Critique of Young People's Societies," *Religious Education* (June 1929), 526-535.

2. Richard G. Braungart, "Historical and Generational Patterns of Youth Movements: A Global Perspective," *Comparative Social Research* 7 (1984), 11.

3. Ivan M. Gould, "Another Milestone: Recent Developments of the United Christian Youth Movement," *International Journal of Religious Education* (November 1940), 17.

CHAPTER 5

Batteries Not Included:
The Spread of a Christian Youth
Movement

I stared at the large orange manual with a certain degree of disbelief. Before me were 565 pages of "how to's" prepared by Inter School Christian Fellowship, the high school ministry of Inter Varsity Christian Fellowship of Canada. "Complete" would understate the material. It covered everything from purpose to publicity, from planning to program ideas, from Bible study to evangelism. To the casual observer the manual would appear to be a key tool for having an effective ministry to young people in Canada.

The irony of the situation was that ISCF was at that very moment going through a gut-wrenching process of restructuring their entire high school ministry in Canada. The manual may have been an excellent tool when it was first published in 1976, though some insiders wondered if it were not outdated when it came off the press. Now it represented the ideas of a bygone era of youth ministry. Major changes were being made.

Publishers are both the best friend and the worst enemy of Christian youth movements. Manuals and program materials, whether produced in-house or by an established publishing firm, take the best thinking the movement has to offer and make it available to even the least creative or insightful people in the movement. This usually raises the quality of ministry to young people. But at the same time, the resources standardize what happens in the movement and diminish creativity and entrepreneurial activity.

The training materials are much like the automatic camera I bought for my wife one Christmas. On the outside of the box in clear view were the words, "Batteries not included." Ruth is not mechanically inclined so I knew she would enjoy the camera. It was about as automatic as a camera could be. All I needed to do was install the batteries — not just any AA batteries such as might be stashed away in the house somewhere. The new Minolta required a specifically designed battery. It took a quick trip to the store on Christmas afternoon to put the camera in working order.

Christian youth movements are much like Ruth's camera. The batteries are not included. They may look like a youth movement but, unless there is energy to drive it forward, nothing happens. Scripture teaches that the Holy Spirit is the *dunamis*, or power, of God which accomplishes His ends in history. Yet consistently the Spirit of God has used committed people working through human relationships to accomplish His ends. In this chapter we will look at the human actions which bring about the spread of a Christian youth movement.

A Visionary

The story of youth ministry is filled with people who had great ideas and used them in a local context but did not see them spread farther than the immediate neighborhood. Others are visionaries whose ideas go far beyond their communities. Theodore Cuyler was one of the former; Francis E. Clark, one of the latter.

Pastor Cuyler's concern was for the young people of his Presbyterian church in Brooklyn. He started a youth society which adapted the methodology of the Y.M.C.A. and used it within his church. What Cuyler's group did and what his ideas were for helping other people use his concepts are not clear. The only scrap of history that is clear is that a Congregational pastor from Portland, Maine, heard about what the Presbyterian minister was doing and visited him.

The young Congregational pastor was *Francis E. Clark*. After trying a number of unsuccessful approaches to working with the youth of his church, Clark came across Cuyler's ideas and blended them with some his wife had been using with girls of Williston Church. Adding the Methodist idea of a class-meeting, which he called the consecration meeting, he formed the Society for Christian Endeavor. Clark, like Cuyler, was an innovator but the former was also a visionary. Within a year the young pastor began sending information about the society to other pastors in New England.

From the early years Francis Clark's vision was ambitious. Though most of his objectives had to do with the piety of individuals, he had dreams about the impact the society might have on the church and the world. His desire for interdenominational fellowship manifested in conventions and conferences illustrates this dream. Less than 18 months after the Young People's Society for Christian Endeavor was founded Clark hosted a conference at his Williston Church. The gathering became an annual event and grew in number, registering 56,435 endeavorers at the 1895 convention in Boston. Similar meetings are being held a century later.

Clark was instrumental in promoting the organization around the world. Traveling and writing while still a pastor became too much for him so, on 4 September 1887, only six years after the first meeting of the society in Portland, Maine, the young husband and father resigned his pastorate, stepped out in faith, and became the first full-time employee of Christian Endeavor. By the turn of the century there were close to a million people associated with the movement.

Each movement has a visionary who sees beyond what his peers think possible and then attracts capable people to put legs on the vision. In most cases the vision is progressive and grows in response to opportunities, usually against the advice of more experienced voices.

Jack Wyrtzen, founder of Word of Life Fellowship, is a classic example of a visionary. While still in his twenties, Wyrtzen experimented with radio broadcasting and mass evangelism of youth. Against the advice of most seasoned churchmen in the New York area, Jack felt led of God to begin Saturday night rallies in the heart of Times Square and broadcast the meetings over WHN, which became a 50,000 watt station about the time of the first transmission. Only 250 people showed up for the first rally, but within a few weeks crowds had swelled to over 1,000.

From those bold steps of faith in 1941 came Word of Life rallies and broadcasts around the world. Gil Dodds, an early participant in Wyrtzen's meetings and later a chronicler of the Youth for Christ movement states, "It was not until Jack Wyrtzen stepped out to [follow] God's call that the reality of Youth for Christ caught fire in the hearts of other . . . Youth for Christ leaders. Had he failed, it is safe to say that there would be no Youth for Christ as we know it."[1]

Another visionary was Young Life's *Jim Rayburn.* Like Wyrtzen, Rayburn had an instinct for ministry which others saw as folly. The purchase of Star Ranch near Colorado Springs in late 1945 seemed absurd to the Young Life board members since the organization had been unable to pay staff salaries and had ended the fiscal year in the black only as a result of a last-minute gift of $2,500 from board chairman, Herbert J. Taylor. The idea of investing $50,000 they certainly did not have into a camp they really did not need and then banking on attracting students from as far away as Texas, New York, and Bellingham, Washington, to that camp in Colorado seemed like a fantasy.[2]

Yet industrialist Herbert J. Taylor was captured by Rayburn's idea. Selling his preferred stock in Club Aluminum, Taylor bought the campsite himself and then leased it back to Young Life at a minimal cost. From that vision for ministry came the entirely new concept of resort camping to reach students for Christ. Camp began playing a key role in the evangelization of nonchurched young people. Students came by the bus load, first to the Star Ranch and other Young Life camps in Colorado, and then to facilities located in picturesque locations across the continent. By the late 1980s, close to 20,000 students enjoyed one of the camps annually. The vision shaped the ministry.

Evelyn M. McClusky was a visionary of a different kind. Her idea of teaching the Bible to high school young people caused her to found the Miracle Book Club in 1933. In the process she formed the first parachurch high school youth ministry in the United States. The timing was right. People from Wapato, Washington, to De Land, Florida, shared McClusky's vision. Women spearheaded the movement from which Young Life, Youth for Christ, and Hi-C clubs would eventually grow. Numbers vary regarding chapters associated with the club during the 1930s. In 1938 *The Sunday School Times* claimed there were as many as 1,000 worldwide though it was uncertain how many of them were active.[3] A count of the chapters within the United States a year later suggests the number to be closer to 300, but in either case the idea of a non-denominational club to reach young people on or near the high school campus, rather than in church buildings, was revolutionary.

History is filled with visionaries whose brilliance died with them and extended no further than their individual capacities could carry them. To create a Christian youth movement, systems were needed for spreading these dreams. To complicate matters, the systems had to be simple enough to tolerate the leadership of people who were not as insightful as the originator.

A Simple System

Most of the people who have done youth ministry over the years have been lay people. Even those who have been paid a stipend for their efforts, such as the early Sunday School teachers, were not professionals in any sense. Their time for working with youth was limited. What they needed was a method compatible with their abilities, training, and time constraints.

The Sunday School is the earliest example of a simple system which was used to reach and hold young people. Though there were a number of variations on how to organize a Sunday School, the basic components remained the same: an adult used free time on Sunday to teach Biblical truths to *a small group of children.* Even without curricular materials or training as a teacher a dedicated person could use this formula and feel good about the work she was doing.

D.L. Moody was not an educated man nor was he a trained theologian. The nineteenth-century evangelist started his ministry by gathering children from the streets of Chicago and teaching the Bible to them. Children were delighted to be a part of Mr. Moody's class because they felt loved by the bearded shoe salesman. The more Moody taught the Bible, the more children and adults responded. In time this group grew to become the Moody Church which now stands at Clark Street and North Avenue in Chicago.

Another example of simple organization was Francis E. Clark's Young People's Society for Christian Endeavor. The activities of the organization were built around a simple *pledge.* It required each individual in the society to testify for Christ, participate in the society's committee work, pray and read the Bible daily, as well as support the church and its services, unless a person had an excuse which Christ would accept.

Accountability was high. Once a month, at a consecration meeting, a roll call was held to allow every member to report on his Christian endeavor. Daily prayer and Bible study were assumed to be part of that process which reminds a person of his consecration to God made once and for all. Committee work was another visible way of demonstrating loyalty in one's growth process and at the same time learning skills of church leadership.

The pledge concept was simple. If young people were willing to live up to the pledge, they remained members. If they did not, they were "weeded out." Though the idea seemed rather legalistic to many people, it remained the core of the society and distinguished

Christian Endeavor from what was described as "the old type young people's meetings that made so manifest a failure."[4]

Evelyn M. McClusky's Miracle Book Club, founded a half century later, provided a simple formula of a different sort. Instead of being located in churches, under ecclesiastical sponsorship, and held on Sunday afternoons, the chapters met as neighborhood study groups during the week for the express purpose of knowing what God has to say in the Bible. Adults were the leaders, but young people were the ones who were responsible to get their friends, both churched and nonchurched, to attend.[5]

The *parachurch club* was entrepreneurial in character. Leaders did not have to wade through layers of bureaucratic red tape in order to begin their ministries. Most merely read about Mrs. McClusky's idea and quickly organized chapters in their own communities. The concept was made simple when Mrs. McClusky began publishing Bible study materials for these teachers. Though the lessons were criticized as being "prepared by a woman who has a penchant for 'lilies and lace' that make her writing not only feminine but absurd," they captured the imagination of such figures as Francis and Edith Schaeffer, who became the Pennsylvania State Chairmen for the movement in 1939.

Percy B. Crawford pioneered a fourth simple delivery system for youth ministry. This was the radio rally. Actually it was an old idea with a new twist. For years evangelists had held revival services as they traveled from town to town. But with the advent of commercial radio in the late 1920s, a new generation of preachers could address entire regions of the country and eventually the whole country through the new medium. The radio audience demanded a different set of communication skills. Sermons which droned on and on were not tolerated by youthful listeners. Crawford became known as the master of the seven-minute sermon. Jack Wyrtzen, who began the longest-running series of radio rallies 10 years after Crawford originated his broadcasts in Philadelphia, was said to have forbidden anyone on his broadcasts to speak longer than 45 seconds. This, of course, excluded his messages, which carried much of the staccato rhythm learned from Percy Crawford.

The radio rally before a live audience became the focal point for the Youth for Christ movement in the 1940s. Torrey M. Johnson and Robert Cook used the idea to give birth to Chicagoland YFC Rallies and then described how such efforts could be made successful in communities across the nation in the book *Reaching Youth for Christ.*

These "simple systems" may seem passé today. But in the day in which they were introduced, each was enthusiastically received by a loyal band of followers who had been looking for a workable way to touch the lives of young people.

As good as these ideas were, a Christian youth movement would not have been created without a rapid distribution of the systems, and so the media became the third link in the development of a cycle of youth ministry.

Media Coverage

When we think of media today our minds focus on television, music, and the movies. The media of the first three cycles of youth ministry was far less dynamic but still powerful and persuasive. Newspapers and magazines were the agents which stimulated movements and communicated trends.

Robert Raikes was not the first person to teach or sponsor what came to be known as a Sunday School. Such efforts had been happening in scattered pockets all over England. Raikes was a journalist, however, and when he began describing the work of Sunday Schools in the *Gloucester Journal* the response was swift and gratifying. People who thought themselves to be alone in their efforts discovered they were part of a grassroots movement. Others who had never attempted to reach young people were challenged by the ideas and became involved in the Sunday School movement.

The formula repeated itself with the coming of the Christian Endeavor movement. After Francis E. Clark had been successful in reaching the youth of his community and other churches in the region had experienced similar achievements, he wrote an article for *The Congregationalist* entitled "How One Church Looks after Its Young People." The response was dramatic. Letters came from all over the nation and as far away as Foochow, China, inquiring about the Society.

In order to keep up with the flood of mail, Clark wrote a book which placed in manual form the procedures for molding a Christian Endeavor Society. The book standardized the development of the Society while keeping the spotlight on the essential elements of the movement.[7] By 1887 it was essential to provide a regular publication to tie the rapidly growing movement together and so *The Golden Rule,* later called *The Christian Endeavor World,* was begun. It was both a constant source of programming ideas and a means of cross-pollinating ideas.

Fifty years later the cycle duplicated itself with the Miracle Book Club. After the first six chapters were formed in the Portland, Oregon, Charles G. Trumbell, editor of the *Sunday School Times,* heard about the club and asked Mrs. McClusky to write several articles for his nationally circulated paper. They appeared during the summer of 1935 and the mail came pouring in. McClusky, who like the founder of Christian Endeavor, was an excellent writer, determined to set the criterion for Miracle Book Club chapters and so wrote *Torch and Sword* in 1937. At about the same time she began publishing *The Conqueror,* a monthly report of ideas and news from chapters as far away as Adelaide, Australia.

Unlike the spread of Christian Endeavor, which combined strong male leadership with outstanding organizational ability and an ability to use the media effectively, Mrs. McClusky's abilities were primarily in writing and public speaking. As radio began to supersede the printed page as the primary means of stimulating a Christian youth movement, and men with stronger organizational skills absorbed the fragmented Miracle Book Club chapters into new club systems, Mrs. McClusky's publications faded from sight. Yet her imprint had been left primarily through a very effective use of media.

It was the Youth for Christ movement that made the switch from the passive medium of the printed page to the more active channel of radio. No longer were leaders dependent upon adults to read youth ministry ideas and then translate them into ministry for young people. Young people of the 1930s and 1940s became the consumers. Percy Crawford, Jack Wyrtzen, and Billy Graham spoke directly to the youth of the nation. It was like having a national youth group.

The peak of the radio rally era was in the late 1940s. If the third cycle of youth ministry was to be sustained, resources had to be provided to youth workers on the local level. Adults were still central to continuity and leadership. Again magazines were the key to exchanging ideas and feeding the grassroots movement. *Youth for Christ* magazine and *Young Life* magazine became a virtual bulletin board of ideas. Then *Moody Monthly* magazine got into the act. Hazel Goddard, Wally Howard, and later Tom Bade left Young Life to edit the young people's section of the magazine, while Youth for Christ people like Jack Daniel, Gordon McLean, and Warren Wiersbe later contributed articles.

But media coverage alone was not enough to sustain the new Christian youth movements. There had to be face-to-face contact in large group settings.

A Spokesperson
Enthusiasm for a movement is seldom maintained in isolation. In each cycle of youth ministry there have been people who have traveled extensively in order to spread the vision and reinvigorate the people already committed to the movement. "Mail order" clubs do not last very long.

Jack Hamilton, the father of the Youth for Christ clubs, received hundreds of letters in response to his articles about high school clubs in *Youth for Christ* magazine during the early 1950s. Since there were relatively few materials available, all Jack could do was send out a few mimeographed sheets and keep their addresses on file. Then when he had a trip scheduled, instead of taking public transportation, the master club man would obtain a drive-away car from an agency which wanted a car moved from Chicago to the East or West Coast and set up a route which would allow him to meet groups of these young people face-to-face without risking automobile breakdowns in his aging car. Sometimes Hamilton's stop-over would be no longer than an hour or two before he was off to meet the next group of students 100 miles down the road.

Hamilton was the spokesman for YFC Clubs. His constant travel enabled him to both spread and strengthen the vision held by students of reaching their high school peers for Christ through their clubs. The pace was exhausting and yet personal contact was essential if the club strategy was going to work.

Incessant travel appears to be essential during the early day of a movement. The Wesleyan movement was weaned as John Wesley traveled by horseback preaching several times each day. The Sunday School movement was extended into the Mississippi Valley as missionaries sent by the American Sunday School Union traveled to "every desolate place" in the midwest planting Sunday Schools.

Before his death in 1927 it was estimated that Francis Clark traveled over a million miles doing the work of Christian Endeavor. Though he served as statesman for the movement, his primary responsibility was addressing every level of the movement from the great conferences to individual societies.

Evelyn McClusky and Maurice Jacques, the national president of

Miracle Book Club, traveled constantly in the late 1930s addressing MBC rallies, conferences, and chapters. There appears to be a relationship between the strength of the movement and the travels of its leaders.

Billy Graham, the first employee of Youth for Christ International, reported that he traveled 135,000 miles during the 1945-1946 school year and that he "got a little note from the United Air Lines saying that [he] had traveled on United Air Lines more than any other civilian in the United States last year." Graham was only one of many Youth for Christ speakers of that era but it was the slender North Carolinian who captured the attention of the media and inspired the Saturday night rally movement until in 1949 the *Minneapolis Star* would assert that Youth for Christ covered 1,450 cities.

Face-to-face contact between youth leaders and their constituency in the field is essential for a Christian youth movement. This personal contact in turn stimulates the last vital organ which goes into the anatomy of a Christian youth movement — the sense that God is doing something special. Some people would call it revival.

Revival

To this point, the social scientist might point out, the description of a Christian youth movement could be explained entirely in sociological terms. It might even be depicted as mechanical or contrived. But to the participants and those who have studied them over the years, there is an entirely different perspective. They were convinced they were part of a special working of God.

"Revival is here!" wrote Harold J. Ockenga in *Youth for Christ* magazine describing the meetings held by Billy Graham in Boston as the second half of the twentieth century began.[8] In a city which was 76 percent Roman Catholic, was traditionally hostile to revivalism, and was a mecca for the 100,000 students who came to Harvard, M.I.T., Boston University, and a host of other great institutions of higher learning, the pastor of historic Park Street Church could explain the overflow crowds in the city's largest arenas in no other way.

A sense of revival was the mood of the movement. Reports from college campuses to major cities, from rural communities to private high schools were constantly published in evangelical periodicals. As early as 1944 the *Sunday School Times* linked Jack Wyrtzen and Percy Crawford to "The Revival in Our Midst."[9] Conservative Christians were convinced that God was doing something special and the

Youth for Christ movement was near the heart of it.

So convinced were leaders of the revival that one person documented a prayer meeting on movie film before a Chicago Stadium rally which would see 28,000 people attend during October 1944. There was a sense of destiny. These young visionaries wanted to document for history not only the large events but the smaller events which led up to them.

This same sense of revival was associated with the earlier cycles of youth ministry. R.P. Anderson, in reflecting back over the first 50 years of Christian Endeavor, commented, "The church was ripe for such a movement. Christian Endeavor . . . brought to young people of the world a new and easily comprehended ideal: 'What would Jesus do if He were in my place?' It opened up new fields of service. It stimulated the spiritual life of the multitudes, and above all, it enthroned Christ."[10]

Robert W. Lynn describes the role of revival in the American Sunday School movement in the nineteenth century. "At the very heart of the educational ecology of the evangelical Protestants was Revival. Around this center clustered an array of enterprises, propelled into existence and maintained by a determination to convert the whole population. The Sunday School, as embodied by the American Sunday School Union, was one of the first offshoots of the Revival."[11]

A report from a section of New Jersey during the 1820s speaks of just such a revival atmosphere.

> No sooner were [Sunday] Schools commenced in destitute places than a change was visible in the morals of the children and the inhabitants of the neighborhood. Profane swearing, intemperance, and Sabbath breaking, which formerly prevailed to an alarming extent, in a great measure ceased. . . . This was not all; from a number of reports of [Sunday] Schools belonging to this [Sunday School] Union, it appears that many teachers and scholars have been made recipients of divine and saving grace.[12]

Speaking at the Yale Divinity School in 1888, H. Clay Trumbull tied the Sunday School movement with the great religious reforms of the Church since the days of John the Baptist and the Apostle Peter. Though such revivals have been brought about by preaching, "religious training of any people has been attained, and the results of any great reformation have been made permanent, only through . . .

81

teaching such as forms the distinguishing characteristics of the
. . . Sunday-School."[13]

In each cycle the participants and observers sensed that God was
doing something exciting and they felt privileged to be a part of that
moving of the Spirit. Extended times of prayer were common in the
early stages of each movement along with the sense that there was a
fresh wind of the Spirit blowing.

Conclusion

In each cycle of Christian youth ministry the "batteries" are included. Participants and observers agree that God is doing something
special for a new generation of young people. Every 50 years or so
the component parts of youth work have been repackaged and have
appeared in new forms. Yet the components are the same: a visionary, a simple system, media coverage, a spokesperson, and of course,
the batteries — a sense of God's special working in a new generation.

---

1. Gilbert L. Dodds, "A Survey of Youth for Christ" (M.A. Thesis, Wheaton
College, Wheaton, Illinois, 1948), 18.

2. Char Meredith, *It's a Sin to Bore a Kid* (Waco, TX: Word Books, 1978), 41-45.

3. Evelyn M. McClusky, "The Miracles Worked in 'Miracle Book,' " *The Sunday
School Times* 80 (22 January 1938), 62.

4. Amos R. Wells, *The Officer's Handbook* (Boston: United Society of Christian
Endeavor, 1900), 9-15.

5. Evelyn M. McClusky, *Torch and Sword* (Oakland, CA: The Miracle Book Club,
1937).

6. Torrey Johnson and Robert Cook, *Reaching Youth for Christ* (Chicago: Moody
Press, 1944).

7. F.E. Clark, *The Children and the Church* (Boston: Congregational Sunday
School and Publishing Society, 1882).

8. Harold J. Ockenga, "Revival is Here!" *Youth for Christ* magazine 7 (April
1950), 8-13f.

9. James E. Bennet, "The Revival in Our Midst," *The Sunday School Times* 86
(25 March 1944), 218.

10. W. Knight Chaplin and M. Jennie Street, eds., *Fifty Years of Christian Endeav-
or* (London: The British Christian Endeavor Union, 1931), 30.

11. Robert W. Lynn and Elliot Wright, *The Big Little School* (Nashville: Abingdon,
1980), 150.

12. Edwin Wilber Rice, *The Sunday School Movement and the American Sunday
School Union* (Philadelphia: The Union Press, 1917), 67.

13. H. Clay Trumbull, *The Sunday School; Its Origin, Mission, Methods, and Auxil-
iaries* (New York: Charles Scribner's Sons, 1911), 67.

PART TWO

Three Revolutions

O ne way to understand what the future might look like is to make a careful review of history. Most of the New Testament teachings about the fulfilling of Old Testament Scriptures, for example, are based on the Hebrew idea that what God has been doing in the past, He is still doing in the present and will continue to do in the future. History changes but God does not.

Students of the Bible are first and foremost historians. To understand the New Testament, people must have insights into what God did in the Old Testament. If they want to gain perspective on the Second Coming of the Lord, they must first comprehend Christ's Advent two millennia ago and before that, the Old Testament prophecy which prepared the way for those 33 years on planet earth. Bible students must look back in order to look forward.

Thus, it seems rather perplexing that Christian leaders, especially younger people, are so hesitant to learn from history. For years I have attended conferences for youth workers and listened as workshop leaders provide principles of ministry. Most will put their philosophy of youth work into biblical perspective but few will even attempt to connect their thoughts with anything that happened between the end of the first century and their current experience. It seems as if the Holy Spirit must have played hopscotch with history, and the only place where He landed was where the canon was still open and Scripture was being written.

Obviously, history must be interpreted in the light of biblical revelation, but for the most part this philosophy of exegeting history has led to an absence of studying the past. We have either lowered ministry history to a series of anecdotes which reflect the subjective choices of the current generation more than the actual movement of history, or we have made our record of historical events so dreadfully boring that few people were able to remain awake during its recitation.

Yet there is a more interesting way to write history than a recitation of disjointed facts, people, and dates. In Part II I will paint a picture of the revolutions of youth ministry which have taken place in the past two centuries by looking at three stories, each set in the middle of one of the cycles.

Mark Twain's classic *The Adventures of Tom Sawyer* describes life in the early 1840s at St. Petersburg, Missouri. Tom and his friends live right in the middle of the first cycle of youth ministry in the United States, 1824-1875. This period was dominated by two agencies from England, the Sunday School (which Tom hated) and the YMCA (which came after the period covered in Twain's book).

Meredith Willson's musical comedy *The Music Man* is set in the summer of 1912, when the second cycle of youth ministry is beginning to stagnate. Stretching from 1881-1925, the cycle is dominated by the Young People's Society for Christian Endeavor and its denominational counterparts such as the Epworth League in the play.

The third cycle is represented by the rock musical *Grease.* The reunion for Rydell High class of '59 sets Jim Jacobs and Warren Casey's show at about the high point of the cycle, which stretched from 1935-1987 and featured the Youth for Christ movement. Unlike Tom Sawyer and The Music Man, Patty Simcox and Danny Zuko and the crowd from Rydell make no mention of youth ministry agencies. Yet the musical reflects the era.

The end of the third cycle is typified by the movie *The Breakfast Club* in which young people from all strata of the high school society find themselves isolated from authority figures. They struggle for relationships, but there is no hint of religious feelings or agencies which touched their lives.

In each chapter we will look at the predictable crises outlined in chapter 4, from the disruption in society through the emergence of an acknowledged leader in youth ministry, and an outside event which draws the cycle to a close. Though the years given are not exactly 50 years in length, they come very close.

CHAPTER 6

Tom Sawyer and the British Invasion: Two Ideas from England (1824-1875)

om Sawyer hated Sunday School passionately. It was down-right unnatural. Aunt Polly made the boy wash himself with soap and water, then he had to put on the "other clothes," clothes used only on Sundays. They were complete with his neat roundabout buttoned up to his chin, shirt collar turned down over his shoulders, and shoes thoroughly coated with tallow adorning his feet.

Mr. Walters, the superintendent, was a very earnest man with a sincere and honest heart. He had set up a system by which a student could earn different colored tickets for reciting Bible verses. When the tickets collected indicated that a person had memorized 2,000 verses he would be honored by the superintendent and be awarded with a Bible. It was not the Bible Tom wanted, only the honor of being acknowledged. To that end Tom had traded his treasures such as fish hooks and licorice for enough tickets to obtain the award. Then, to the amazement and dismay of the adults present, Tom proudly paraded to the front and claimed his prize.

Usually, it was the older children, the teenagers, who had learned enough verses to be acknowledged by Mr. Walters. Tom, by contrast, was not old enough to have lost his first tooth. But in St. Petersburg, Missouri, during the 1840s there was little distinction between grade school and adolescents. Yet even at his young age Tom Sawyer had learned to play the Sunday School game.

The Sunday School Tom Sawyer attended was a vital part of the first cycle of youth ministry in the United States. This cycle received its initial boost in 1824 when the American Sunday School Union was formed in Philadelphia and became the first national parachurch agency dedicated to establishing Sunday Schools throughout the west. Of course, "west" at that time meant anything beyond New York's Hudson River. It was stimulated during the middle of the century by the introduction of the Young Men's Christian Association and Young Women's Christian Association, two parachurch agencies which, like the Sunday School, had their roots in England. The first youth ministry cycle began to wane following the Civil War and came to a conclusion in 1875 with a Supreme Court decision which was instrumental in establishing the modern-day public high school.

Westward Expansion of the Nation

Tom and his buddies, Huck Finn and Joe Harper, peered at the ferryboat from the bushes on Jackson's Island. Playing out a fantasy of childhood, the three boys had run away from home to become "pirates" and had set up camp on the island three miles below their hometown of St. Petersburg. While the steam-driven ferryboat was being used to look for the "lost" boys, it and many like it were key factors in the settlement of little towns all along the Mississippi River and beyond. The boys were viewing not only a search for themselves but also for a national destiny.

As long as the nation was nestled along the eastern seacoast of North America in relatively isolated pockets, the Christian education of each generation of young people was not of great concern to the broader Christian community. The responsibility was fulfilled by the family and such school systems as were available.

But as the west began to open to settlement and people moved beyond the Allegheny Mountains of western Pennsylvania, concerns were expressed about the undisciplined frontier environment and the damage which it might inflict upon young people. Enormous changes were taking place within society which set the context for the first cycle in American youth ministry.

The technology of the steam engine and the beginnings of the Industrial Revolution in America altered the patterns of people's lives and the manner in which they earned their living. Factories started to replace family-run shops for the production of goods. Informal patterns of support and education found in the established communities of the east were shattered as families migrated west and young people moved to the cities in search of jobs.

The slavery issue alienated brother from brother and divided the nation. Tension was increased in 1828 when Andrew Jackson, an unrefined frontiersman and military hero, was elected President of the United States. Though popular with the common people, Jackson was feared by the eastern business interests. These fears were further agitated in 1832 when the President vetoed a bill and effectively killed the national bank, giving the impression that he was not in favor of sound economic policies.

Change surged like a wave across the nation, breaking briefly along the banks of the Mississippi and then cresting again as the tide of events continued to carry a new generation westward. Left in the backwater of the nation's expansion, however, were the children of the frontiersmen whose values were shaped more by a desire for adventure and wealth than by historic Christian convictions.

Grassroots Movements

Efforts to protect the youth of America from the evils of society and build Christian character sprang up all over the nation. Tom Sawyer joined the new order of Cadets of Temperance, being attracted primarily by their flashy regalia rather than their promise to abstain from smoking, chewing, and profanity as long as he remained a member. Immediately a problem arose. He found himself suddenly tormented with a desire to drink and swear which only the hope of wearing the Cadet's red sash on the Fourth of July temporarily could allay. Even with such motivation, Tom could only endure the agony for a few days. He resigned only to discover that once he was free to drink and swear, he had no desire to do so.

Throughout the 1830s and 1840s, young men's temperance societies came into being in the cities of the land. Many were sponsored by employers who were concerned both with the moral standards of their employees and the loss of productive labor which would result from a lack of sobriety. The activities of the societies would indicate, however, that the primary objective of these groups were not the redemption of lower-class workers so much as the preservation of literate, respectable, and evangelical youth.[1]

Such were the dynamics of grassroots associations which sprang up all across the nation during the first half of the nineteenth century. Most featured a type of pomp and ceremony which would attract young people to participate and then attempted to stimulate an interest in accepting the Christian values being advocated. Frank Otis Erb documented a number of such endeavors formed during this period, of which the temperance societies were but one example.[2]

Singing-schools, though dating back to the previous century, became more popular during the early years of the nineteenth century. The schools, which some people feel were the forerunners of the modern church choirs, provided a place where young people could meet together in a socially acceptable manner apart from most adults and participate in an activity which they found enjoyable. It was an activity which youth could claim as their own.

The significance of singing-schools was that they were essentially parachurch functions in which young men and women could gather in a natural setting and join in a common enterprise. It should be noted that even after youth societies were established later in the century, choirs remained in existence by becoming a part of the church's program.

Young people's missionary societies were another expression of the era. While college students were highly influential in beginning the modern missionary movement early in the century, by the time the first cycle of youth ministry was well under way, young people's missionary societies had followed the model of similar women's groups in the church and were attracting young people to donate money, study, and pray for the heathen of the world.

Denominationally sponsored "Union" or city-wide societies further enhanced the effectiveness of these efforts. The Missionary Assistance Society of London was composed

> chiefly of young persons of both sexes. Their officers are young men, whose ages according to their constitution must not exceed a certain limitation. They must be of the Baptist persuasion and in good standing in some church of that denomination. . . . They hold a monthly meeting for business, which is opened and closed by prayer and singing appropriate hymns. They also have a monthly prayer meeting.[3]

The definition of "young people" was far different in the nineteenth century than it is in the United States at the end of the twentieth century. The phrase referred to people from puberty to their late twenties. Thus leadership for such parachurch type union societies were drawn from what we would consider young adults today.

As early as the 1840s and 1850s local churches began experimenting with more generalized *youth societies* on a local basis. Some were designed only for young men, such as the Lutheran *Juenglinggaverein* headed by Johann Buenger in St. Louis. But most were coeducational efforts in isolated churches scattered throughout Baptist, Presbyterian, Lutheran, and Brethren in Christ denominations. Instead of being as task-oriented as temperance societies, singing-schools, or missionary societies, these imitate the cultures of the sponsoring churches.

The Sunday School and YMCA

The first cycle of youth ministry was solidified by the Mississippi Valley Enterprise of the American Sunday School Union. Though grassroots ministries had developed, the vision of the Philadelphia based Union in 1830 was that, "in reliance upon divine aid, will, within two years, establish a Sunday School in every destitute place where it is practicable throughout the Valley of the Mississippi."[4]

The campaign was an enormous success. It was computed that over half of the 8,000 to 10,000 new communities in the Mississippi Valley were provided with Sunday Schools in a two year period. In addition, over a million volumes supplied by the American Sunday School Union were put into circulation through libraries in order that the young scholars would have something profitable to read. Professions of faith during the effort exceeded 30,000 scholars.

Encouraged by the response to the Mississippi Valley venture, the Sunday School Union accepted an invitation to attempt the same type of enterprise in the south. While hampered by financial problems, limited personnel, and less than adequate facilities, the effort still had an impact upon the youth of the region.

As the first cycle of youth ministry progressed, the Sunday School emerged as the most widely spread agency for working with youth. Many of the key elements of the other grassroots movements were enfolded into the curriculum of the Sunday School. Singing, missions, and temperance all became part of the lay-led teaching program.

By the time Tom Sawyer arrived on the scene in the mid 1840s, the Sunday School had fallen into some counterproductive ruts. The American Sunday School Union had found it impossible to provide leadership or supervision for the thousands of new Sunday Schools which they had established during the 1830s and before long the lay-led agencies had degenerated into oral recitations of memory verses and presentations of ill-prepared Bible lessons. The "Union" or community Sunday Schools had fragmented according to denominational lines and the influence of the Sunday School began to wane.

Many youth workers may have a problem making Sunday School synonymous with youth ministry. For many youth pastors the Sunday School, if the church maintains one on the high school level, is the least productive part of the ministry. But in the mid-nineteenth century the situation was far different. The Sunday School and church services may have been the only place in town where Christian young people could socialize in an acceptable manner. Few were in school. In most communities formal schooling ended before puberty began.

Young people of the mid-nineteenth century experienced a vacuum. They were neither children nor adults, yet they were expected to work and live like adults. The problem was that society was changing so rapidly that no one knew exactly how adults should live. The discovery of gold in the Sierra Nevada mountains doubled the nation's wealth during the decade leading up to the Civil War. Plank roads, canals, riverboats, and short rail-lines were replaced by more than 30,000 miles of rails connecting every region of the country except the West Coast. Steam-driven factories continued to centralize job opportunities in cities and attract young people from the spiritual and social insularity of their home communities.

It was into this vacuum that the Young Men's Christian Association (1851) and later the Young Women's Christian Association (1858) came to America. Like the Sunday School before them, the movements began in England and then quickly spread to Canada and the United States. The purpose of these parachurch agencies was to help Christian young people retain their Christian commitments after they had moved into the urban jungles where jobs were available.

The constitution of the Boston YMCA describes the vision of the early ministry. It hoped to become

> a social organization of those in whom the love of Christ has produced love to men; who shall meet the young stranger as he enters our city, take him by the hand, direct him to a boarding house where he may find a quiet home pervaded with Christian influences, introduce him to the Church and Sabbath school, bring him to the Rooms of the Association, and in every way throw around him good influences, so that he may feel that he is not a stranger, but that noble and Christian spirits care for his soul. . . ."[5]

Anxious that their vision for ministry spread, the Boston YMCA, as would happen with the major agencies of the next two cycles of youth ministry as well, actively promoted their idea. Ten thousand copies of their constitution were distributed to clergymen and denominational leaders throughout New England and beyond. Soon membership in Boston reached 1,600. The idea spread and by the following year the number had swelled to 49. By the end of the decade there were said to be 205 YMCAs and 25,000 members.

The idea was simple and easily reproducible. Young men were responsible for reaching their peers while a room was provided by the local organization where young men could gather with friends to read, relax, be trained as Sunday School teachers, and participate in Bible studies and weekly prayer meetings. Evangelical convictions that the Bible was the unique, supernatural repository of all truth, knowledge, and morality drove the movement not only to protect young men from the wiles of the city, but also to seek the reformation of character and the improvement of human relationships.[6]

Despite the regional efforts of the Boston YMCA, the associations across North America were for the most part localized efforts. One man, William Chauncy Langdon, co-founder of the Washington YMCA and founder of the Confederation of American YMCAs, was the prime mover in bringing about a national movement.

The climax of the Confederation orchestrated by Langdon came at the 1859 gathering in Troy, New York, at which 237 delegates from 68 YMCAs were present. At the request of the delegates the young minister wrote a document which would clarify the relationship between the Associations and the church. In the paper Langdon advocated that Associations not pursue any course which violated the denominational principles of any of the supporting ecclesiastical organizations. This specifically included a ban on doing evangelistic work while stressing the formation of Christian character. The rejection of the proposal was nearly unanimous. The delegates wanted no limits placed on their future initiatives.

The YMCA in the United States was not an association built around one man's or woman's vision, but within the movement different people arose to fulfill specific needs at appropriate times. William Langdon was only the first of many such national leaders.

Revival of 1857-1859
What happened next few could have anticipated and still fewer remember. Young men active in the YMCA became leaders for a

revival which swept across the nation. Unlike other spiritual awakenings in the United States, the revival of 1857-1859 found its momentum in prayer rather than in preaching. Churches and YMCAs became places where men would gather during their noon hours for prayer and the Spirit of God would drive them to repentance and public confession of sin.

While the nation was experiencing a period of unparalleled economic prosperity, the internal dissention over slavery caused an undercurrent of anxiety. The economic and social structures of the nation were not prepared for the stress brought about by the dynamics of the financial and political climate. So when the Ohio Life Insurance and Trust Company failed during August 1857, panic swept the nation. Thousands of businesses were affected. Banks closed and railroads went into bankruptcy. The extreme optimism of the nation was shattered.

In this context a few members of the YMCA got the idea for a noon prayer meeting from the London Association. Jeremiah Lanphier, at the urging of Association member, Richard C. McCormick, gave an open invitation for prayer in the Consistory building of New York's North Dutch Church at noon on 23 September 1857. Six showed up the first week, 20 the second, 40 on the first Wednesday in October, and soon the prayer meeting was being held daily. Within six months 10,000 businessmen were gathering each day for prayer in New York and within two years a million converts had been added to the churches of America.[7]

Though the revival embraced men and women of all ages, members of the YMCA were active participants. A young man from Philadelphia attended the New York prayer meeting and upon his return home enlisted his friends from the YMCA to begin a similar noon prayer meeting in the United Methodist Episcopal Church. In Louisville the prayer gatherings were held in the YMCA room until crowds forced them to employ larger quarters. The role of the YMCA in Chicago in the prayer movement left such an impact on D.L. Moody that it became his favorite organization.

J. Edwin Orr, the premier authority on evangelical revivals, concluded,

> The Young Men's Christian Associations were already in existence when the Great Awakening began. Out of the Revival of 1858 came the introduction of the YMCA to American cities, and the flowering

of the movement in the United States. The influx of concerted men into Christian churches found an outlet in the evangelistic activities of the early YMCA.[8]

Then came the Civil War. The nation was shredded during four years of bloody struggle. Though at times the revival continued, especially in the southern camp meetings, the loser in the conflict was the youth of the nation. Over 600,000 soldiers died and another half million were wounded during the carnage. The majority of the casualties were not much older than children.

The methodology employed by YMCA leaders after the war reflected the entrepreneurial spirit of the day. Though prayer meetings and Bible studies were thought to be central to the movement, the strategy was much more successfully employed in Canada and abroad than in the United States. By the early 70s only one out of seven or eight YMCAs reported having Bible studies.[9]

Crisis: The Birth of the Public High School

Though the Sunday School and YMCA continued to have an influence on the youth of America as the nation recovered from the war, an event took place in 1875 which completely changed the nation's definition of youth. Until then adolescents were either older children or younger adults. There was no category in most people's thinking for "adolescence" until G. Stanley Hall popularized the concept with his book by that name published 30 years later in 1905.

The crisis which brought to a close the first cycle of youth ministry was the decision by the United States Supreme Court which permitted tax money to be used to fund public high schools. Prior to the *Stuart V. School District No. 1 of Kalamazoo* decision, the primary way in which to educate young people prior to college had been in private academies.

Slowly, the public high school began to take shape. By 1880 more students were enrolled in public high schools than in academies. At the turn of the century public high school enrollment had jumped from the 80,000 in 1870 to a half million. These were people who, as G. Stanley Hall would point out, had adult bodies but were still undergoing a transition from childhood.

The discovery of adolescence both from a legal perspective and from an educational point of view meant that youth work would have to change. If the school system now had to provide educational services for people in their middle adolescence, the church would have to respond in a similar manner.

Conclusion

Tom Sawyer and his friends lived in the middle of the first cycle of youth ministry and were part of the Sunday School movement after its effectiveness had peaked. Had Mark Twain written of Tom 10 or 15 years later he probably would have included references to the YMCA and its influence on the lives of young men. The first cycle of youth ministry was an adaption of British evangelical efforts to reach and hold the youth of the day. Social dislocation caused by the westward expansion of the nation set the stage for a number of grassroots movements, which then were superseded by the Sunday School and YMCA movements, before stagnating as effective evangelical tools and eventually giving way to new movements in the second cycle of youth ministry, when the public high school became a viable option in society.

It should be noted, however, that the various agencies and grassroots movements of the first cycle still exist at the end of the twentieth century. Singing schools have become church choirs. Temperance societies have been succeeded by Students Against Drunk Driving. Young people's missionary societies now are agencies like Youth with a Mission and Teen Mission. While Sunday Schools have become centers for students to socialize and learn in the church, the YMCA has settled for an educational and athletic focus in the young person's life.

---

1. Ian R. Tyrrell, *Sobering Up: From Temperance to Prohibition in Antebellum America, 1800-1860.* (Westport, CN: Greenwood Press, 1979), 140-145.

2. Frank Otis Erb, *The Development of the Young People's Movement* (Chicago: The University of Chicago Press, 1917), 196.

3. Ibid, 21.

4. Edwin Wilber Rice, *The Sunday School Movement and the American Sunday School Union* (Philadelphia: Union Press, 1917), 196.

5. C. Howard Hopkins, *History of the YMCA in North America* (New York: Association Press, 1951), 18.

6. Ibid, 45-46.

7. J. Edwin Orr, *The Second Evangelical Awakening in America* (London: Marshall, Morgan, and Scott, 1952), 21-26; Hopkins, 81.

8. Orr, 119.

9. Hopkins, 184.

CHAPTER 7

Trouble in River City:
The Period of Accountability (1881-1925)

T here is hardly a high school in America which at one time or another has not produced Meredith Willson's musical comedy *The Music Man.* The delightful story describes how a traveling salesman who calls himself "Professor" Harold Hill arrives in River City, Iowa, on 4 July 1912, intending to sell band instruments and uniforms by forming a boys band and teaching them to play. Hill does not expect to stick around the town of 2,212 people long enough to train the reluctant musicians. All he wants to do is make a quick sale and then skip town.[1]

Professor Hill's strategy was simple. First, he found something in River City which he could portray as a threat to the youth of the city, then he connected it to other fears of moral corruption which Hill knew parents harbored, and when enough hysteria was whipped up, the "Professor" presented the idea of a Boys' Band as an immediate solution to the problem. Of course, this meant that the parents would have to buy band instruments and uniforms, but that was a small price to pay to save their children from "the road to the Depths of deg-ra-Day[tion]."

In one of the most creative songs ever included in a Broadway musical, Harold Hill plays on parents' fears to describe the "trouble right here in River City" which was indicated by the presence of a pool table in their community. Hill's song gives a classic "slippery slope" argument for the way that young people slide into a life of sin. First, their boys play pool. Then they gamble on their games which in turn leads to betting on horse racing. From there it is all downhill:

95

they become cigarette fiends, dance at the armory with libertine men and scarlet women, and listen to shameless ragtime music.

By the time the salesman is finished with the song, the entire community is clamoring for a way to keep the young ones moral after school. Harold Hill's suggestion is the formation of an adult-sponsored youth movement in the form of a boys' band. Though Hill's motivation is purely selfish, the church-sponsored youth societies, which arose during the second cycle of youth ministry and spanned this period around the turn of the century, were sincere responses to similar concerns. Parents wanted to keep their children moral. They wanted to keep their children evangelical.

The second cycle of youth ministry in the United States has the most clearly marked starting point of the three cycles which span the nineteenth and twentieth centuries. It began on 2 February 1881, in Portland, Maine, when Francis E. Clark formed the Young People's Society for Christian Endeavor. With a growing middle class in America and a spirit of optimism in the air, the evangelical church was ripe for a new method of doing youth ministry. Response to Clark's ideas was enthusiastic and this support for an evangelically based philosophy of working with young people continued until the Scopes Monkey Trial made a mockery of Bible-believing Christians in 1925.

The Progressive Era

By the time Harold Hill arrived in River City, America had undergone a fundamental change. Cities had become the focal point of expansion. The value of manufactured goods had surpassed that of farm products in the United States. Whereas 53 percent of the labor force in 1870 were engaged in farming, by 1920 73 percent held non-agricultural jobs. If the first cycle of youth ministry was associated with the social dislocation caused by the move of people from the east to the west, the second cycle is related to a mass movement from rural to urban America. Educational historian Lawrence A. Cremin refers to the period from 1876-1980 as the "metropolitan experience."[2]

The flood of people into American cities was a result of the Industrial Revolution and the jobs, especially in factories, which were available in the cities of the land. Some workers came from rural areas and settled in the cities looking for a better living than was available in agricultural communities, but more than 25 million entered the United States from Europe and after the turn of the century a majority of these newcomers settled in cities.

The nation was optimistic. Despite occasional recessions the American economy grew at an amazing rate and became the world's foremost producer of manufactured goods. Railroads stretched from coast to coast carrying products over nearly a quarter of a million miles of track by 1910. Technical innovation as evidenced by new patents propelled the economy forward. Educational institutions were captured by the progressive flavor of the national psyche and John Dewey emerged as a champion of teaching methods which were centered on the child and responsive to her needs rather than on traditional curricular materials.

The Christian church was affected by the spirit of the day. "In almost every major American denomination, sometime between the late 1870s and World War I, serious disagreements broke out between conservatives and liberals."[3] The more liberal elements de-emphasized historic Christian doctrines in favor of interdenominational unity whereas the conservatives stressed holding to the fundamentals of the faith and living in a manner which reflected traditional evangelical values.

William Jennings Bryan, three-time presidential nominee of the Democratic Party and Secretary of State under Woodrow Wilson, represented a blending of Christian piety and ideals of progress and American democracy. While maintaining an unshakable faith in the authority of scripture and advocating a lifestyle based on that conviction, Bryan also stood for progressive ideas which would "protect the people in their social, economic and political rights, and promote the general welfare of the country."[4] His national popularity and the consequent demand as a speaker made the orator a spokesman for evangelical concerns throughout the second cycle of youth ministry. Unfortunately, his performance as prosecuting attorney at the Scopes Monkey Trial in 1925 later brought about the demise of this era in working with youth.

Bryan's combination of concerns was not shared by the ordinary church member. The parents of River City better typified the values of the average evangelical church member at the turn of the century. They were more concerned with issues of conventional morality than national progress. Sloth, drinking beer from a bottle, reading dime novels, memorizing jokes out of Captain Billy's Whiz Bang, and using words like "swell" and "so's your old man" alarmed the people of Meredith Willson's comedy, while they were urged to maintain a discrete distance from the likes of Tommy Djilas whom Mayor Shinn described as a wild kid whose father was one of the day laborers living south of town.

To help protect young people from the evil influences so much present in the changing culture at the turn of the century, youth societies came into being, first within the church and then independent from ecclesiastical controls. Before Harold Hill arrived in River City the Methodist Church already had a chapter of the Epworth League. Each of the other Protestant denominations had similarly formed youth societies during the closing years of the nineteenth century. After the turn of the century Boy Scouts and Girl Scouts, 4-H Clubs, Future Farmers of America, Future Homemakers of America, and Campfire Girls would become agencies of socialization based on a Judeo-Christian ethic.

Francis E. Clark and the Society for Christian Endeavor

On 2 February 1881, the second cycle of youth ministry was born. It was revolutionary in its simplicity and yet profound in its impact. What Francis E. Clark did on that Sunday afternoon set the stage for youth groups around the world.

For several years the young pastor of Williston Church in Portland, Maine, had been looking for a way to assist the young people of his church to continue in their Christian faith after an initial salvation experience. His wife had been somewhat successful with the girls of the church through a missions oriented group which she called Mizpah Circle, but this was not enough. Contacts with a Brooklyn pastor, Theodore Cuyler, the YMCA, and the "class meeting" used by the Methodists contributed to his thinking, but still something was missing.

Francis Clark was not trained in youth ministry. His was the standard preparation for pastoral ministry, but during his formal education there were hints of the effective ministry to come. While at Dartmouth College (class of '73) and Andover Seminary (class of '76), the young man manifested both writing and oratorical skills. Though chosen one of the student speakers at his college graduation, Clark had a equal love for journalism and vacillated between the ministry and a writing career until three months before graduation. Collegiate journalistic experiences included being an editor of *The Dartmouth* and serving as a correspondent for the *Boston Globe* and the *Congregationalist*. The latter provided a contact which brought his fledgling youth society to public attention.

For five years the ministry to youth at Williston Church seemed ineffective. Though the church grew from 50 in attendance to over 400, Clark expressed frustration at the bottleneck which parents provided by allowing young people to join the church. Then, after a week of prayer and special meetings in January 1881, an idea came to him. The concept would demonstrate to parents, church leaders, and the community the capacity of young people for sincere spiritual commitments.

The idea was accountability. Clark created a society whose primary purpose was to reinforce the desire of young people to grow in their walk with God—to strengthen their Christian endeavor. Accountability took the form of a pledge which required two commitments. Every member was expected, "unless detained by some absolute necessity," to be present at every meeting and take part, "however slight" in each meeting. Then, once a month, an "experience meeting" was to be held, at which "each member shall speak concerning his progress in the Christian life for the past month." Failure to do so meant removal from "active" status in the society.[5]

Though the language of the pledge was masculine, the society was comprised of young people of both sexes. Harriet A. Clark had balked at the idea of girls speaking in front of the boys when her husband first suggested the idea but soon affirmed the wisdom of the mutual accountability.

The actual formation of the Society for Christian Endeavor took place in the pastor's home. Seventy young people heard the constitution read and signed the pledge. Officers were elected and a new chapter of youth ministry was begun.

Word of the new society spread rapidly. In October 1881 a second society was formed by Rev. C.P. Mills at Newburyport, Massachusetts. By June of the following year, six societies were known to exist. When the second conference for Christian Endeavor was held in June 1883, representatives from seven denominations were present. These included Congregational, Baptist, Free Baptist, Presbyterian, Methodist, Dutch Reformed, and "Christian" churches.

After Clark published an article about the new venture in the *Congregationalist,* requests for information flooded his office. To answer the questions which clogged the mails, the founder wrote a book, *The Children and the Church,* which was a manual for beginning new chapters. This simple tool enabled the Society to spread across

America and as far away as Foochow, China.

The number of delegates at the annual conventions dramatically outlined the multiplication of the movement. The Philadelphia convention in 1889 brought together 6,500 delegates; the Minneapolis convention of 1891 registered over 14,000 Endeavorers; while the Boston convention of 1895, only 14 years after the first meeting of the society, saw 56,435 persons attend.

Though each society was under the authority of the host church and pastor, the international conventions, regional conferences and "union" or area rallies brought an interdenominational flavor to the movement creating an interesting cross section of support. For those who were concerned with biblical values and personal piety, the pledge attracted them. For those who wished for interdenominational cooperation, the rallies and conferences served their purposes.

Denominational Youth Societies

Saturday night was Epworth League night in River City. Zaneeta Shinn, the mayor's daughter, and most of the young people ages 10-34 from respectable families of the town attended every meeting. The League was divided into three sections: the Junior Division for children ages 10-12, Intermediates included youngsters ages 13-17, while the Senior League grouped everyone from age 18 to 34 in a young adult fellowship. The Saturday night meeting was a "sociable." It was held only once a month and was designed to provide a good time for Methodist young people in a healthy environment.[6]

The normal Epworth League met on Sunday nights during the school year and emphasized the missionary efforts of the Methodist church. Evangelistic efforts and social concerns were addressed. Opportunities for personal involvement in local missions were provided through visits to hospitals, orphanages and old folks' homes. Frequently, even the Saturday night sociables had a missionary flavor as money was raised for a Methodist outreach activity.

The Epworth League, formed from a merger of five district Methodist youth societies in 1889, was the oldest denominational youth program in the United States. Baptist Young People's Union followed in 1891 and was quickly followed by denominational youth programs in the other major Protestant denominations—Westminster League (Presbyterian General Assembly) in 1891, Walther League (Missouri Synod Lutheran) in 1893, Young People's Christian Union (United Brethren) in 1894, Young People's Christian Union (United Presbyterian Church) in 1895, Keystone League (United Evangelical Church in America) in 1895, and Luther League (Intersynodical Lutheran) in 1895.

Each denominational youth program started from a grassroots effort which was then stimulated by the dramatic success of the Society for Christian Endeavor. Fearing the loss of denominational distinctives and a diffusion of denominational loyalty while seeing the potential for what they were already doing, each religious body formed its own youth society and began generating program materials. Though each of the denominational societies retained a pledge associated with membership similar to that of Christian Endeavor, the contents of the pledge changed and focused much more on denominational priorities and less on issues related to accountability in one's endeavor to live as a Christian.

The Baptist Young People's Union provides an interesting illustration of how a national denominational youth program began. The first stage was the spontaneous efforts of local churches to meet the needs of their youth. Most of the records of these are lost, yet there were primitive youth ministries in the First Baptist Church of Rochester, New York (1848), under D. E. Holtemann in Marengo, Illinois (1858), and at First Baptist Church in Troy, New York (1863), under the leadership of George C. Baldwin, D.D.[7]

The second stage began when manuals were developed in order to spread the ideas across a state or throughout the nation. Oliver W. Van Osdel, D.D., began the "Loyalist Movement" in Ottawa, Kansas, in 1886. Though the motto called for "Loyalty to Christ, in all things, at all times" the object of the movement was "to encourage the doctrinal study of the Bible, the adoption of direct proportionate giving, and missionary work." The denominational character was clear. Quickly, Van Osdel developed and published a comprehensive plan for organizing Baptist young people. Two years later the plan was adopted by Kansas Baptist State Convention.

Dr. Alexander Blackburn wrote about the "Loyalist Movement" in a national Baptist publication and soon other pastors became interested. About the same time Rev. J. M. Coon of Whitewater, Wisconsin, published "The Self-Help Handbook for Young People" and urged its use in Wisconsin Baptist churches. The manuals enabled the "technology" of youth ministry to spread.

The third stage happened when the grassroots and regional ideas were formalized into a national program. The Baptists put their organizational wheels into motion in 1889 and the following year a committee was set up to assist churches, associations and states to establish Baptist young people's groups. By the end of 1890, 14 states had held young people's meetings or had provided for such gatherings.

On 22 April 1891, a national Baptist young people's organization was established which was broad enough to include all Baptist youth groups, no matter what their name or constitutional structure. This inclusiveness was an attempt to embrace groups like Christian Endeavor which were already established in Baptist churches and incorporate them into the national organization. Yet all societies were urged to subscribe to *The Young People at Work*, the Baptist national publication, in order to provide continuity within groups with Baptist distinctives.

From this point onward, denominational allegiance became primary. Youth groups of different Protestant affiliations seldom associated with one another. This organizational separation was instrumental in the rapid spread of youth ministry. Rather than having only one youth ministry organization (Christian Endeavor) about which some pastors had doubts regarding its understanding of religious living and ecclesiastical control, the United States now had close to a dozen church-based youth ministry agencies, two of which rivaled the mother organization in size. The denominational youth societies were safe places for young people to socialize and prepare for leadership in the local church and the national denomination.

By the end of the twentieth century's third decade there was a mood of optimism about what was being accomplished in youth programs sponsored by the major denominations. Summer conference attendance, money raised for missionary projects, publication of comprehensive programming materials for the four years of high school, and generalized statements for leadership development were cited by denominational publications as reasons for confidence.[8]

Reports such as these were justified. Denominational involvement in ministry to young people had increased dramatically from the humble beginnings of a few years before. Community, state, and national organizations had been developed and many were staffed with capable and concerned adult leaders, many of whom were paid for their efforts. The place most likely for youth specialists to be employed, however, was in the denominational publishing houses.

A blizzard of printed materials swept from denominational presses. Following the example of Christian Endeavor, they marketed training materials which provided step-by-step descriptions of every aspect of the youth program. Program materials quickly followed, allowing a local youth society to put together a variety of Sunday evening meetings with a minimum of work on the part of students or adult leaders.

With this direct link between youth societies and denominational headquarters, programs became increasingly generic. It was simply impossible to be in touch with the local needs of thousands of young people's societies and tens of thousands of adolescents. The consequent result was that denominational youth workers, influenced by denominational priorities, began establishing the agenda for youth societies rather than local pastors or adult sponsors. World missions, stewardship, social issues, and denominational distinctives dominated the topics for weekly meetings.

Activities in which denominational youth workers participated were effective. Camps, conferences, and area-wide meetings were too great an effort for volunteer youth workers to accomplish by themselves and so into this vacuum stepped professional youth workers. Two campgrounds in North Carolina, Montreat for Presbyterians and Ridgecrest for the Southern Baptists, were examples of locations where specialists assumed responsibility for national and regional programming.

Despite the growing superstructure in the young people's society "industry," there is little evidence that local church programs shared the excitement or dynamism of denominational or interdenominational efforts. Robert and Helen Lynd, in their classic study published in 1929, of one Midwestern town, concluded that the young people's meeting had remained "fundamentally unchanged since the 1890s" while high school extracurricular activities had become conveyers of social prestige.[9] Katherine Evelyn Niles came to similar conclusions after studying 18 young people's societies in Portland, Oregon. In an article published that same year she concluded "their forms and techniques, which remain much the same as they were in the beginning (i.e. the last decade of the nineteenth century) are no longer suited to modern society."[10]

The clearest indicator that church-based youth societies were losing their influence over middle-class young people was the rise of youth associations which emphasized wholesome activities designed to build character in boys and girls. These agencies, such as Boy and Girl Scouts, Camp Fire Girls, 4-H Clubs, and Boys Clubs of America, had little to do with the church but shared an ethic based on a Judeo-

Christian heritage. These activity-oriented clubs required young people to have enough free time to participate in the club functions and sufficient financial resources to pay for the uniforms, equipment and activities. Free time and discretionary cash were not available to the poorer classes of people and so the youth movements of the second cycle remained solidly within the middle class.

Crisis: The Scopes Monkey Trial

While youth societies remained static in what they did and how they did it, the public high school made radical changes. Schools were larger. By the 1929-1930 school year nearly 5 million students were enrolled in secondary schools. This was 51.3 percent of the age group between 14 and 17 years of age.

High school curriculums changed as well. Instead of concentrating exclusively on the old liberal arts curriculum, high schools of the 1920s were including courses which were socially relevant, such as business education, agriculture, household arts, music, and physical education. Along with this "progressive" education came a decrease in the influence of religion and an increase in the sway that science and specifically the concept of evolution had upon the curriculum.

The most important change was the role which the high school played in the community. The school, rather than the church, had become the focal point of community life. Education functioned as the religion of day. Salvation from life's problems (no longer viewed as sin) was acquired through knowledge applied to life. Teachers served as priests. Science was the Bible.

Even in Meredith Willson's River City the change was evident. The community "sociable" at the conclusion of the musical was set, not in a church, but in the high school assembly room. The changing nature of the public high school had set the stage for the decline of the youth society and with it the second stage in youth ministry.

It is fitting that the crisis which brought to a conclusion the second cycle of youth ministry found its context in the high school science education in Tennessee, with the key role being played by an aging William Jennings Bryan. The former presidential candidate was a staunch opponent of the teachings of evolution and in his waning years traveled extensively addressing the issue.

When the state of Tennessee, influenced by a ground swell of support from fundamentalist Protestants, passed a law which forbade the teaching of evolution in public schools, the American Civil Liberties Union offered publicly to finance a test case of the law. Even though school was already out for the summer, John Thomas Scopes, a substitute science teacher agreed to be charged with the violation of the law in Dayton, Tennessee. The stage was set for one of the most highly publicized trials of the twentieth century.

Clarence Darrow, the foremost criminal lawyer of his day, and Dudley Field Malone were the lawyers for the defense financed by the ACLU. Bryan, at the urging and support of the World's Christian Fundamentals Association, agreed to act as prosecuting attorney. For 11 days in the heat of July 1925 the nation followed newspaper accounts of the drama in what came to be known as the Scopes Monkey Trial. The trial climaxed when Darrow called Bryan to the witness stand. The aging statesman, wearied by his many years of crusading and slowed by diabetes proved no match for the younger man. Wilting in the summer heat, Bryan was made a laughingstock by the media which covered the trial and along with Bryan, the belief in the authority of the Bible became a scandal.

Though John Scopes was convicted and fined $100 by the jury, his conviction was later reversed by the State Supreme Court on a technicality. The impact on the credibility of Bible believers across the nation seemed to have been destroyed. Fundamentalists were relegated to the intellectual scrap pile. Science as taught in the public school had replaced the Bible as preached in the church. The very existence of youth ministry was in jeopardy.

Conclusion

The people of River City, while being the creation of a playwright, were typical of the environment in which the second cycle of Protestant youth ministry flourished and then floundered. The Epworth League which had been stimulated by Christian Endeavor and put down roots in River City was part of the wave of church-based young people's societies which had swept the nation starting in 1881. But by the summer of 1912, after 30 years of helping young people learn skills of church leadership and personal piety, the denominational youth societies had passed their prime and parents were looking for something else to keep their children "moral after school."

The boys' band which "Professor" Harold Hill proposed filled that need and captured the dynamics of the youth associations which came into being during the early years of the twentieth century. It was non-sectarian and yet shared the values of church people. The band was limited to children whose parents could afford uniforms and band instruments or who were motivated enough to earn money and pay for the required equipment themselves.

If there was a tether which held young people's movements to the church, it was the desire by parents to have their children discover God and the truths of the Bible. Scouting organizations and 4-H Clubs were excellent activities but they were not active in teaching the Bible or calling young people to Christian conversion. But when the Scopes Monkey Trial made a scandal out of the evangelical faith, it appeared as if the era of Christian youth ministry had come to an end. Now it was time for the public educational system to assume the responsibility for building the character of the nation's youth.

---

1. Meredith Willson, *The Music Man* (New York: G.P. Putnam's Sons, 1958).

2. Lawrence A. Cremin, *American Education: The Metropolitan Experience, 1876-1980* (New York: Harper and Row Publishers, 1988).

3. George M. Marsden, *Fundamentalism and American Culture* (New York: Oxford University Press, 1980), 102.

4. Paolo E. Coletta, *William Jennings Bryan: Political Puritan, 1915-1925* (Lincoln: University of Nebraska Press, 1969), 105.

5. W. Knight Chaplin, *Francis E. Clark: Founder of the Christian Endeavor Society* (London: The British Christian Endeavor Union [1927], 30.

6. J. Warren Smith, "Youth Ministry in American Methodism's Mission." *Methodist History* (19 June 1981), 224-230.

7. John Wesley Conley, *History of the Baptist Young People's Union of America* (Philadelphia: The Griffith and Rowland Press, 1913), 16.

8. Mark H. Senter III, "The Youth for Christ Movement as an Educational Agency and Its Impact upon Protestant Churches: 1931-1979" (Ph.D. Dissertation, Loyola: University of Chicago, 1989), 96-97.

9. Robert S. Lynd and Helen Merrill Lynd, *Middletown: A Study in American Culture* (New York: Harcourt, Brace, and World, Inc., 1929), 216-7, 398.

10. Katherine Evelyn Niles, "A Survey and Critique of Young People's Societies," *Religious Education* (June 1929), 534. Parenthentical information supplied.

CHAPTER 8

Reunion at Rydell High:
Reaching Youth for Christ (1935-1967)

W elcome Back: Rydell High, Class of '59," read the large sign trimmed in green and brown. It could have been a class reunion anywhere in the United States and have looked very much the same. Former cheerleaders, honor society students, and athletes, along with that majority of average students, gathered to see if life after high school had been kind to their classmates.

But the Rydell High School reunion was different. Instead of focusing on the leaders of the student body, Jim Jacobs modeled the story after his experience as a "greaser" at Chicago's Taft High School and used the musical *Grease* to tell an idealized story about the people who never bothered to show up for a class reunion.

The movie version, released in 1978, depicted a flashback to their senior year. It featured John Travolta as Danny, the leader of the Burger Palace Boys and the archetype of a 1950s greaser, and Olivia Newton-John playing the role of Sandy, a sweet, wholesome, "Gidget" type of girl who has just arrived in the community and is about to identify with the high school's "in crowd" but instead is attracted to Danny's charm.

The setting for Grease is the apathy of the 1950s. A nation wearied by a World War and the Korean Conflict has enjoyed the security and conservatism of the Eisenhower years. High school students were divided into three groups. The first was student body leaders, which consisted of athletes, cheerleaders, and student body officers. The second was a collection of people called "greasers" who flaunted their rejection of the symbols of status in the high school community.

Though the two groups varied from school to school, the combined groups seldom exceeded 30 percent of the student body.

The last and by far the largest group in the public high school of the 1950s was the nameless group which existed between the two cliques which have been stereotyped so often in movies like *Grease*. These average students were like Sandy who merely wanted to have friends and a place to belong in the social structure of Rydell High. These students were the primary participants in the third cycle of youth ministry. Though Young Life and to a lesser extent Youth for Christ Clubs attempted to attract student body leaders (they seldom targeted the "greasers"), the ordinary participant was drawn from the middle section of the student body.

The late 1950s to the late 1960s was the high point of the parachurch contribution to the third cycle of youth ministry. As in the previous two cycles, ministry agencies came into being in the context of social disruption, solidified as one, or in this case two organizations, moved to the front before their strategies were imitated by the church, and ultimately lost their cutting edge of effectiveness.

The Depression and World War II
Rydell High School was a product of two major events of the twentieth century—the Great Depression and World War II. The high school experience was a relatively new episode in America when the stock market collapsed on "Black Thursday," 20 October 1929. The number of young people enrolled in secondary education had doubled each decade of the century until 4.4 million high school students filled publicly financed classrooms that fall day.[1]

The 1920s had been a period of social liberation for young people, but just when adolescence began to be fun, the Depression came. Survival became the concern of both parent and child. In some industries unemployment ran as high as 30-40 percent. Banks closed. Homes, farms, and businesses were lost to foreclosure. With a scarcity of jobs, young people stayed in school longer and by the end of the decade high school enrollments had increased by another 50 percent to 6.6 million.

The quality of high school education improved as the adolescent population increased. One trend concerned conservative Protestants, however. Religion in general and Bible teaching more specifically was being removed from the classroom. By 1941, 12 states, mostly in the

East, required Bible reading in the public schools, while an equal number in the West and Midwest had outlawed the practice. This trend was finalized when the United States Supreme Court, in the *McCollum v. Board of Education* decision of 1948, held that a program permitting religious instruction within public schools during school hours, and excusing students attending such a class from a part of the secular school schedule, was unconstitutional.

The dual movements of students out of the home and into the high school while religious instruction was being removed from the public school left a vacuum of religious and moral instruction. The trend which gradually increased during the period set the stage for a response on the part of Christian adults.

World War II was the second disruption of the social order in the nation. The attack on Pearl Harbor brought the United States into the war and rallied the nation around one massive task — a military victory on two fronts. Fifteen million servicemen and women went to war. With a shortage of men on the homefront, thousands of women went to work in defense plants. The economy, though military in focus, was functioning at or near capacity. There was not much time to relax or socialize except as a means to prepare for the war effort.

The impact of the war on youth ministry was twofold. From the inception of church youth groups, leadership for youth societies had come from young adults in the church. Fellowships included people in their early and middle twenties who in turn served the role of sponsors for the younger groups. When the war came, this pool of leaders enlisted in the military, leaving the church to find a new group of adults to reach young people for Christ.

The war created a crusade spirit. Young Americans who entered the war discovered their abilities to lead and drew on the resources of their homeland to rid the world of the fascist threat of Germany and imperialist ambitions of Japan. With victories on both fronts, American service personnel returned home convinced they had saved the world. Soon Christian young adults were ready to participate in another crusade—a campaign to change the spiritual convictions of the nation and the world. The worldly wise young believers returned home to lead the church in cooperative efforts of evangelism.

Into this setting came the Youth for Christ movement, a scattered assortment of young adults who took as their task the evangelization of their peers and those young people a few years younger than themselves. Only later, as the war was drawing to a close, did one group of these youth evangelists band together and call themselves Youth for Christ International.

Initial Strategy: Youth Rallies

For Washakie High School in Worland, Wyoming, 22 November 1952 was an exciting day. Led by halfback Dick Harkins' four touchdowns, the Worland squad downed rival Douglas, 26–13, to become the state class A football champion.

The thrill was even greater for Wendy Collins, Youth for Christ Director for southern Montana and northern Wyoming. The night before the victory, 14 of those gridders had gathered in the home of their team physician, Dr. L.S. Anderson, for a time of Bible study and prayer. Then on the evening of the championship victory, 16 newly crowned state football champions lined the platform at the Worland Youth for Christ rally to give testimony of their personal relationship to Jesus Christ.

An isolated occurrence? Not really. By 1952, thousands of communities, large and small, were feeling the impact of the Youth for Christ movement. *Newsweek* reported on the most dramatic evidence of the movement's success when it described the Memorial Day Youth for Christ Rally attended by a reported 65,000 "sweater-topped bobby soxers, adult civilians and servicemen" at Chicago's Soldier Field. By 1959, there were similar rallies covering as many as 1,450 cities across the nation.[2]

As World War II moved toward an Allied victory, America was ready to celebrate. Ten years of depression followed by six years of war had put a damper on the nation's capacity to enjoy itself. All that was needed was an excuse and a bit of organizational "know-how." The Youth for Christ movement provided both.

The excuse was captured in the "Youth for Christ" slogan, as enthusiastic young ministers from a fundamentalist tradition became concerned about the moral and spiritual condition of America's youth. Where the phrase was first used is difficult to determine. According to the movement's earliest historian, Mel Larson, the motto was first used in 1934 when Paul Guiness, a young Australian evangelist, used the title at a Sunday night youth meeting held in a theater in Brantford, Ontario.

Oscar T. Gillan apparently was the first person in the United States to use the slogan in any official manner. In 1938, Gillan's

Detroit based "Voice of Christian Youth" used "Youth for Christ" as their motto. The year 1940 found Jack Wyrtzen, an insurance man turned evangelist, using the phrase for rallies in New York's Times Square. By 1943 Roger Malsbary had launched regular "Youth for Christ" evangelistic meetings in Indianapolis. Soon St. Louis, Chicago, and a legion of other cities picked up on the theme and the idea of Saturday night rallies.

As the war wound down, the response to the Youth for Christ meetings increased. Thirty thousand crowded into Chicago Stadium for a "Victory Rally" in the fall of 1944. Twenty thousand packed Madison Square Garden for one of Jack Wyrtzen's "Word of Life" rallies as another 10,000 people were turned away. Minneapolis drew 7,000 to Municipal Stadium on two occasions while Kiel Auditorium in St. Louis seated 5,000 people to hear the Gospel focused on bringing youth to Christ.

The movement spread so effectively and rapidly that one might look for a master strategy formulated by a few people and implemented by others in their organizations. But such was not true. The youth rally idea was a grassroots movement which spread like a grass fire on a parched August day.

Lloyd T. Bryant and Youth Centers

Lloyd T. Bryant of New York City appears to have been the originator of a youth-targeted mass evangelization effort in the United States. After graduating from New York's National Bible Institute in 1932, Dr. Will Houghton of Manhattan's Calvary Baptist Church named Bryant as the church's first full-time minister to youth. His motto was "Training through Participation" and student involvement in evangelistic efforts was the key. His young people, ages 12 through the mid-30s, were involved in hospital visitation, radio work, literature distribution, and open-air preaching. Bryant would use just about any means to get high school and college-age youth under the sound of the Gospel. Popular speakers, symposiums, debates, dinners, conferences, and retreats were all part of his strategy. A decade later, Bryant would be so innovative as to open the nation's first "Christian Youth Theatre" in the Times Square district of New York.

Youth centers were at the heart of Bryant's approach to youth ministry. Using his own New York Youth Christian Center on West 57th Street as a base, Bryant was instrumental in developing 14 or 15 youth centers throughout the East by 1936. When their number reached 40, Bryant founded the Association of Christian Youth Movements of America to spread the ministry.

Starting in the late 1920s Bryant sponsored three evangelistic meetings each week for seven years in Manhattan's Christian and Alliance Tabernacle, placing the gatherings on weeknights so as not to conflict with normal gatherings of churches in the community. Outstanding speakers and gospel musicians were featured along with "unusual" testimonies from young and older people who witnessed to God's saving and keeping power. Lively singing as well as a youth choir and orchestra added to the appeal of the meeting.

There was another factor contributing to the success of Bryant's youth centers. The Depression had left young people few options for social life after school. Youth center evangelistic meetings were a socially acceptable manner to get out of the house during the week. Bryant's ministry met both social and spiritual needs.

Percy Crawford and Radio

More than anyone else, Percy Bartimus Crawford influenced the style of youth evangelists during the 1930s and 1940s. Reacting against the boring religious meetings he had attended in his childhood, Percy came to be described as the "master of the seven-minute sermon," and insisted on a fast-moving, lively service. Every rally was entertaining. Even the quartet traveling with the evangelist knew to laugh on cue to stimulate audience response.

Crawford's background, like many of those who led the Youth for Christ movement, was economically deprived. Abusiveness on the part of Crawford's father caused the teenager from Minnedosa, Manitoba, to leave home to seek his fortune in Southern California. Instead of material wealth he discovered a spiritual dimension to his life and by 1931 had made his way through the Bible Institute of Los Angeles, University of California at Los Angeles, Wheaton College, and Westminster Seminary in Philadelphia.

When the Missionary Board of the Presbytery of Philadelphia asked the recent seminary graduate to assume the responsibility for the dilapidated Albert Barnes Memorial Presbyterian Church, the young visionary took to the streets in order to reach the community. Outdoor meetings held on the steps of the downtown church drew hundreds of people. Then the young pastor began the "Young People's Church of the Air" in 1931. The ministry multiplied rapidly and soon the broadcast had a network of 275 stations.

Radio forced a discipline on public meetings. Competition from variety shows and radio drama forced the rapid pacing of the rallies. "Dead air" would weary listeners so meetings moved with the precision of a Swiss clock. The response to Crawford's evangelistic appeals suggested the validity of this new concept in youth ministry.

Invitations to speak at evangelistic rallies followed. His staccato speaking style became a standard on the rally circuit. As Youth for Christ evangelistic meetings multiplied during the '40s, Crawford traveled and spoke on a regular basis. Mel Larson suggests that "unconsciously many Y.F.C. speakers patterned their messages after Crawford's preaching." Among those influenced were a budding evangelist named Billy Graham and a New York insurance man named Jack Wyrtzen.

Jack Wyrtzen and Saturday Night Rallies

If there was one person at the center of the Youth for Christ movement, it was Casper John Von Wyrtzen, better known as Jack Wyrtzen. The assessment of Gil Dodds, the world-class miler and 1944 Sullivan-Award winner who gave his testimony at rallies across the nation, was that there would have been no Youth for Christ movement as it was known in the mid-1940s without Jack Wyrtzen. In all probability he was correct.

Born in 1913, Jack spent his childhood in Brooklyn where he developed the musical interests which provided the setting for his involvement in the Jamaica High School dance band. His interest in horses and sports combined with the trombone talent were instrumental in Wyrtzen's joining the 101st Cavalry Band. It was there as a young adult that the personable young man met George Schilling who would later be instrumental in Wyrtzen's spiritual conversion.

Though his parents were Universalists, young Wyrtzen did not associate with any church consistently. Thus, when a spiritual turbulence was aroused within him during his late teenage years and a Christian conversion took place, Jack turned not to the church but to a group of friends, and together they sought to discover and serve God, calling themselves Chi Beta Alpha. From this group came Word of Life Fellowship (Wyrtzen's organization), Brandt Reed's High School Evangelism Fellowship, and a director for the already existing Pocket Testament League in the person of Alfred Kunz.

Though all of the young men enjoyed preaching, Jack Wyrtzen emerged as the most effective in attracting and holding audiences.

Like his conversion experience, his audiences were not conventional. Prisons, rescue missions, open-air meetings, and evangelistic banquets were all sounding boards for the budding youth evangelist. Stimulated by Percy Crawford, Jack and the "fraternity" began radio broadcasts beamed at youth over Brooklyn's WBBC in 1940.

The boldest steps in those early days were 28-year-old Wyrtzen's twin decisions to try Saturday night rallies in New York's bustling Times Square and to broadcast the evangelistic messages over 50,000-watt WHN, one of America's most powerful independent radio stations. Two hundred fifty people attended the first "Word of Life" broadcast. Within four months the numbers would swell to 1,000 each Saturday night.

Within five years the Saturday night rally broadcasts were packing the major auditoriums of New York City and the nation—20,000 jammed into Madison Square Garden, Carnegie Hall was packed with youth and adults each week, 3,000 gathered in Chicago, 4,000 came to rallies in Philadelphia, and 5,000 attended in Boston.[3] Three thousand boarded a Hudson River Dayline boat for a cruise. At the conclusion of each meeting an invitation was issued by the youthful evangelist for young people to "come to Christ." Weekly scores, even hundreds, responded, walking forward to be counseled by a battery of volunteer youth workers.

Wyrtzen's ministry expanded after World War II. Evangelistic tours to Mexico and the British Isles were followed by the purchase of a resort for young people in upper New York State. But it was the Saturday night rallies that were most frequently imitated by youth workers across the nation.

Jim Rayburn and the Young Life Campaign

Jim Rayburn stood in stark contrast to Jack Wyrtzen. Whereas Wyrtzen was raised in Brooklyn, Rayburn's home was Newton, Kansas, or wherever in the West his evangelist father planted his tent for meetings. Wyrtzen's parents were Universalists; Rayburn's were Presbyterians. Wyrtzen began evangelistic work at age 19, while Rayburn was weaned on his father's evangelistic meetings and was imitating his father as early as age two-and-a-half. Wyrtzen had to drop out of high school during the Depression, by contrast Rayburn was a graduate of Kansas State University and Dallas Theological Seminary. The most evident difference was in speaking styles. Wyrtzen used a rapid-fire delivery while Rayburn pioneered a conversational approach to evangelistic communication. Yet as different as the two men were, Wyrtzen and Rayburn serve as bookends for the Youth for Christ movement's approach to youth ministry.

Though Jim Rayburn is best-known for the incarnational club strategy which he pioneered, his early efforts utilized a mass evangelism approach to youth ministry. The name of the organization he founded, Young Life Campaign, was borrowed from the National Young Life Campaign of Great Britain after founders, Rev. and Mrs. Frederick Wood, visited Dallas Seminary and described their British ministry. With their permission, the 30-year-old Rayburn used the campaign motif to promote week-long evangelistic efforts in the Texas towns of Galveston, Houston, Dallas, Fort Worth, and Weatherford. On 25 February 1941, a Dallas newspaper proclaimed "Young Life Pep Rally Draws 2,000." Rayburn's approach was beginning to look like the efforts of Bryant, Crawford, and Wyrtzen. The ingredients of these rallies were similar to those in the East—large auditorium, enthusiastic music, and preaching which appealed to young people. Yet there were two differences. Rayburn's rallies were attended nearly exclusively by young people whereas meetings addressed by the others had an adult population as high as 50 percent of the audience. Without the adults and the donations they made through campaign offerings, rallies never became a means to provide financial support for the movement. This fact alone may have given Rayburn the freedom to scrap the mass approach to youth evangelism in favor of a club- and camp-based strategy by the mid-1940s.

The second difference was that radio was never a significant part of Rayburn's ministry. Whether this omission was by design or by oversight is not clear. Rally-based youth ministries needed radio coverage to spread the news of meetings and events. Rayburn seldom used the media in that manner. It was not part of his vision. Instead, he preferred to feature what was happening in Young Life clubs. Consequently, the Young Life Campaign rallies peaked in 1943 and thereafter played a secondary role to the blossoming club program and the camping ministries which became part of the movement with the purchase of Star Ranch in 1945.

Torrey Johnson and the National Vision

A person who taught Greek at a seminary would not seem to be the most likely candidate to serve as a leader in the Youth for Christ movement, and yet Torrey Maynard Johnson, teacher at Northern

Baptist Seminary, became the first president of Youth for Christ International. At age 36 Johnson was a product of Chicago—Carl Schurz High School, Northwestern University for two years, then Wheaton College, and Northern Baptist Seminary; finally he became the pastor of Midwest Bible Church, which claimed to be the fastest growing church in Chicago during the early 1940s.

Though Johnson was an evangelist in his own right, his contribution to the movement was his national vision for evangelizing youth. This dream began in Chicago where he began a radio program which became "Songs in the Night," and was later turned over to a young pastor in suburban Western Springs whose name was Billy Graham. Evangelistic boat cruises similar to those sponsored by Jack Wyrtzen were hosted by Midwest Bible Church. Twenty-two hundred young people crowded on board. Invitations to speak at evangelistic meetings flooded his desk. One of these invitations was to speak at Roger Malsbary's Indianapolis Youth for Christ rally. "This can happen in Chicago," was the guest speaker's thought.

Happen it did. For 21 weeks in the spring of 1944 Chicago's Orchestra Hall was packed with over 2,000 young people of all ages. WCFL, Chicago's powerful "Voice of Labor," broadcast the Saturday evening extravaganza. Then on 21 October 1944, Chicago Stadium hosted a "Victory Rally" sponsored by Johnson's Chicagoland Youth for Christ. Twenty-eight thousand people attended to witness the same type of high-powered program as Wyrtzen would sponsor in Madison Square Garden a little over a year later.

The movement gathered size and momentum. Torrey Johnson and Robert Cook's book, *Reaching Youth for Christ,* did for Youth for Christ what Francis E. Clark's book, *The Children and the Church,* had done for Christian Endeavor 60 years earlier—it took what was happening in one location and briefly explained how it could be done elsewhere. Letters again covered Johnson's desk. The need for a national organization seemed apparent.

At the invitation of Arthur W. McKee, director of the Winona Lake (Indiana) Bible Conference Grounds, Roger Malsbary, Torrey Johnson, and a half dozen other youth leaders met in August 1944 to plot a strategy. By November the group had expanded to include 35 men from 21 cities who met and elected Torrey Johnson chairman of a "Temporary Youth for Christ International Committee." Offices were set up in Chicago to promote the first Youth for Christ International Week at Winona Lake during the last week of July 1945.

When 22 July 1945 arrived, 42 delegates representing different rallies were present at the Winona Lake Conference Grounds. A roll call of those attending read like a who's who of the leadership of evangelicalism for the years to come. Most prominent among those present was a young pastor/evangelist named Billy Graham, the first nonclerical employee of the fledgling organization.

None of the other evangelists mentioned in this chapter were present, however. Wyrtzen distrusted structures other than his own. Crawford was headed in a different direction as he prepared to found the King's College. Rayburn had already left the rally emphasis in favor of club and camp work. The net result was that, although Youth for Christ International was voted into being on 29 July 1945 and a structure was provided for the movement which would provide a tidal wave of missionary and evangelistic ministries focused on young people, organizational unity was not and never would be achieved.

Though Torrey Johnson was an outstanding evangelist in his own right, the contribution he made to the movement was more visionary and political in nature. It took a skilled hand to bring together such a diverse group of Protestant fundamentalists who still had a tendency to distrust bureaucratic structures, which many of them viewed as being one of the factors which brought about the slide of mainline denominations into theological liberalism a generation earlier.

A Sense of Revival

As the decade of the 1950s began "revival" was the dominant theme of the evangelical church in general and the Youth for Christ movement in particular. *Youth for Christ* magazine released a quotation from the President of the United States under the caption, "Truman Longs for Revival." The President was reported to have said, "Many times during the past decade the conviction has come to me with increasing force that a revival of the spirit of old-fashioned religion is what the world needs most."[4]

Dr. Harold J. Ockenga, pastor of Boston's Park Street Church, told the 1949 midsummer Youth for Christ Convention that it was time for a spiritual revival. By the following March, Ockenga reported in *Christian Life* magazine that "America's revival is breaking" followed by the proclamation in April that "Revival is here."[5]

With youth evangelists in the forefront of the spiritual awakening, the revival took two forms. The best-known had to do with the evangelistic preaching of such people as Billy Graham (in Los Ange-

117

les and Boston), Bob Jones (Vancouver, British Columbia), Merv Rosell (Des Moines), and others. The response to the invitations was so great that the word "revival" was appropriate.

Billy Graham's eight-week campaign sponsored by "Christ for Greater Los Angeles" in the fall of 1949 brought the revival to national attention. More than a third of a million people flocked to hear the youthful evangelist in a tent which seated 6,280 people. Thousands responded including people from the movie industry. The resulting publicity was spectacular. *Time, Life, Newsweek,* The Associated Press, The United Press, The International News Service, *London Daily Mail,* and many local papers carried the reports of the hand of God working in Los Angeles. The reports were instrumental in the spread of the mid-century awakening.

At the same time a different type of revival was happening on the campuses of the nation. The best known was the spiritual movement which took place at Wheaton College for 38 hours between 7 p.m. on Wednesday, 8 February 1950, until 9 a.m. on Friday, 10 February. In a quiet, at times unemotional manner, students stood to give testimony of God's working in their lives. Many confessed sin and asked for forgiveness from fellow students. There was no preaching and little singing as students and faculty members waited their turns to witness to the working of the Holy Spirit in their lives.

Huntington College, Greenville College, Pasadena College, North Park College, John Brown University, Houghton College, Asbury College, and Northern Baptist Seminary experienced similar workings of the Spirit. Similar revivals were reported on the high school level at Wheaton Academy (near Wheaton College) and in Columbus, Ohio, where under the encouragement of Hi-B.A. (High School Born-Againers) several hundred junior and senior high school students met before school twice a week to pray.

The revival of 1950, especially as it related to youth ministry, was short-lived though its impact continued for years to come. By the fall of 1950 all that was being reported in Christian periodicals were evangelistic meetings which continued to be described as revivals but which lacked the spectacular dynamics of the previous year. Yet no one whose life had been touched by a special working of the Spirit of God could return to life as usual. From the ranks of young people involved in the revivals of 1950 came many of the leaders for the youth and missionary movements which emerged in the following years.

Where Did All the Rallies Go?

Youth for Christ rallies had their most effective years in the late 1940s. As the apathy of the Eisenhower years took hold of the culture, the weekly Saturday evening evangelistic effort went through a period of decline only to be revived by student participation in a national quizzing program and talent contests in the late 1950s and early 1960s before being discontinued as part of the national strategy in the late 1960s.

If the *Minneapolis Star* report that 1,450 cities had Youth for Christ rallies in 1949 was accurate, the decrease to 255 chartered rallies reported to the organization's 1958 Mid-Winter Convention was dramatic. Even granting the difference between newspaper "hype" and the conservative numbers which may have resulted from an official chartering procedure, which was resisted at the grassroots of this entrepreneurial-type organization, the decrease was significant.

The next five years saw a reversal of the number of chartered rallies reported until the numbers peaked in 1963 with 327. Then the slide began again with the number reported in 1967 reaching a low of 232 before the rally concept was discontinued in all but a few cities. Some of these rallies later left Youth for Christ to form the Youth Evangelism Association.

The number of people attending the Saturday night meetings was similarly declining. Saturday night evangelistic rallies were not the attraction they once were. Times had changed and so would the methodology of youth workers.

Another Strategy

Sandy Dumbrowski was just the type of girl to whom Saturday night Youth for Christ rallies might have appealed had Rydell High School had a rally nearby. If Grease had been set in the 1940s or early 1950s there would have been a distinct possibility that Sandy and possibly even Danny Zuko may have been invited to a YFC rally. The Saturday night rally was on the wane by 1959 and in Chicago where Jim Jacobs, the creator of Grease, had attended high school, the weekly rally was but a shadow of the glory days of the 1940s.

It is questionable if the rally idea ever reach the "greasers" of the high school society. For that matter, with a few highly publicized exceptions like future Olympic decathlon champion Rafer Johnson and the football team of Washakie High School, not many student body leaders were included in the thousands of young people who

119

attended the rallies. Most were just the average teenagers who were by far the majority of the high school population.

For the people who look only at the rallies as characteristic of the third cycle of youth ministry, the cycle would seem far shorter than the fifty-year cycles previously observed. In reality the rallies merely set the stage for and gave visibility to a much more influential form of youth ministry.

Already an alternative was being employed in the Young Life movement. It was the high school club. Youth for Christ had used clubs starting in 1950 as a delivery system to get high schoolers to attend rallies but as the larger meetings began to loose their luster a club strategy which could be the primary tool for evangelism on the public school campus began to take shape.

---

1. To put the 1929 high school enrollment into perspective, the number of students attending public secondary schools in 1989 was approximately 12.4 million or about three times the enrollment of 1929. Had the rate of growth continued from the first three decades of the century there would be more high school students today than there are citizens of the United States (318.4 million students).

2. "Wanted: A Miracle of Good Weather and the 'Youth for Christ' Rally Got It," *Newsweek* (11 June 1945): 84; "Youth for Christ Now Covers 1,450 Cities," *Minneapolis Star* (12 February 1949), 8.

3. Jack Wyrtzen remembers these rallies to have been better attended: 15,000 in Philadephia and 16,000 in Boston Garden.

4. "Truman Longs for Revival," *Christian Life Magazine* 12 (November 1949), 33.

5. Harold John Ockenga, "America's Revival Is Breaking," *Christian Life* 12 (March 1950): 20-22f; Harold J. Ockenga, *Youth for Christ* (April 1950): 8-10ff.

CHAPTER 9

Behind the Scenes at Rydell High: Teens Telling Teens (1935-1987)

E ven if Jim Jacobs, the creator of *Grease*, gave no hint of religious activity at Rydell High or YFC rallies on Saturday nights, Taft High School, after which Rydell was fashioned, had a active Youth for Christ Club in 1959. Weekly club meetings were used to stimulate interest in the Saturday night rallies held at historic Moody Church on Chicago's Near North side.

It was not that greasers were not wanted, it was just that young people, like adults, tend to invite friends and natural acquaintances to religious activities. Thus it was that clubs consisting primarily of middle-of-the-road high school students focused on telling other middle-of-the-road high schoolers about club meetings and rallies but seldom reached beyond into other social groupings within the school.

The opportunities for one teenager to tell another teenager about Christ were enormous. The baby boomers were reaching high school age amid the turmoil caused by the launching of Sputnik I into earth orbit by the Soviet Union and the corresponding fear on the part of many that Communist technology might bury the United States. Yet the rally strategies which had flowered in the summertime of the late 1940s had faded in the autumn of the late 1950s. In its place had blossomed an array of parachurch club programs designed to provide an incarnational presence on the high school campus.

Incarnational Strategy: High School Clubs

While large evangelistic meetings which appealed to youth were capturing the attention of both the popular and religious press in the

1940s, another approach to youth ministry was beginning to happen. In apparently unrelated settings across the country, adults who shared a concern for young people began experimenting with a form of youth ministry which outlived the Saturday night rally.

In Chicago, for example, as one glances through the pages of *Schurzone 1941*, the annual yearbook of Carl Schurz High School, page 112 is distinct. Pictured are 21 students and two faculty sponsors of the Miracle Book Club. The description of the club calls it a "strictly non-sectarian" organization which met on Friday afternoons in a conveniently located church. The club, however, was not an isolated phenomenon. It was a chapter of a national club program based in Oakland, California, which was founded some eight years before.

Two years earlier in Long Beach, California, high schooler Bob Hopkins was invited to attend a Dunamis Club. He had recently made a spiritual commitment to Jesus Christ through the influence of two sailors associated with the Navigators, an organization founded by Dawson Trotman, so he consented. The Dunamis meetings centered on the memorization of Bible passages. To most people these activities may have seemed dull but not to the students involved. Even parents had a difficult time believing their children would get up early in the morning just to study the Bible in preparation for the club meetings. It was something to which they were not accustomed in their churches.

Even earlier a ministry to high school students modeled after an Australian group called Crusaders was begun by Noel Palmer of Canada's Inter Varsity Christian Fellowship. At the suggestion of Howard Guinness the work was begun in Victoria, British Columbia and Toronto in 1931, to evangelize high school students and channel them into Inter Varsity chapters on university campuses.

Across the continent, John Miller began High Light Clubs for high schoolers in Washington, D.C., during 1942. The reason was simple. He knew some kids who wanted to grow in their Christian faith. Apparently something was missing in their family and church experience. Soon others heard about the idea and wanted clubs in their schools as well. In time four clubs met in homes on weeknights to study the Bible. There was little outreach to students who did not share their spiritual convictions, but along with a friend, Wade Seaford, Miller led the clubs and helped students bring meaning to their faith.

"Ever attend a meeting on a bus?" asked Kansas City's Al Metsker in a 1949 *Youth for Christ* magazine article. Most people have not. Yet for Bible clubbers in Kansas City the experience was common. Following the Supreme Court's McCollum decision removing religious instruction from public schools, innovative measures were employed by those Christians who wanted to maintain a Christian presence on the high school campus. Consequently, a school bus was bought for $4,000 and fitted like a clubhouse for the "Youth on the Beam" clubs of the city.

The common denominator of these stories is an innovation which began to happen in youth work during the 1930s and 1940s. High-school-based Bible clubs began springing up with the express purpose of becoming an incarnational presence for Christ on the public high school campus. Without ecclesiastical roots, the clubs came to be known as "parachurch" agencies from the Greek preposition "para" which means "alongside." Club leaders considered themselves to be alongside and thus complementary to the church. Many clubs were the response of one person to a perceived need. Others were initiated by local committees or people affiliated with agencies whose primary function was to conduct Saturday night rallies. For the most part these Bible clubs were initiated by church members outside the domain of the church. Yet the methodology and curricular approach would influence church youth ministry for years to come.

Evelyn M. McClusky and the Miracle Book Club

In a movement as diverse as that which spawned the rallies and clubs of the second third of the century and in a nation as sprawling as the United States, it would be folly to suggest that one club gave birth to the other Bible clubs which dotted the land. Yet one high school club did originate earlier than any other in the United States, was widely publicized in *The Sunday School Times,* and can be found in the records of club programs like Young Life, Youth for Christ, Chicago's Hi-C, and Detroit-based Voice of Christian Youth. It is the Miracle Book Club founded by Evelyn McClusky in 1933.

While living in Portland, Oregon, Mrs. McClusky, who was in her forties and whose husband had divorced her, was asked by a friend to teach the Bible to a class of high school students meeting in her home. The daughter of a Presbyterian minister consented and for the next two years taught the Washington High School Bible class.

Enthusiasm for the class spread to other schools and by June of

1935 five other schools had chapters of what had come to be known as the Miracle Book Club. *The Sunday School Times* ran an article entitled, "Winning High School Students for Christ" and two well-crafted stories by Mrs. McClusky about individuals to whom she had witnessed.

The effect was much the same as the article written by Francis E. Clark in *The Congregationalist* over 50 years before. Within a year more than 100 chapters were in place as the founder continued to promote the club. In 1937 her book, *Torch and Sword,* was published for the purpose of explaining the club's structure. By then chapters had been formed in every state of the union and various foreign countries. Though the exact count of clubs is suspect, *The Sunday School Times* proclaimed that the number of chapters chartered by the organization which had moved its headquarters to Oakland, California, was over 1,000 by the end of the year.

The growing club movement attracted quality people into leadership positions. Edith Schaeffer along with her husband, Francis, became the Pennsylvania state directors in 1939. Mrs. Charles J. Woodbridge served as the state director for North and South Carolina while Jim Rayburn served in a similar position for Texas in 1940.

Located in neutral locations near public high schools and taught primarily by women, the chapters of the Miracle Book Club had four goals: they wanted to invite young people first to salvation in Christ; then to realize that Christ lives in them; which in turn enabled them to be victorious in Christian living; followed by becoming Christian "conversationalists." Mrs. McClusky was convinced that young people could be taught to weave a Christian witness into any conversation without alienating the listener. Today this might be referred to as "lifestyle evangelism."

A typical meeting was divided into two parts: Student officers led the first 15 minutes and included singing, some club rituals, and "minutes" from the previous meeting. This was followed by 45 minutes of teaching from a book of the Bible given in a lecture/storytelling format. Such invitations for salvation as were given were low key and were never stated in a manner in which a student might be embarrassed.

Jim Rayburn, the founder of Young Life, was the most effective of the Miracle Book Club teachers. His chapter in Gainsville, Texas, built around his own communication skills rather than McClusky's materials, grew from 3 to 123 members in 13 months and by the spring of 1940 reached 170 students. He later became the Texas State Director before forming the Young Life Campaign in 1941 and adopting the Texas chapters into his newly formed organization. Al Metsker and Jack Hamilton, who were the founding fathers of the Youth for Christ Club program, got their start in Kansas City's first Miracle Book Club chapter. It was during his term as chapter president in 1941 that Metsker first expressed his desire to see a group started near every high school and college in greater Kansas City, a dream which he realized in cooperation with his former Miracle Book Club vice president, Jack Hamilton, after founding Kansas City Youth for Christ. From these beginnings grew the national YFC club program.

Mrs. McClusky's organization was the first parachurch organization in the United States to focus on high school youth. She stands as the mother of parachurch youth ministry as it is known in the nation today.

Jim Rayburn and Young Life Clubs

If Evelyn McClusky set the stage for the parachurch high school club program, Jim Rayburn forged the high school club methodology which would be perfected in the Young Life movement in the 1940s and 1950s. A nearly identical strategy was adopted by the Youth for Christ International club division in the 1960s and then found its way into church youth groups during the decade of the 1970s. Rayburn's contribution was at the heart of the parachurch contribution to church youth ministry.

Jim Rayburn's split with the Miracle Book Club in 1941 was not the beginning of the Young Life club strategy. Rayburn's approach to youth ministry was fundamentally different from anything that had preceded it. Unlike Miracle Book Club, it was not designed for Bible study. Distinct from Baptist Young People's Union, Epworth League and Walther League, it claimed no denominational ties. Different from the Christian Endeavor Society, it was not based in the local church. Distinguishable from YMCA efforts, it was focused exclusively on high school students. Rayburn's approach to youth ministry was essentially a missionary effort by Christian adults to win uncommitted high school students to a personal relationship with God through Jesus Christ.

There are five distinct contributions that Jim Rayburn and the Young Life movement made to youth ministry. The first and perhaps most significant was that clubs were *leader-centered*. From the first training manual produced in 1941, it was evident that the adult leader would be in charge of the weekly club meeting and would be the primary speaker:

> The Leader is it! A Young Life Club does not begin and grow by [having] a group of young people sending for materials and methods. It gets results as the LEADER meets his qualifications and is HIMSELF effective in conducting the meeting and teaching young people to do so.[1]

Even the singing was led by adults in most meetings. Students participated in the club "minutes" which were usually skits or humorous announcements.

The philosophy of adult-led meetings was an extension of McClusky's approach and was in stark contrast with the approach of church youth groups which helped shape Jack Hamilton's strategy for Youth for Christ clubs and the Inter Varsity influenced Inter School Christian Fellowship in Canada. Both of these club systems viewed the leader as training and coaching students to lead meetings and do the work of evangelism on the high school campus.

A second distinctive of Young Life was that it was *evangelism-focused*. Jim was influenced by his father who was a Presbyterian evangelist and later by Rev. Clyde Kennedy of Gainsville Presbyterian Church. When Kennedy asked Rayburn, then a student at Dallas Theological Seminary, to minister to students in Gainsville, his concern was outreach-oriented. "Jim," the minister explained, "I'm not particularly worried about the kids who are in [church]. They're safe. As far as they're concerned I don't need your services. To you I entrust the crowd of teenagers who stay away from church. The center of your widespread parish will be the local high school."[2]

Perhaps the best-known contribution of Rayburn's Young Life Campaign was its emphasis on "winning the right to be heard" by secular high school students. By this slogan Young Lifers meant they needed to gain the friendship and respect of students before expecting them to listen to the claims of Christ. This had to be done on the young person's own turf—football games and practices, high schooler's hangouts such as soda fountains, school events and, when permitted by school authorities, the high school cafeteria.

It was not enough, however, for the staff person or volunteer leader to merely establish contact with students and build relationships. The whole process, which came to be known as "incarnational theology" led to a point at which the Christian Gospel was presented. The club meeting was the initial place to call for commitments to Christ, but with the purchase of resort camps starting in 1945, a second and even more effective delivery system was discovered. Students came from across the nation for a week at a time and found the Gospel not only spoken but lived out 24 hours a day.

Jim Rayburn's *conversational approach* to public speaking was a third distinctive of Young Life's ministry. He was different from the preachers of his day. He did not shout or pound the pulpit. He just talked. Fellow staff member George Sheffer described Rayburn's style:

> He really wowed kids. He had such a shy, quiet approach. He was marvelous building up to a punch line. Like, "High school isn't so bad, is it? It's just the principal of the thing."
>
> Kids would cheer and whoop and howl. . . . He was corny as could be [for] the first half. Then he'd talk about the fact that our nation was based on the Christian faith and there was a heritage in our country that a lot of kids didn't know anything about. "You're doing yourself a disservice," he'd say, "if you don't at least find out what you're missing."[3]

This style was perpetuated by leaders who followed Rayburn.

Young Life clubs spread from Texas to the Pacific Northwest, the Chicago area and Memphis, Tennessee. From there the movement branched out into other areas of the nation with strongholds in affluent communities near major cities. Statistics were not well kept under Rayburn's leadership. It is clear that by the time Bill Starr followed Rayburn as executive director of the movement in 1964 there were over 400 clubs in existence. This number grew to the 1,000 mark by 1973 where it has continued through the 1980s.

Jack Hamilton and Youth for Christ Clubs

Judy Raby was a homeless girl who lived with a high school friend. Loaded with talent and creative energy, she would be a senior in a Kansas City high school during the 1946-1947 school year. Already active in the highly popular Saturday night Youth for Christ rallies, she decided to attend the Second Annual Youth for Christ Convention with rally director Al Metsker. At the Medicine Lake conference near Minneapolis, Metsker shared an idea with Judy, "Maybe we could get some Bible clubs going and challenge kids to bring their unsaved friends to the rally. If you're interested in this sort of thing, let me know when we get back."

Shortly after school started, Judy showed up at Metsker's office wondering when the clubs could get started. For the next several weeks the idea was presented at the rallies. Twelve high schoolers from ten high schools responded and the club program was under way. One problem existed, however. Metsker was far too busy with his other responsibilities to head up a club program.

The leadership problem was solved when Jack Hamilton, Metsker's vice president from Miracle Book Club days, walked into the Youth for Christ office and volunteered for full-time Christian ministry. The director "hired" his friend on the spot with the stipulation that Hamilton would raise his own salary. Thus began the Youth for Christ club program, known first in Kansas City as Youth on the Beam, according to Hamilton, "They had a 'YOB' to do."

Unlike Young Life clubs, Youth on the Beam's stated purposes were not evangelistic. Christian fellowship among the students, spiritual growth through Bible study, higher Christian living as a means of fighting juvenile delinquency, and inter-club activities were their purposes. Yet all of this was part of a larger delivery system intended to encourage Christian students to bring their non-Christian friends to the Saturday night rallies.

By the spring of 1947, 12 thriving clubs had been established. The number swelled to 20 by the end of the following school year.

The kids planned and led the programs. Everything from special music and skits to emceeing and selecting speakers was left for them to do. One factor which made it easy for the student leaders to obtain speakers was that there was a great number of traveling evangelists and performing artists on the circuit just after World War II. Some would speak in the Saturday night rally and then address club meetings during the week. Pastors, businessmen, and missionaries were also available for club meetings.

In time the club program began to influence YFC rallies. Bible quizzing, which originally was designed to help new believers grow in their Christian faith, became a fixture in the rallies and made the club-rally delivery system even more effective. Students from various high schools came to the rallies to cheer for their quiz teams and in the process made or renewed spiritual commitments.

By 1950 it was obvious that Youth for Christ International needed to develop a nationwide club program. Torrey Johnson, the first president of YFCI, had seen the success of Miracle Book Club and Hi-C (High School Crusaders) from Chicago's Carl Schurz High School, for they had met in the building of the church he pastored. But it was the organization's second president, Bob Cook, who brought Jack Hamilton from Kansas City and gave him the mandate to start a national club program.

Hamilton went first to Detroit to get a program rolling. Next it was Portland, Oregon, and later San Diego, all the while spreading the word through *Youth for Christ* magazine. By the summer of 1951 the high-energy Hamilton reported 700 clubs had been established. By year's end 1,000 were reported and that number stretched to 1,956 by the time of the annual convention in 1955. Though some insiders question the accuracy of the annual reports, the official record shows that the club program reached a peak of 3,073 clubs in 1962 before declining along with the Saturday night rallies.

Campus Life Strategy of Youth for Christ

During the middle of the decade of the 1960s, Youth for Christ International made a bold shift in philosophy. Clubs were severed from the rallies and redesigned to stand entirely alone. Rallies were discontinued in most places. Bible quizzing and national music competition, which were related to the rally concept were phased out. New staff members were recruited to minister on two or three campuses instead of coaching student leaders in 25 or 30 schools. The primary leadership of the clubs switched from student leaders to trained Youth for Christ specialists.

Three factors made the change possible and even necessary. Baby boomers had come of age as high schoolers. They were living in the Benjamin Spock/post-Sputnik era where the emphasis in education was on dialogue and understanding rather than the older educational idea of lecture and retention. A second generation of Youth for Christ leaders who were not married to the rally idea took a hard look at the scope and effectiveness of the ministry and concluded that changes had to be made. About the same time the organization's structure was changed, making the decision-making process much more functional.

At issue in Youth for Christ was an understanding of the religious make-up of the American teenage population. It was discovered that only about 5 percent of American adolescents claimed to have had a

Christian conversion experience, while another 35 percent claimed to have some sort of religious affiliation. This left 60 percent of the high school population whom YFC staff described as "unchurched," meaning that they claimed no regular contact with a church or synagogue.

The new generation of leaders took these findings and asked a hard question. "Which of these groups are we reaching?" The answer was most disconcerting. Most of the teens identified with YFC clubs were in the first category — students who already claimed to have had a conversion experience. The next largest group were those associated with a church or synagogue followed by a very low number of students who claimed no active religious affiliation.

A readership survey of those who subscribed to *Youth for Christ* magazine in 1960 supported this finding. Of those responding to the non-scientific poll, 96 percent said that their church had a youth group of some kind while 85 percent indicated they attended that group regularly. Only 6 percent said they never attended a church youth group at all. Later research done in cooperation with the Human Learning Research Institute at Michigan State University further validated these findings.

If these findings were true, then something was very wrong with the YFC ministry philosophy. The very people whom the organization was claiming to reach were remaining outside of the program's influence. Thus was ushered in the Campus Life philosophy of ministry.

Salt Lake City was the unlikely place for a meeting in 1962 at which six club leaders discussed a club philosophy which could reach beyond students already committed to Jesus Christ to the non-churched, non-Christian student. Bill Eakin, Willie Foote, Jack Hamilton, Bob Kraning, Ken Overstreet, and Bruce Washburn spent two days together and conceptualized a new shape for campus ministry. Still realizing that the teenagers themselves were the key to high school evangelism, they drafted a teen-to-teen philosophy whereby Christian teenagers could properly and successfully communicate in action and words their personal faith in Jesus Christ to their friends, their campuses, and their world.

Over the next several years innovative approaches to club ministry were field-tested. A "2-plus-2" format emerged. Two meetings each month would be focused on outreach while the other two meetings would concentrate more on biblical content. In San Diego, under the leadership of Ken Overstreet, Jim Green and Mike Yaconelli pioneered ways to attract and hold non-Christian youth at club meetings. This included limiting a club leader to a few campuses in order to allow him (the vast majority were male) to meet and build relationships with campus leaders in a manner similar to that employed by Young Life leaders. The outreach meeting came to be called Campus Life Impact.

In Fresno, California, and Arlington Heights, Illinois, Larry Ballenger and Clayton Baumann explored methods for aiding students who wanted greater spiritual formation. This discipleship aspect came to be called Insight. Impact and Insight together came to be known as Campus Life. About the same time the organization's magazine changed its name from *Youth for Christ* to *Campus Life* magazine.

Insight meetings were the first to be initiated. Though designed to attract the YFC club crowd, the adult leader was now in charge. He guided the meeting to address three questions: "Who am I in relationship to God?" "Why should I communicate my faith to others?" and, "How can I best carry out my responsibility for Christian witness?" The format for each session as described in the Insight/Impact Manual first published in 1968, included four components: instruction (biblical and psychological insights from the leader related to needs which called for help in Christian students), inspiration (prayer, challenges from leaders or students), involvement (discussions and testimonies), and initiative (gentle but firm encouragement to put his or her faith to work on the high school campus).

The second part of the Campus Life strategy was the Impact meeting. It was designed to be

> an informal evening meeting of one hour centered on a YFC Campus Life Director. It contains a significant amount of involvement by students who participate in both informal preliminaries of the meeting (icebreakers and games) and in the discussion/talk-to before the wrap-up. The make-up of the audience should comprise at least a one-to-one ratio of non-Christian to Christian, and the meeting should be at a comfortable place for the non-Christian to be.[4]

The reception to the Campus Life strategy in those places which adopted the ideas was outstanding. Special relational skills were needed to implement Insight/Impact. Some of the staff had these naturally. Others were trained in interpersonal and small group dynamics. But some leaders simply could not master the new style of doing youth ministry. Nationally, the average attendance at Campus Life clubs remained about the same as the older YFC clubs. For the next two decades the number of Campus Life Clubs hovered at about the 1,000 mark, though both the number of clubs and average attendance dipped significantly as the 1980s drew to a close.

Fellowship of Christian Athletes

The one organization ministering to high school students which appears to be gaining momentum as the end of the twentieth century approaches is Fellowship of Christian Athletes. Established in 1954 by Don McClanen with the blessing and financial support of Branch Rickey, then the general manager of the Pittsburgh Pirates, and a group of Pittsburgh businessmen, the organization immediately began to fashion a ministry to and among professional athletes and coaches. National conferences starting during the summer of 1956 quickly gave the organization visibility and credibility within the sports fraternity.

Actually, the idea of a ministry focused on high school students was not formalized until 1966 when the name "huddle" was given to the growing numbers of groups springing up among young men in the high schools of the nation. From the beginning huddle groups have been a grassroots movement. Led by coaches or other faculty members and parents interested in sports, huddle groups include singing, announcements, and a talk or Bible study led by the adult sponsor or a guest from the world of sports.

Huddle groups were not an end in themselves. FCA provided very little training for huddle group leaders but a great number of options for students through area rallies and weekend and week-long summer conferences. Thus the huddle groups became a delivery system for getting student athletes, many of whom knew very little about Jesus Christ, to attend conferences where they met well-known athletes and coaches as well as received instruction in the truths of the Christian faith.

As with most other parachurch ministries, numerical records in the early days of the movement were more like guesses than accurate data. Reports show 1,000 huddle groups in 1969, a figure which if accurate, placed the FCA high school program on numerical par with Young Life and Campus Life after just three years in existence. The figure is a bit misleading because some of these huddle groups were on college campuses. Yet the sudden growth was impressive.

By 1972 there were 1,500 huddles, and 2,000 in 1977.

The March 1990 report from Richard F. Abel, President of FCA, called 1989 a "miracle year." According to Abel, 18 percent of the high schools in the nation had FCA huddle groups during the past year. The August 1990 report on high school huddle groups showed 3,357 chartered units on the campuses of the nation. Total high school membership in FCA was just over 19,593 for the same period of time, an increase of 53 percent over the previous year.

The question could be asked as to why the high school ministry of the Fellowship of Christian Athletes appears to have grown so rapidly while all of the other high-school-based ministries were going through a period of malaise. Four factors should be considered: First, FCA had just completed its first 25 years of ministry to high school students and historically that period is the time of most rapid growth in all parachurch ministries. Second, the whole concept of a huddle group has a built-in point of contact for adults with students. Whereas most other ministries have to find a way to enter the student's world and build relationships, the huddle group leader already had that contact through his or her role as coach, faculty member, or parent with a common love for athletic competition.

A third reason for the growth of FCA's high school ministry was the fascination which young people had for successful athletes and the willingness of Christian men and women in highly visible positions in the sports world to give of themselves at camps, conferences, and even at the huddle group level. The last reason may be the cement that holds the others together, namely, finances. Since huddle groups are staffed by volunteers, most of the fund-raising activities go into the very types of projects to which donors like to give—highly visible activities and facilities. Though finances will always weigh heavily on the shoulders of the professional staff, volunteer leaders have the joy of serving with their only paycheck being written in the lives of high school students to whom they have ministered.

Two problems with FCA should be noted, however. The organization has been very weak in providing training for huddle group leaders and this has led to an unevenness in the effectiveness with which Christian truth is taught. Though camps and conferences help correct some of this randomness, much needs to be done to raise the methodological and theological effectiveness of the lay leaders.

A second problem grows out of the training deficiencies of FCA.

The organization may have bought into the American mystique that "winning isn't the most important thing, it is the only thing." A constant emphasis on sharing the victory, and on "no pain, no gain," tends to teach impressionable high school students a value system contrary to the concepts of yielding, sacrifice, and humility, which are major themes in biblical teachings.

Other Club Programs

To put the parachurch club movement into perspective, one must be careful not to leave the impression that the four organizations mentioned in this chapter were the only shows in town. In reality, there were probably hundreds of localized club programs but only a few spread widely enough to merit mention.

High School Born-Againers (Hi-BA), founded by Brandt Reed in metropolitan New York in 1938 was designed to train Christian students in the "know how" of personal evangelism on the high school campus. Like Young Life, all meetings were led by adult staff members, though a staff person may have led as many as 10 meetings each week and, as a result, did not have much time to spend on the campus "earning the right to be heard." For Hi-BA this was no problem because it was the trained student who was to be the evangelist anyway.

Two other distinctives set Reed's organization apart from the others. Staff people were placed in an area only at the invitation of the local churches. They were seen as an extension of the churches' training ministry. This was further enhanced by including a world missions emphasis in every meeting. In addition, a high school missionary conference was held as one of the two or three major events planned for clubs throughout an area.

The ministry remained a regional high school agency operating primarily in the New York/New Jersey metropolitan area but with a missionary extension in Japan. Kenn Clark, who led the ministry in Japan for years, took over the leadership of the organization in 1982 after the death of Brandt Reed.

High School Crusader Clubs (Hi-C), sponsored by Christian Teachers' Fellowship, was an outgrowth of the Miracle Book Clubs in Chicago. When, in 1943, the teachers' group felt they were no longer being serviced by Mrs. McClusky's organization, the new organization was formed utilizing primarily Moody Bible Institute and Wheaton College students to lead the clubs. Though Hi-C was also a regional organization, students returning home after college planted clubs as far away as Hampton Roads, Virginia, and Portland, Oregon.

When the switch was made from the Miracle Book Club affiliation, board member C. Stacey Woods suggested the name High School Crusaders after an organization he had seen in Australia. With the new name came new concepts of ministry. Instead of merely focusing on Bible studies, Hi-C clubs under the leadership of Gunner Hoglund and later Daniel Ankerberg began to sponsor activities which would build bridges to other teenagers. Basketball leagues were formed in various parts of the city, Saturday morning radio broadcasts aimed at Christian teenagers, and area-wide social activities such as banquets added to the list of outreach activities. The most spectacular event, however, was the formal concert given each year by the 125 voice Hi-C Chorale in Chicago's Civic Opera House. At its high point Hi-C had 78 clubs in the Chicago area.

Hi-C remained a vital part of youth ministry in the Chicago area until 1959 when Bill Gothard, Jr. became the director. A product of the club program, Gothard felt that significant changes needed to be made both in club strategy and in the organization's approach to fund-raising. The idealistic young man refused to depend on promotional letters to generate financial support, choosing instead to "trust the Lord to provide." Funding sources began drying up and the whole program began to deteriorate rapidly.

With Hi-C in decline, Chicagoland Youth for Christ began establishing its own clubs in high schools. Competition developed. At one point, Schurz High School had both a Hi-C and YFC club with cousins Arnold Mayer and Alan Aiger serving as presidents of the respective organizations. The final demise of Hi-C did not come until the late '60s when Chicagoland YFC absorbed the once dynamic club program.

Dunamis Clubs were the creation of Dawson Trotman for high school students in the Los Angeles area beginning in 1939. Tired of what he described as the "take-it-easy" philosophy of ministry, the founder of the Navigators decided to set up a new system which would lay out stiff requirements and make membership a privilege. What students did between meetings was the key to the weekly gathering. When the boys gathered (later there was a similar group for girls called Martures) there would be spirited singing and then what was called an "oral check-out" on Bible portions which had been memorized during the week. This was followed by reports on

TNT (Tackle 'n' Trust) assignments in which fellows told their peers about their Christian faith. The meeting was concluded by a Bible study or challenge from the leader.

By 1941, 35 clubs were sprinkled across southern California. Lorne Sanny, a student at BIOLA College, was given responsibility for the clubs, which boasted as leading members Ralph Winter, who later directed the United States Center for World Mission, and Dan Fuller, best known as Professor of Systematic Theology at Fuller Theological Seminary. The organization did not last long under Sanny's leadership primarily because the young man's skills were soon needed in the broader leadership of the Navigators.

Jack Wyrtzen had developed an evangelistic delivery system which drew young people to local rallies and camps where commitments to Christ took place, but he was not happy with the way in which local churches were following up on the declarations of faith. Joe Bubar shared Jack's frustration and in 1959 Word of Life Bible Clubs were born.

The clubs were designed to guide young people in their spiritual development through a doctrinal study, a daily quiet time, Scripture memory, a reading program of Christian literature, and evangelism. Unlike the other club programs highlighted in the chapter, Word of Life Clubs were sponsored by Bible-believing churches and led by youth leaders trained by Word of Life field staff. Curricular materials and evangelistic area-wide events were provided by the 50 field staff to over 750 churches in 1989.

Wyrtzen's rallies of the 1940s and 1950s have been replaced by evangelistic events frequently associated with sports activities. Frank Roe, the North Central States Regional Club Director, reported that 19 such events took place in Illinois, Indiana, and Wisconsin during the 1989-1990 school year, resulting in an average attendance of 403 people with 31 professions of faith. What one local youth group could not do in an evangelistic effort, the staff worker could accomplish through combining the energies of many smaller churches.

Campus Crusade for Christ started a high school extension of its rapidly growing college and university ministry in 1966. Bill Bright, the founder of Campus Crusade, had observed college students who had made commitments to Christ on campus returning home and starting high school versions of the college ministry. While consulting with his seminary friend Carl Wilson, Bright conferred with Bill Starr of Young Life and Sam Wolgemuth of Youth for Christ International to see if there was room for another high school ministry in the United States. Starr's response cut to the heart of the matter. "We are reaching perhaps 1 percent of the high school students of America. It would be naive of us to say there is no room for Campus Crusade for Christ to reach high school young people. We just ask that you cooperate with us, that you work with us, that you move carefully into what you are doing so as not to make unfortunate mistakes."[5]

Student Venture, as the ministry came to be known in 1982, mirrored the college strategy. It included personal evangelism by staff members, small group discipleship groups, and periodic evangelistic blitzes by staff evangelists including Pat Hurley, Bill Reif, and Dawson McAllister. Major training conferences or ministry projects during vacation periods were likewise part of the ministry.

As the decade of the 1980s drew to a close, Student Venture had 250 full-time staff serving in 18 metropolitan areas nationwide, with the largest staff teams in Minneapolis and Houston. Though staff members stress evangelism, their emphasis on discipleship is underscored by the fact that 6,500 students were engaged in discipleship groups during the 1988-1989 school year. The ratio of student to staff, 26:1, placed the movement squarely within the range of average size youth groups in the nation, where the normal group leveled off with an average attendance of about 30 students.

While parachurch ministries to high school students were the most influential club programs of the third cycle of youth ministry, churches staffed and sponsored club activities with the help of a different type of parachurch agency. Most were an extension of children's club programs. Christian Service Brigade, established by Joseph Coughlin in 1937, was an evangelical alternative to the Boy Scouts. Brigade's sister organization, Pioneer Girls (now Pioneer Clubs) came into being under the leadership of Betty Whitaker two years later. AWANA Youth Association, incorporated in 1950 with roots in the urban setting of Chicago, was the product of Lance Latham and Art Rorheim. In each case the children's portion of the program was much more successful at attracting and holding members than was the high school version of the program.

Later Jack Wyrtzen established church-based Word of Life Clubs which have been better received by high school students in the church. The program has been most successful in churches where lay leadership needs a curriculum to follow and high schoolers want a youth group which reaches beyond the church's youth club.

There were other club programs as well. The Key to Life Clubs, based in Oakland, California, in 1940 had an emphasis on reaching the student who did not seem to fit anywhere else. King's Teens, founded by Mike Martin in 1944, spread throughout the Pacific Northwest and up into Alaska in the decade following World War II. But most of the smaller regional clubs were eventually absorbed by the national parachurch club programs.

Conclusion

As the decade of the 1990s begins, Taft High School, the model for Grease's Rydell High, is without a Christian parachurch ministry. No Campus Life club, no Young Life club, no Fellowship of Christian Athletes huddle group. Nothing. Unlike 1959 when a Christian presence was felt by some students, if not by the greasers, today there is little possibility that the Jim Jacobs of the student body will be exposed to the Christian Gospel.

Why the demise of incarnational witness at Taft High School and the other secondary schools of the nation? In the next chapter we will look at the factors which are bringing to a close the third cycle of youth ministry.

---

1. "Young Life Leaders' Manual," 2. Folder 26, Box 69, Collection 20, Papers of Herbert J. Taylor.

2. Char Meredith, *It's a Sin to Bore a Kid* (Waco, Texas: Word Books, 1978), 20.

3. Meredith, 36; An example of a Rayburn talk is found in Jim Rayburn III, *Dance, Children, Dance* (Wheaton: Tyndale House Publishers, 1984), 122-129.

4. *Campus Life Impact* (Wheaton: Youth for Christ International, 1968), 1.

5. Bill Bright, *Come Help Change The World* (Old Tappan, NJ: Fleming H. Revell Co. 1970), 107.

CHAPTER 10

The Breakfast Club at the End of an Era

T he Shermer High School library, 7:00 on Saturday morning, 24 March 1984, was the setting for John Hughes' movie, *The Breakfast Club*. Five students seen by "Vern" Vernon, their assistant principal, as a brain, an athlete, a basket case, a princess, and a criminal, are set to serve eight-hour detentions.

The five students, who would never socialize together given normal circumstances, start the day by defending their self-perceptions and blasting the social groups represented by each of their companions. Angry critiques of the five cliques fill the morning hours, but gradually the flow of conversation strips away the facades and an empathy, even a bonding occurs among them. By the afternoon they have begun protecting each other from a common foe—Vern Vernon, bemoaning a common affliction—parents, and exploring their common nemesis—pressures, either internal or external.

As the movie ends, "The Breakfast Club," as Brian Johnson, the intellectual of the group, describes them, is wondering what will happen to them on Monday. Will they revert to their old friends and exclude these new confidants? The eight-hour experience has brought about an honesty and vulnerability which is unique in their high school experience. They have tasted what it is like to be healthy young adults. Yet as they head home the song, "Don't You Forget about Me" is playing in the background, leaving the audience with the haunting question, what will happen on Monday morning?

There is a quote from rock singer David Bowie which appears on the screen at the start of the movie. It sets the tone for the day of detention and critiques the adolescent culture of the 1980s:

> ... And these children
> that you spit on
> as they try to change their world
> are immune to your consolations.
> They're quite aware
> of what they're going through.

Producer John Hughes, along with a majority of the current genre of teenage films, in an educational concept that stretches back to Jean Jacques Rousseau, is suggesting that young people can handle their own world if left to their own devices and not get messed up by the adults that surround them.

Such is the mood for a generation of high school students who have lived in a land of prosperity unthreatened by military or economic forces. They live their lives expecting to enjoy personal satisfaction based on economic stability. Even their efforts to serve other people are based upon the desire for self-gratification. Singer Cyndi Lauper illustrates the point. When asked why she participated in Live Aid, a concert designed to raise money for the starving peoples in the sub-Sahara of Africa, she reportedly replied, "Because it makes me feel so good." Her motivation was based on the internal rewards which she received by participating, not because it was the right or just thing to do.

Despite scattered signs which may be considered optimistic for the field of youth ministry among the Breakfast Club generation, the overwhelming evidence is that the third cycle is rapidly coming to an end. The first chapter of this book provides extensive evidence that the evangelical movements which have served young people during the middle of the twentieth century have stagnated in their ministries. This is in keeping with the pattern established in the previous two cycles. Several factors have dulled their cutting edge for youth ministry, leaving youth groups, both in the church and in parachurch settings, with little that would represent a significant movement of the Spirit of God. Those influences are the subject of this chapter.

The Rise of the Professional Youth Worker

The sudden visibility of the Youth for Christ movement towards the end of World War II captured the imagination of thousands of servicemen who would soon reenter civilian life. Choices were made about education and careers. The war effort had liberated the youth of America from the normal process of career selection by postponing the crucial decisions until after they had been exposed to the world. From the Christian perspective, this included seeing spiritual commitments made at Youth for Christ rallies around the world, which they placed in contrast with the spiritual vacuum they saw in the lives of so many people in the United States and abroad.

The Youth for Christ rallies created a movement toward Christian service. Just as the American military had been the saviors of the Western world, now American evangelicals viewed themselves as the saviors of the spiritual world. Not all Christians, not to mention other religious groups, agreed with this assessment, but the men and women influenced by the movement were not deterred by such sentiment.

During the years following the war, thousands of people influenced by the movement either went directly into the ministry or enrolled at Bible institutes and colleges, Christian liberal arts schools, and seminaries. A ferment of spiritual revival on college campuses kept students from sliding into spiritual apathy induced by the material benefits of the rapidly expanding American economy. Meanwhile, the success of the evangelistic efforts of Billy Graham, who came to national prominence in the Los Angeles crusade of 1948, and by a host of youthful speakers featured in Saturday night rallies across the nation, confirmed to the Youth for Christ enthusiasts that they were part of something that God was doing and solidified their commitments to ministry.

By the early 1950s, thousands of people were committed to doing professional youth ministry. The vast majority of these people found places of service in the emerging parachurch youth ministry agencies. Exact figures of those being paid by evangelical groups to work with youth in those early days are hard to obtain and highly inflated when available. Yet by the 1970s when personnel records were kept with greater care, Youth for Christ International and Young Life Campaign each employed over 1,000 staff members. When adding the staffs of other parachurch agencies such as Word of Life Fellowship, Hi-BA and Campus Crusade's high school ministry, the numbers mounted. Local churches, similarly, had begun employing youth specialists as had denominational organizations, camping ministries, and publishing houses.

The number of people employed to do Christian youth ministry suggests that the youth movement had become a profession. But there was a problem. Most church people, lay as well as pastors and professors, saw the position of youth worker as a transitional one. Youth specialists were viewed as novice ministers who were gaining enough experience to qualify them for "real ministry," that is, the preaching pastorate. Youth ministry was considered an extension of one's education, a type of internship. The old prayer, "Lord, we'll keep 'em poor; you keep 'em humble" appeared to be the philosophy of the 1960s and 1970s. This was especially true of the parachurch agencies where a third of the workweek spent on fund-raising was not uncommon. Despite the financial hardships, the ranks of youth ministers continued to swell.

The post-war baby boom caught the church without a strategy for dealing with the sudden influx of people whom the media began to call "teenagers." The idea of having someone employed by the church to work primarily with young people was foreign to the vast majority of churches. Prior to the 1950s only major and usually urban churches such as Calvary Baptist Church in Manhattan (1932), Vista Community Church in North San Diego County (1948), and Moody Memorial Church in Chicago (1949) hired "youth directors." As Young Life and YFC clubs flourished across the nation, the idea that smaller churches might employ youth workers came into being as well.

The majority of the early youth ministry "professionals" were students employed part-time to help with the youth of the church. Since no real training was available, many merely imitated what they had seen happening in parachurch club programs. The Youth for Christ movement had begun spawning a new approach to youth ministry.

During the years between the middle of the 1950s and the end of the 1960s, the position of "youth pastor" became established as an important part of a pastoral staff in evangelical churches. The position was slower to develop in mainline denominational churches. Much like the sudden appearance of the rock 'n roll disc jockey, the youth pastor was a response to the vocal presence of middle class adolescents as factors in the American way of life. So compelling was the teenage generation that, had Young Life and Youth for Christ not been present, youth pastors would have appeared on the scene anyway, but their ministry values and philosophy would have come from a different source. The parachurch agencies were there, however, and as a result played a formative role in the development of the profession.

Financial consideration made the role of church-based youth pastor much more attractive to a new generation of would-be professionals than ministry with a parachurch agency. Since the church paid the youth pastor's salary, he did not have to waste his time raising support. In addition, salaries were generally higher, thus allowing married youth workers to support their families more easily and so sustain their ministries over a longer period of time. He could use the same skills necessary for campus ministry sponsored by Campus Life or Young Life and focus on the church youth group and their friends at school. From the mid-1970s until the end of the 1980s the bulk of youth ministry shifted from parachurch to church-based operations.

It should be noted that youth ministry has been predominantly a masculine profession. This is ironic because the originator of the parachurch club concept was a woman, Evelyn McClusky. Yet from the time people started being employed to minister to youth, the names on the payroll have been male by an overwhelming majority.

Of the 23 staff members listed in the 1943 annual report of the Young Life Campaign, only six were women, and five of those were listed as secretaries while the other person was described as the wife of a staff member. An early brochure of Hi-BA staff listed 7 women among the 25 staff members, but all of them were office staff or wives of staff members. *Youth for Christ* magazine, in reporting the job Mrs. Morris Anderson was doing directing Kish Valley YFC in Stillman, Illinois, commented that she was one of the few lady directors of Youth for Christ rallies.

Over the years parachurch ministries have become more open to including women on their professional staffs, yet men still dominate all leadership positions and most field staff leadership appointments. Churches from an evangelical tradition are even more closed to women in youth ministry. Few will hire a women no matter how qualified unless she is teamed with, and accountable to, a male youth minister. Even the writers and editors of youth publications are male to a greater extent than is found in any other genre of Christian literature. Only in mainline denominations has the door been opened to women in youth ministry.

The professional youth minister had made the volunteer youth worker either obsolete or a second-class citizen. While some youth ministers have built effective ministry teams and have utilized lay ministers effectively, most have no idea of how to accomplish the task of discipleship through lay leaders. The professional has merely replaced the volunteer without necessarily increasing effectiveness.

The Professionalization of Youth Ministry

The picture of what has happened in the Youth for Christ movement and especially over the past 20 years (the last portion of the 50-year cycle) is that a dynamic organism has gradually become institutionalized through what sociologist Max Weber described as "the routinization of charisma." The same pattern can be observed in the Sunday School and YMCA movements of the first cycle and the Christian Endeavor organization of the second cycle. All started out with highly charismatic, entrepreneurial leaders and a loose association of followers, which eventually became an organization of managers with few visionary instincts. This process can be seen in four areas as youth ministry changed from a movement to a profession.

Formalization. In the early stages of a movement, certain activities are found to be more effective than other efforts. In an attempt to conserve the energies of people new to the movement, systems are developed and then published to standardize and coordinate the procedures. Bill Bright's "Four Spiritual Laws" brought such formalization to Campus Crusade for Christ; Evelyn McClusky's *Torch and Sword* for Miracle Book Clubs (1939), Jim Rayburn's nine-page mimeographed manual for Young Life club leaders (1941), and Jack Hamilton's Youth for Christ High School Bible Club Directors' Manual (1954) were all instruments, of bringing about conformity within the various movements.

Unfortunately, many people, including the leaders of the movements saw the formalized process, whether it was a Saturday night rally or a weeknight club meeting, as the end of the creative process rather than the beginning of new strategies. Efficiency became the emphasis as leaders sought to direct rallies, lead club meetings, and conduct camps more competently. To many observers the formalization of youth ministry amounted to production of buggy whips for a generation of people who had begun to purchase cars.

One of the best illustrations of formalization was the development of Bible quizzing in youth ministry. Though the use of Bible quizzing in Sunday School or on radio programs had been going on for years, Jack Hamilton came up with an entirely different use for the idea. YFC rallies in Kansas City were bringing young people to Christ who were from churches where the Bible was not taught. Rather than antagonize the pastors of those churches by advocating that these young people join churches where they could learn biblical truths,

Hamilton created a system for discipling new believers through Bible quizzing.

The idea caught on and soon spread to Detroit. During the 1950 Youth for Christ conference in Winona Lake, Indiana, the two rallies put on a demonstration quiz and the idea spread like wildfire. Within months hundreds of quiz teams came into being in YFC programs across the nation. The system of quizzing remained basically the same, but its function in YFC began to change. Young people who had been raised in Christian families soon dominated the quizzing program. Though still intended for discipleship, quizzing was reaching a different target audience.

Soon quizzes were being contested in Saturday evening rallies and the role of quizzing changed again. With all the excitement generated by the competition between clubs from different high schools, the program became like another type of athletic league with Saturday night rallies becoming the "stadium." Quizzing became a drawing card for attracting young people to rallies.

One look at the YFC club committee minutes from the 1950s reveals how formalized Bible quizzing had become. Rule modifications dominated the energies of the group which was supposed to provide leadership for the entire club ministry. For many, Bible quizzing had become an essential part of the club concept.

Thus it was in 1972, after Youth for Christ had initiated its Campus Life club strategy making Bible quizzing an obsolete methodology, it was discovered that Bible quizzing had a life of its own. Denominations had already copied the system, but something more was wanted. The World Bible Quiz Association was founded in the mid-1970s by former YFC Bible quiz coaches in hopes of linking denominational efforts and promoting additional programs. What had started as a means to an end had become an end in itself. Bible quizzing had been formalized.

Self-maintenance and Conservation. As youth workers increased in number, certain activities became an accepted part of the role played by people in the profession. At first the music employed to communicate with secular young people, the public relations tricks used to attract attention to the evangelistic efforts and the financial risks taken by idealistic youth workers were assumed to be a part of being on the cutting edge of youth ministry.

With success came followers. Some, such as Herbert J. Taylor of

Chicago's Club Aluminum Corporation, C. Davis Weyerhauser of Tacoma's Weyerhauser Lumber Company and Robert C. VanKampen of Hitchcock Publishing Company, provided financial support and brought about a bit more businesslike approach to the endeavors of youth workers. These spiritually-minded leaders in industry wanted to see decisions made which would benefit youth ministry for years to come and not just die in a flash of sincere but ill-advised flames. With the millions of dollars invested by these and others over the years came a conservatism which was focused on perpetuating the ministries.

Another set of followers were the imitators. These were equally sincere people who were not the entrepreneurers that the early youth workers had been and who were not by nature risktakers. They wanted to invest their energies in approaches to working with young people that were known to work. Thus, as the profession grew in size it became more conservative.

Finances have much to do with this conservatism. When the youth ministry pioneers began working with young people, most of them had to raise their own salaries in much the manner a missionary associated with a faith mission did. Most of his supporters were friends and believed in what he was doing no matter how radical. But when a large church in the latter part of the 1980s offered a youth pastor a salary which exceeded $30,000 per year, the person tended to be a bit more conservative and conform to the expectations of his constituency.

Infusion of Value. As certain methodologies were effective and youth work professionals closely identified themselves with these activities, many had difficulty separating themselves from the specific systems even when those endeavors had ceased to be productive. Rallies, Bible quizzing, one-on-one discipleship, and student leadership in clubs are examples of values which, though proper in certain contexts, have become institutionalized as youth ministry has become the habitat of professionals.

A classic example of value infusion is the idea that students should or should not lead clubs. YFC clubs and Canada's InterSchool Christian Fellowship both nearly died fighting for the idea that students had to lead club programs. The idea had worked very well on the college campuses where students had organized and led Inter Varsity chapters for years. Though YFC gave up the idea in the 1960s, ISCF tenaciously clung to the idea until the end of the 1980s. To some leaders the idea of turning leadership over to adults or pursuing some other strategy was tantamount to leaving the faith.

By contrast, Campus Life's resistance to using lay leaders as the primary focus of their club programs had bottle-necked their movements because they placed such a high value on trained staff developing and leading campus ministries. Chartering systems, academic requirements and in-service institutes all have brought about a sense of professional competency which may have limited the capacity of these agencies to extend beyond a specific base.

Distinctive Social Composition. There is a certain conformity which takes place within a profession as it institutionalizes. People begin to look or act alike. For youth professionals the uniformity has been in a certain craziness of lifestyle.

The classic illustration of the social composition associated with youth workers was seen in the "Wittenburg Door Awards" dinner held for years on the Friday night of the Youth-Specialties National Youth Workers Convention. Though located in the grand ballroom of a major convention-oriented hotel, the 600 to 1,000 youth workers present came dressed in their casual working clothes and used table etiquette more suited to summer camp than to the surroundings in which they found themselves. Only the waiters were shocked (perhaps amused would be a better word). To everyone else the craziness which transpired was simply the way youth workers acted.

There are other, more serious distinctives that have come to identify the youth ministry profession. Middle-class orientation, a commitment to biblical teachings, an emphasis on personal salvation, and a sensitivity to the felt needs of students tend to be common denominators in the profession.

Most youth work professionals belong to a network of youth work professionals where they can go for in-service training, encouragement, and ideas. The National Network of Youth Ministries, Sonlife Ministries, *Group* magazine, and Youth Specialties, as well as denominational and informal regional gatherings, service the needs of youth work professionals. All of these activities go into the formation of youth work professionals as a distinct social group.

The Youth Specialties/*Group* Magazine Phenomenon

The demise of effective youth ministry in the first two cycles was closely associated with the cooperation of the parachurch agency's ministry technology by the church and denominational structures. In both cases the methodologies were adapted for use in the church while the core rationale was either discarded or significantly modified. Once incorporated into the church's program, the Sunday School became a spiritual nursery for church families rather than remaining an evangelistic arm of the congregation. When denominational bodies imitated the Society for Christian Endeavor, the result was a watered down pledge which required little accountability from individual members.

The same pattern has emerged as youth ministry nears the end of its third cycle. Once again the church copied the technology of parachurch agencies, this time Young Life and Campus Life, and employed their methods to maintain youth groups of Christian adolescents in church settings while practically ignoring the vast majority of young people who had not made a commitment to the Christian faith. The primary agents for providing that transfer of information were Youth Specialties and *Group* magazine.

Youth Specialties arrived on the youth ministry scene in the fall of 1968. Campus Life had just launched its Impact/Insight strategy while Young Life was recapturing some of the momentum it had lost when its founder Jim Rayburn became ill and new leadership took over the reins of the organization. Though there was a growing host of youth pastors, no one seemed aware of how many there were and what their needs happened to be.

Wayne Rice and Mike Yaconelli had worked together for several years on the staff of San Diego Youth for Christ. Both were active in formulating the Campus Life strategy for Youth for Christ before resigning to finish college. To support their education, the two men served as part-time youth ministers, Wayne at San Diego First Church of the Nazarene, and Mike at Lemon Grove First Baptist.

To further supplement their incomes Rice and Yaconelli took some of their programming ideas which they had generated both in their Youth for Christ days and later in their church ministries and published a 52-page youth program manual which they cleverly called *Ideas*. To market their product they rented a booth at the Greater Los Angeles Sunday School Convention and sold their initial run of 200 copies. Quickly another 500 copies were printed and followed in 1969 by *Ideas No. 2*. Thus, Youth Specialties was launched.

One of the awkward aspects of the early days of Youth Specialties was the fact that many of the ideas which were published and copyrighted by the young entrepreneurers had been developed while they were still associated with Youth for Christ International. YFC leaders felt the organization owned the material though it had never been copyrighted. Consequently, Campus Life leaders found themselves in the touchy position of having to secure permission from Youth Specialties to use programming ideas they had helped generate.

By 1970 there were four *Ideas* books and the two men took a major risk by sponsoring an event which came to be known as the National Youth Workers Convention. Using primarily old YFC buddies like Jay Kesler, Bill McKee, and Bob Kraning, the conference attracted approximately 300 people, and, even though the company lost money, a youth ministry training tradition had begun.

The following year they picked up an underground Christian newspaper called *The Wittenburg Door.* Published by two youth workers from the Los Angeles area, Paul Sailhamer and Gary Wilburn, the paper's motto was, "There is no public reform that was not first private opinion." The satire and humor as well as the dissatisfaction with the local church were an appropriate match for Rice and Yaconelli's perspectives on the current state of ministry. Youth Specialties acquired the publication for its debts and $600 worth of unfulfilled subscriptions and promptly misspelled the name of the expanded magazine. Sticking by their mistake, the new name became *The Wittenburg Door* when it was issued in June 1971.

The fledgling organization gained national attention because of the 1971 convention which attracted 650 people to hear such speakers as Francis Schaeffer, Hal Lindsay, Lyman Coleman, Larry Richards, John MacArthur, Jr., and others. The following spring the two men and their new associate, Denny Rydberg, went on the road with what they called "National Youth Programming Seminars." These seminars became a way to take youth ministry "ideas" to the people and at the same time market *Ideas.*

Though Yaconelli and Rice fought against the inconsistencies of the religious establishment continually, their visibility, creativity, and insights in the world of youth ministry soon made them part of a newly established power block. "Ideas" were their commodities. Consistently, they generated programming ideas which had once been the domain of the parachurch agencies and marketed them to every church youth worker in the nation. The net effect was a rapid and broad distribution of parachurch ministry technology to people who were more interested in methods for keeping students active in youth groups than in full-cycle discipleship. The final phase of the third cycle of youth ministry had begun.

During the summer of 1974, Thom Schultz, a youth pastor in Loveland, Colorado, became frustrated with the lack of programming ideas for church youth ministry available in magazine form. *The Wittenburg Door* had settled on a diet of humor, issues, and renewal-oriented interviews. *Campus Life* magazine focused on the individual high school student and his or her world. Sunday School materials were, well, Sunday School materials.

Finding a niche in the post-Jesus Movement church youth ministry market created by Youth Specialties, Schultz created *Group* magazine which masterfully gathered the youth ministry technology from any source available and sold it first in article form and later in books compiled from the best pieces in the magazine. The circulation grew from 450 in 1974 to 20,000 in 1979 and 54,000 in 1984. Growth then leveled off and there were 57,000 subscribers in 1989.

With the growth of the magazine leveling off, Schultz's organization increased its emphasis on book publication and events for youth groups. Unlike Youth Specialties, which focused on adult leaders, Group Publishing attempted to reach the student leader in the church youth group. A "Colorado Flood Disaster Recovery Camp" in 1977 followed by the first "National Christian Youth Congress" convened in Estes Park, Colorado, in 1978, were the first steps in that direction. By the end of the 1980s it was estimated that over 15,000 young people were involved in group-sponsored events during the year.

Thom Schultz's organization had found a way to provide services to the local church similar to the manner in which Youth for Christ had served local YFC clubs and rallies in the 1950s and 1960s. "Youth Congress" type events were a throwback to the old Winona Lake Conventions which had ceased in the early 1970s, while the work camps provided for church youth groups what "teen teams" of young musicians had previously supplied within Youth for Christ.

Some might conclude that the Youth Specialties/*Group* Magazine phenomenon had breathed life back into church youth ministry. Rather than facing the end of a cycle of youth ministry, the church had become the rallying point with youth ministry publishing house conglomerates as the catalyst. A new generation of youth ministry had already begun. The contention might further be supported by the rise of the two Sons—Son City (later called Student Impact) and Sonlife Ministries with their broad followings in youth ministry circles (see chapter 1).

Unfortunately, the conclusion is far too optimistic in light of the facts. The entire publishing/training system is based on one factor—money. Youth ministry as defined by Youth Specialties/*Group* magazine or exemplified by Son City/Sonlife is built around the assumption that church youth groups will have professional youth ministers and interns who will in turn have the discretionary funds available to buy materials, attend seminars, and take young people halfway across the nation to attend conferences or participate in work projects. The market is stratified within a middle-class and upper-middle-class clientele from which women and minorities are functionally excluded from leadership.

While the bulk of the youth population in the nation is found in urban settings or in communities which have little contact with Christian youth work, the vast majority of youth ministry is taking place in groups of 30 people or less located in upper-middle-class suburban settings. The Youth Specialties/*Group* magazine phenomenon has merely allowed an increasing number of youth ministers to communicate more effectively to an ever-decreasing population. It is the last gasp before the death of the third cycle of youth ministry.

Crisis: Televangelist Scandals

Then came the crisis. Only a year before *Time* magazine had proclaimed "Power, Glory—and Politics: Right-wing preachers dominate the dial."[1] Televangelists were reported to have amassed viewing audiences ranging from 16.3 million for Pat Robertson's "700 Club" to 5.6 million for Jerry Falwell's "Old Time Gospel Hour." Ranked in the middle were programs featuring Jimmy Swaggart (9.3 million), and Jimmy Bakker (5.8 million), both of whom were ordained by the Assemblies of God and appeared to have won a place for the traditional Pentecostal denomination in the mainstream of American life.

On 19 March 1987, the bubble popped. The boyish-faced Jimmy Bakker admitted to having committed adultery and resigned from the presidency of his PTL Club. Less than a year later, on 21 February 1988, a tearful Jimmy Swaggart confessed to his congregation and a national television audience that he too had committed a "sin." Like Bakker, the violation was sexual and as a result both men were disciplined by their denominational leaders while their ministries withered overnight.

Though the actions of Bakker and Swaggart did not directly affect youth ministry, the impact of their deeds created a new climate for conservative Christians in America. Bible believers were caught up in the greatest religious scandal since the Scopes Monkey Trial in 1925. A new cynicism toward conservative Christians developed. The summer of the "born-again" Christian had quickly faded into the winter of individual religion and new age mysticism. National newspapers and magazines as well as ABC TV's "Night Line" had a field day exploring the many facets of impropriety attributed to the televangelists. No longer was it popular to be known as a believer. The scandal had begun to exact its toll. The third cycle of youth ministry had ended.

Conclusion

As the movie *The Breakfast Club* ends, Brian Johnson writes a letter to the assistant principal on behalf of the friends he discovered during the eight hours of detention. It reads:

> Dear Mr. Vernon:
> We accept the fact that we had to sacrifice a whole Saturday in detention for whatever it was we did wrong, but we think you are crazy making us write an essay telling you who we think we are.
> You see us as you want to see us, in the simplest terms, with the most convenient definitions. But what we found out is that each one of us is a brain and an athlete and a princess and a basket case and a criminal. Does that answer your question?
> Sincerely yours,
> The Breakfast Club

The third cycle of youth ministry has ended with high school students refusing to give respect to adults who are trapped by their own insecurities in roles as parents or educators and other authority figures. Instead, they hope the taste of honest relationships they have had will last and their peers will not forget about them on Monday. The alternative may not be much of a bargain, but to the Breakfast Club and millions of other "breakfast clubs," it is the best they have.

---

1. "Power, Glory—and Politics," *Time* (February 17, 1986): 62-69.

PART THREE

The Coming Revolution

S everal obvious questions come to mind after reading of the demise of the current system of youth ministry: "When will the revolution happen?" "What will the coming revolution in youth ministry look like?" "What will become of the current youth ministries?" and "What role will the local church play in the coming revolution in youth ministry?"

In each of the previous revolutions in youth ministry, the advent of a new era caught people by surprise. The leaders of the existing youth ministries were busy maintaining their pieces of ministry machinery while focusing their attention on how to make them more efficient. Consequently, they were not looking in the right place when a new movement sprang to life.

In the past year I have been asked to describe the coming revolution to gatherings of youth leaders in the United States and Canada. Patiently they wait for me to set the stage and then eagerly participate as I attempt to draw a picture of the future. Their comments and insights have given greater definition to the picture which will be sketched in this final section of the book.

Though Part III is the shortest section of the book, it is designed to foment the coming revolution as much as describe it. It is my hope that people who are already experimenting with innovative approaches to youth ministry will be encouraged to go beyond the existing agencies, programs, and published materials to seek connections with other ministry entrepreneurs and thus build a youth ministry mafia for a new generation.

The look into the future will be divided into three chapters. The first will look at the evidence that the revolution is already underway. The second will identify megatrend-like indicators which will be found in the coming revolution, while the final chapter will sketch several scenarios which might paint a picture of the coming revolution in youth ministry.

CHAPTER 11

Pump Up the Volume:
The Revolution Is Under Way

L oud and Clear," was the way high school student Aaron Campbell reviewed the movie *Pump Up the Volume* for the *Chicago Tribune*. The film tells the story of Mark Hunter, the son of a fast track school administrator, who moves to Arizona from the Northeast and attempts to find a niche in the highly rated Hubert H. Humphrey High School. His efforts are frustrated by his shy personality, anger toward his parents for moving to the Sun Belt, and the pressure placed on students by administrators and peers alike.

The clarity of the motion picture is seen in Hunter's understanding of the issues which crowd high school students in the 1990s. As the new kid on the block, the senior feels alienated from parents, peers and school administrators. To relieve the tension, Mark Hunter retreats into his bedroom and creates a pirate radio station which goes on the air each evening at 10 o'clock to vent his frustrations, using tirades of abusive language to make his point.

Within days the word spreads throughout the student body that "Hard Harry," as he calls himself on the air, is describing the problems of the high school world as they really exist. Invectives dominate the broadcasts, hurled at educators more concerned with career development than in true education or meeting student needs. Issues concerning drug usage, alcohol abuse, pregnancies, loneliness, rejection, and suicide are raised by fellow students who call or write the pirate disc jockey.

The movie was violent, not because of murders and mutilations as in *Nightmare on Elm Street,* but because of the manner in which profane language was used to lash out at authority figures. Unfortunately, the ferocity of Mark Hunter's broadcasts stemming from his quiet anguish and loneliness in the uncaring world of H.H.H.H.S. might depict the feelings of a generation at risk better than a universe of researchers or social scientists. "So be it!" Hunter's pet phrase, captured the resignation with which a growing proportion of the high school population viewed the situation.

There was no hint of God other than theological words used out of context. The weeks of school had no Sundays. Parachurch youth workers made no appearances. Youth groups absorbed none of the lonely people. High school students were left to their own initiatives to save themselves and their world.

The stage is set for the coming revolution in youth ministry. It must happen. A spiritual vacuum exists. Fewer than one in four public high schools have a Christian presence focused on their campuses. The most effective youth groups in the nation rescue only an average of nine converts each year. The student world is facing a spiritual crisis of gigantic proportions.

If the coming revolution follows the pattern of the previous three cycles of youth ministry, two and maybe three factors should converge during the '90s: social unrest, the multiplying of new grassroots youth ministries, and the emergence of an acknowledged leader for the revolution. Already, the first of these is in place. It is only a matter of time before the others will follow.

Social Unrest: Perestroika/Glasnost and Recession

The stage for beginning a new cycle in youth ministry has been set three times before by a period of social and economic instability in the American culture. In the early nineteenth century, the western expansion of the nation provided that disruption. Toward the end of the century the Industrial Revolution reshaped society, while the Depression, followed by World War II, repeated the process 50 years later. From each of these periods of social unrest, a cycle of Christian youth ministry emerged.

Twin factors are setting the stage for the coming revolution in youth ministry. The first is already under way while the second appears soon to follow.

Nine months after coming to power in 1985, the Soviet Union's Premier Mikhail Gorbachev introduced a pair of reforms which altered the course of history. He called them *perestroika* (economic restructuring) and *glasnost* (openness). Perestroika meant that the economy of the Soviet Union would move away from its bureaucratic, centralized socialist system, which had proved to be a miserable failure since the Russian Revolution in 1917, to a market-oriented-economy. The change in theological parlance might be equivalent to Billy Graham converting to Hare Krishna.

The accompanying change of glasnost meant that for the first time in their lifetime, people under the Soviet rule would have the opportunity to express their opinions on subjects ranging from politics to religion, from art to the economy, from history to clothing. Again using an American religious analogy, this is like Bob Jones University allowing feminist Betty Friedan to conduct a lecture series on campus.

The impact of these changes within the Soviet Union and around the world has been enormous. The Baltic republics declared themselves independent states (roughly equivalent to the South seceding from the Union), dissident Boris Yeltsin was elected President of the Soviet Union's largest and wealthiest republic (like Jesse Jackson being elected governor of California) and began shaping an entirely new economic federation, while Eastern Europe has opened its borders and the Berlin Wall has been dismantled (similar to opening the American borders to all Latin Americans, including Cubans). Though there have been temporary setbacks to the flow of glasnost, such as the suppression of student protests in China's Tiananmen Square and military crackdowns in the Baltic republics (reminiscent of the 1968 Democratic National Convention in Chicago), the Communist world appears to be irreversibly changed.

The changes outside the Communist bloc nations will have a much more immediate effect upon youth ministry. For the first time in over 70 years the church in the West will have access to the churches of the Soviet sphere, a church which has been refined and shaped (not always positively) by suppression and persecution. It is quite likely that when the young Christians of the former Iron Curtain countries look at the teenage Christians of the West, they will see them as decadent and a product of a materialistic society. It is entirely possible that the spiritual leaders of the oppressed church will become prophets for the churches of the western hemisphere.

The barrenness of American Christianity became painfully evident to the world with the moral scandals associated with two television evangelists and one leader of a parachurch youth ministry agency during the second half of the decade of the 1980s. Though not directly associated with high school youth ministry, the revelations of sexual misconduct made a public mockery of the transforming power of the Christian Gospel and the American public moved a step further away from organized religion.[1]

In both of the previous two cycles of youth ministry an event completely outside the realm of the youth movements signaled the end of a cycle. The United States Supreme Court decision in 1875 which established the American public high school as a valid part of the educational system ended the way youth ministry had been done for 50 years. The Scopes Monkey Trial in 1925, which made a scandal of fundamentalism, tolled the death knell for the Christian Endeavor dominance within youth ministry circles. Now another transition is at hand.

There is another piece of the puzzle, however. The current changes probably will not be enough to bring about the coming revolution in youth ministry. The other factor which is associated with revolutions in youth ministry has been a business recession with the hard times which result. The key to this factor is not a recession by itself, for these have occurred with regularity over the years, but the convergence of such economic conditions with the decline of the major parachurch youth ministries associated with a 50-year cycle of ministry.

The question raised by many economists who have analyzed the business climate of the final decade of the century is not "If?" but "When?" University-of-Basel-educated Paul Erdman saw the stock market crash on 19 October 1987 as the starting point for a period of grace which would be followed by a financial crisis in mid-1989. Though his timing was off, the six conditions which he predicted may still bring about a minor depression, if not a crisis. These factors, which Erdman calls his "Convergence Theory" include the following:

1. The end of the marvelous Reagan recovery;
2. The inauguration of the new President;
3. A cascade of domestic bankruptcies;
4. The United States sinks abruptly into a sharp recession;
5. A sudden financial collapse of the Third World;
6. The drop of oil prices to $10 a barrel.[2]

Though the invasion of Kuwait by Iraq on 4 August 1990, made this last point highly improbable, the $500 billion savings and loan crisis of the early Bush administration, along with the bankruptcy of many related businesses, suggest that Erdman's theory might be a factor still.

The ultimate economic pessimist at the beginning of the 1990s might be Ravi Batra, a professor of economics at Southern Methodist University. Using the economic cycle theories and comparing the decade of the 1920s to the decade just completed, Batra concludes:

> The message of cycles must now be crystal clear. Since the 1960s escaped a great depression, the 1990s will experience another cumulative effect—the worst economic crisis in history.[3]

Admittedly, Batra and Erdman offer worst case scenarios which would be refuted by John Naisbitt's optimistic view of the future in *Megatrends 2000,* but still the American economy is faced with certain factors (foreign trade deficit, savings and loan crisis, bank insolvencies, national debt, deteriorating intra-structures of the American society, the Iraq-induced oil crisis, financing of Operation Desert Storm, solid and nuclear waste disposal, and environmental issues, to mention only a few) which are so enormous that escaping without some type of significant recession seems highly unlikely.

George Barna, President of the Barna Research Group, suggests a balance between the two perspectives and yet anticipates problems ahead. He concludes:

> Nationally, many experts forecast a major economic collapse for the early '90s, with 1991-92 mentioned most often as the likely period of the decline .... While it would be mere speculation to assert with confidence that such a collapse is likely, the signs of bad economic health are evident, and require serious response if the national economy is to weather the turbulent times ahead.[4]

When these hard times come, a new cycle of youth ministry will begin. Youth ministries which require one professional youth worker for every 30 or 40 young people will crumble under their own financial burden. Programs which require expensive trips and activities to maintain momentum will become impractical for all but the "high end" youth groups.

Youth for Christ and Young Life will not go out of business. Fifty years from now they will still be around just as the Sunday School, YMCA, and Christian Endeavor still exist today. The parachurch firebrands of the third cycle of youth ministry will merely find useful niches in the ecology of youth ministry and continue to provide those services for years to come.

The cutting edge of youth ministry in the fourth cycle will come from another source. It will be from entrepreneurial people currently associated with existing parachurch youth ministries but who resign out of frustration over the institutional rigidity of the agencies. Church youth pastors, stymied by the multiple layers of expectations in the local church, will be among those who branch out to start something new. College students or high school young people may be the source of the innovation, or even former youth workers who long ago left professional youth work but who in the meantime have made a comfortable living and now can return to their first love, unhindered by the need to look to others for remuneration.

The New Age Movement and Spiritual Hunger

A question must be asked at this crucial point in history. Are the young people of the 1990s open to spiritual matters? Each time America has approached a revolution in youth ministry during the past two centuries, the popular perception has been that "God-talk" had become irrelevant for the current generation.

August Hollingshead in his classic study of "Elmstown" youth during the 1940s found a similar climate. He reported that:

> To young people the church is a place where one goes to Sunday School, to young people's meetings, to a church party; and to a small segment, it is a place to worship or hear a sermon. It is not something special or supernatural as the ministers and some elders would have them believe. It is plain that about 7 out of 8 young people are not troubled by religious questions or problems.[5]

But as his book was going to press, the Youth for Christ movement burst upon the American scene with such force that *Colliers Magazine* declared, "Bobby-Soxers Find the Sawdust Trail" while *American Magazine* proclaimed, "Bobby Soxers Shout Hallelujah."[6]

Researchers of the 1980s reported findings similar to those of Hollingshead. Posterski and Bibby found that only 20 percent of Canadian youth ages 15-19 attended religious services weekly.[7] A poll of Minnesota youth showed 53 percent of ninth graders, falling to 34 percent of high school seniors, reported weekly attendance in church or synagogue.[8] After high school graduation George Gallup, Jr., cites that weekly church attendance slides to 16 percent.[9] This probably reflects attitudes students developed while living at home during middle adolescence but lived out during the independence of their twenties.

It might be assumed from their lifestyle that young people had abandoned their belief in God, but such is not the case. Eighty-four percent of older Canadian youth and 86 percent of young adolescents in America profess a belief in God.[10] It is the church and organized religious activities that appear to be the villain from whom young people are fleeing. This exodus is most pronounced in mainline Protestant denominations other than the Southern Baptist Convention, while smaller, more conservative denominational and independent churches may actually be gaining new youthful adherents.

John Naisbitt in *Megatrends 2000* predicts that religious revival will be one of the 10 new directions in the third millennium. He cites as evidence the increased popularity of religious fundamentalism of all varieties, the rising influence of the charismatic movement and the new popularity of the New Age movement. Though many rightfully fear this latter movement which is most popular among the baby boomers, the phenomenon clearly indicated a hunger for spiritual experiences which stands in stark contrast with the secular humanism of the 1980s.

A related development is the rise in fascination with the occult which closely parallels the popularity of the New Age movement. While police forces have had to cope with a swelling tide of satanic ritualistic behavior on the part of high school and junior high school young people, the enormous appeal to young people of the Frank Peretti books, *This Present Darkness* and *Piercing the Darkness,* demonstrated the intrigue with which the subject has gripped even churched youth in the rising generation.

Though none of these trends signify revival or a revolution in youth ministry in isolation from other factors, the combination of circumstances would suggest the stage is set for the Spirit of God to raise up an entirely new wave of youth ministry in North America and around the world.

Revision: Attempts at Changing the Existing Strategies

As the decade of the 1980s came to an end there was a flurry of activity within existing youth ministries. Church and parachurch alike acknowledged the inadequacy of the current approaches to reaching and discipling the current generation of young people. Doug Burleigh, President of Young Life International, stated the problem clearly:

> What the whole church must face—local congregations and para-church ministries alike—is the enormity of the need. The facts speak for themselves: only 15 to 20 percent of American teenagers are significantly involved in church. Young Life is involved in just over 1,100 of the over 22,500 high schools in America. What we've got to do is figure out how we can become more effective in penetrating this enormous bloc of unreached kids.[11]

The response to this growing realization has been encouraging. Yet as one pastor once pointed out using the analogy of a juggler, "You have to keep one ball up in the air while attempting to get another one up there as well." A church or parachurch agency would have a very difficult time simply discontinuing its current ministry while attempting to implement a new strategy. The idea has been discussed, however. One innovative thinker in a major parachurch agency is reported to have suggested using the organization's fiftieth anniversary year as a Jubilee Year (Leviticus 25) and suspending all ministries for the year while radically rethinking the ministry.

Though no youth ministries have been so bold as to interrupt what they have been doing for teenagers, even for shorter periods of time, efforts at strategic revisions have taken place. Willow Creek Community Church in South Barrington, Illinois, has been the premier church-based youth ministry in the nation during the decade of the 1980s. Under the leadership of Dan Webster, Son City consistently attracted 800 students. Though the numbers were impressive, Webster realized that there was a problem. While the church continued to grow, exceeding 12,000 at Sunday services, the youth ministry had plateaued. It was not merely a matter of demographics (fewer adolescents per capita), Son City had hit a barrier similar to that which hinders the growth of entire churches of a similar size.

Three changes were implemented. The name, which sounded more like a cult (Son Moon of the Moonies) or a retirement community than a youth movement, was changed to Student Impact. Interestingly enough, this was the same name chosen by Youth for Christ in the mid-1960s when they revised their club program.

An additional person was brought onto staff to assist Webster in staff development. "Bo" Boshers' responsibility was to train and disciple the young adults who in turn were to minister to and through student leaders on the 30 or so high school campuses from which Student Impact drew kids. It was a function which had become impossible for Webster to accomplish due to the pressures of preparing the weekly celebration.

Accompanying this second change was the addition of 16 paid interns who served as team leaders and focused attention on individual high school campuses. Under Boshers' leadership these men are making conscious efforts to evangelize and disciple high school students in Chicago's northwest suburbs. Within the first year attendance at the midweek youth program jumped by nearly 40 percent, averaging over 1,100 students. The target number under this new strategy is 2,000 high school students each meeting and ministry on 30 high school campuses.

The philosophy of ministry looks very much like a combination of the best of the Youth for Christ rallies from the 1940s and the cream of the Campus Life club strategy from the late 1960s. Two questions come to mind. The first is, "Can this approach be duplicated elsewhere?" Though the structure is relatively simple, the financial and leadership demands make the probability of successful clones highly unlikely except in very affluent communities. The second question is, "Does it matter if the ministry cannot be duplicated?" The response should be a resounding "No!" Willow Creek's mission is to reach its own community. Other youth workers must discover tactics suited to their unique contexts.

Canada's Inter-School Christian Fellowship, as well as Young Life and Youth for Christ USA have similarly undertaken renewal activities. Stimulated by their national leadership team of David Knight, Neil Graham, and Don Posterski, I.S.C.F. brought together the remnants of the Canadian high school ministry leadership during the fall of 1989 to radically rethink their entire philosophy of ministry. With approval from the national board of directors, changes began to take place and linkages were formed with American-based youth ministries to establish a national strategy for Canada. Though leaders seem encouraged, the jury is still out on whether new life has been breathed into the dry bones, which as early as 1947 reported the need for a thorough overhaul and revision as far as methods and program were concerned.

Realizing that change brings about change, Youth for Christ USA moved its national office from Wheaton to Denver in an attempt to rebuild its national leadership team. President Dick Wynn and his colleague Bill Muir proposed investing $2 million in "Video 390" a high tech approach to small group ministries. At the same time they worked to establish the new headquarters facility as a national training center for youth ministry, with the idea of finding and training 100,000 volunteers by the year 2000. The financial condition of the organization made these dreams impossible. Wynn chose not to accept nomination to another term as president, leaving the hope of new life for the organization in doubt. The history of YFC suggests that innovations which have been initiated exclusively by the national office of YFC have seldom resulted in permanent changes in ministry philosophy or direction. Perhaps this will be different, though now it looks dubious.

Young Life has become a pioneer in church-parachurch relationships by establishing over 250 "Church Partnership Models" in which local churches hire and fund Young-Life-trained youth ministers, who both lead local church youth groups and start evangelistically oriented Young Life clubs in the community. Even more significant in shaping the future of youth ministry is Young Life's commitment to urban ministry. An evidence of that dedication is that the first two denominations with which they have instituted partnerships in ministry consist primarily of black, urban congregations. With a portion of Young Life's funding problems solved by these new partnerships, the organization may have room to establish new directions, which will enable the movement to reach beyond the diminishing clique of people attracted to club by student body leaders and touch the lives of other social groupings within the high schools of the land.

Academic institutions appear to have gotten into the act of shaping the future of youth ministry as well. The 1990 College Issue of *Campus Life* magazine featured 83 Christian colleges, of which 26 advertised majors in youth ministry. An additional 26 offered concentrations in the field. That totals to nearly two thirds of the Christian colleges which provide some type of ministry training for would-be youth workers.[12]

Unfortunately, in reviewing the catalogs of the schools offering Youth Ministry majors, it would appear that the majors are little more than marketing hype with little substance in the various programs. Few of the majors had more than five courses which were distinctly youth-ministry-oriented. The other offerings were cross-listed courses such as recreational leadership, educational psychology, and instructional methodology. Only four of the schools made a serious enough commitment to youth ministry to recruit faculty members and create courses which would begin preparing young adults to minister to adolescents at the end of the twentieth century.

Despite sincere efforts by churches, parachurch agencies, and schools to bring about an effective mission to youth, it would appear that the revisions may be too little too late. The sum total of the renewal efforts of the existing organizations will not produce the coming revolution in youth ministry.

The Entrepreneurial Nature of the Revolution

Where then should we look to see the revolution develop if, in fact, one is already underway? Tom Peters, author of three books on excellence in leadership/management, emphatically states that no quantum leap forward (revolution) has ever come out of the normal research and development departments of major corporations. Instead, he looks to the "skunk works" or entrepreneurial thinkers within the company to bring about the changes necessary for excellence in their fields.[13]

I suspect that the creative ministry minds which will give birth to the revolution are already at work but not necessarily in the places Christian leaders may be looking. Though they may be associated with churches or parachurch agencies, they probably are not the people in the headquarters building or on the youth ministry task force of the denomination. Youth ministry entrepreneurs seldom have the patience or tact to put up with the institutional gobbledygook and political gamesmanship necessary to survive in organizational settings. They may be characterized as impatient and idealistic. Some may be described as angry or malcontents. Yet these are the ones who find the "hidden peoples" within the youth society and then stay close enough to them to meet their spiritual, social, and physical needs. These are the ones who listen to the voice of God rather than the hollow echoes of financial expediency.

Unfortunately, biblical history is littered with the bones of people who attempted to bring about change. Many were called prophets, of whom Stephen raised the question, "Was there ever a prophet your fathers did not persecute?" (Acts 7:52) Radicals and revolutionaries have not been looked upon with favor throughout the history of the church. Lutherans, Mennonites, Huguenots, Methodists, Fundamentalists, and Pentecostals, along with scores of other groups who

165

wanted to bring about change within the established church, have found it necessary to start new movements in order to release a new wind of the Spirit.

Each of these movements, much like the youth movements of the past, share the characteristics of innovation and entrepreneurship. Peter Drucker identifies several such properties, and these will be present in the leaders of the revolution.[14]

The new breed of leaders will constantly be *analyzing the opportunities* available to advance the kingdom of God within adolescent society. When others ask, "Why?" these men and women will inquire, "Why not?" When colleagues are blinded by problems, the new breed youth worker is dazzled by the potential of the situation and the greatness of God. Intermediate failures are seen as essential stepping-stones along the path to spiritual victory. Friends and critics alike are wearied with their dreams, but their visions will be based squarely on opportunities which others have overlooked.

Ridge Burns and the Center for Student Missions expresses an entrepreneurial instinct in youth ministry. While working in three churches he developed a philosophy of ministry which emphasized spring and summer missionary trips as well as local outreach ministries. Beginning with trips to Mexicali with up to 1,500 students from West Coast churches, Ridge took the same concepts and shaped an outreach ministry for Wheaton Bible Church which peaked with 120 students participating in summer missionary activities. Upon their return home students decided that a ministry event once a year was not enough. So they initiated a program called "Sidewalk Sunday School" for latchkey children in a neighboring community.

Seeing the need for assisting other churches to begin such ministries, he began the Center for Student Missions based in San Juan Capistrano, California. The ministry initially focused on Los Angeles, Chicago, and Washington, D.C., but now also facilitates youth groups doing ministry throughout the United States and Canada. In keeping with youth ministry innovators from the past, Burns has created a manual to assist youth groups to move from the church building to a field of service.[15] The Center has focused on an opportunity of discipleship and moved to utilize it.

The ideas of the youth ministry innovator are *simple and focused.* Others can grasp the concepts easily and duplicate them in similar circumstances, or adapt the essential elements to dissimilar settings. They do not attempt to meet every need of each teenager at the high school, but they do address some needs of specific types of students. It is precisely because of the focused nature of the ministry that young people will respond to Christ.

Phill Carlos Archbold, *Group* magazine's "Youth Leader of the Year" in 1990, may be an example of simplicity. The 54-year-old former hospital administrator was honored for his work with young people on the streets of Brooklyn where he is associated with the First Church of the Brethren. The socioeconomic base of the community does not allow Archbold's ministry to become complex. Many of the parents attempt to support their families on incomes of less than $10,000 a year.

Though the second-career youth worker sponsors programs to allow urban kids to breathe fresh air while visiting sister churches in Pennsylvania, and attempts to teach the youth of his church to reach out to the homeless of the city, a large proportion of his ministry is involved in being a surrogate parent to the teens of the community. It is an exhausting job since troubled kids call him day and night. Pregnancies, drug problems, keeping kids in school, and being a friend are all part of a day's work.

Archbold does not seem worried about his career track. He has already worked with youth for 16 years at the Brooklyn church, 10 as a volunteer and 6 as a poorly paid staff member. Perhaps it is his station in life which allows him to keep his ministry simple and focused.

Entrepreneurs start *small and grow*. National programs are never the starting point or goal. Establishing a niche within the ecology of the youth culture is the sole objective as the ministry begins. If the idea is picked up and used elsewhere, so be it, but the small start allows for a lot of tinkering and adjusting as the ministry comes into its own.

In the late 1980s it was difficult for a woman to break into youth ministry, but that did not stopped Kathi Isbell. Rather than wait for a large suburban church where she could work with high school students and receive the respect due a person of her competence, she began working with churches in communities seven miles apart in rural Illinois. It is hard enough to minister effectively in a single church, but Isbell appears to be thriving on the chaos of two youth ministries. In the process she has trained a staff of over 30 adults to assist her in the discipleship of the young people.

For women in youth ministry, starting small is an essential part of serving God's kingdom. Few churches have been willing to employ women, ordained or otherwise, as part of their ministering staff. Some profess theological convictions for such job discrimination, while others admit only to sociological bias. As a result female youth work entrepreneurs such as Kathi have found it necessary to start small and grow.

One final common denominator of change agents in youth ministry is their ability to *focus on leadership.* They are able to attract and hold the loyalty of people who can influence their generation and the generations that follow. Students and adults alike will be drawn to the charisma and dynamism of the youth work innovator. Creative people capable of making good decisions will be the key to the long term impact of the movement.

Dan Webster at Willow Creek Community Church, Dann Spader of Sonlife Ministries, and Jim Burns of the National Institute of Youth Ministry are current illustrations of those concerned with developing leaders. As the 1990s began Webster harnessed the economic resources of his affluent community and worked out an arrangement whereby 20 paid interns each year could be brought onto the youth staff for a year, in order to extend Willow Creek's growing high school ministry while developing leaders to do ministry elsewhere. This internship approach to ministry development may become one of the key shapers of large church youth ministry in the next generation.

Spader's growing organization, by contrast, has become the primary training agency for youth ministers committed to small-to-medium size churches across the United States and Canada. Whereas Youth Specialties and *Group* magazine provide a potpourri of training experiences, Spader's organization features an integrated philosophy of youth ministry, and in 1990 saw more than 15,000 youth leaders participate in some aspect of their training program.

Perhaps the key to Spader's strategy is his minimalist approach to youth programming. Fanatically he advocated reducing activities so that the youth leaders will have the energy and creativity to do the important work of evangelism and discipleship. Though resisted by those with traditional church expectations, Spader's voice will be heard by those on the cutting edge of the coming revolution in youth ministry.

The National Institute of Youth Ministries led by Jim Burns provides training for youth workers in similar size churches, but provides longer training sessions (two weeks at a time) and smaller groups (usually less than 25 at a time). The Institute attracts a clientele from a broader denominational spectrum than does Spader's organization and places its emphasis on bringing novice youth workers into dialogue with well-seasoned youth ministry specialists. While principles of youth ministry are presented, the greatest value of the Institute's philosophy is the training which takes place through informal interactions between experienced and developing youth workers.

It is quite possible that this type of leadership development for youth ministry may be the face of the coming revolution. When young men and women are not forced to break the continuity of ministry and encumber themselves with financial obligations usually associated with classroom settings, ministry skills may be learned far more effectively than in traditional training models. The primary problem, however, will be associated with biblical and theological training. The new delivery systems will need to find ways to provide as sophisticated a theological content as they do methodological insights.

Conclusion

If Mark Hunter's profanities in *Pump Up the Volume* are at all accurate in describing the quiet desperation of the current generation of high school students, they will become a rally cry for Christian ministry. A vacuum is present and the time is right for a new breed of youth workers to step forward and assume the mantle of leadership.

---

1. George Gallup, Jr. and Jim Castelli, *The People's Religion* (New York: Macmillan Publishing Company, 1989), 42-44.

2. Paul Erdman, *What's Next?* (New York: Doubleday, 1988), 71-119.

3. Ravi Batra, *The Great Depression of 1990* (New York: Simon & Schuster, 1987), 132.

4. George Barna, *The Frog in the Kettle*, (Ventura, CA: Regal Books, 1990), 106.

5. August B. Hollingshead, *Elmtown's Youth: The Impact of Social Class on Adolescents* (New York: John Wiley and Sons, Inc., 1949), 246.

6. *Colliers Magazine* 115 (26 May 1945): 22-23; *American Magazine* 141 (March 1946): 26-27.

7. Donald Posterski and Reginald Bibby, *Canada's Youth: Ready for Today* (Ottawa: The Canadian Youth Foundation, [1988]), 47.

8. *Minnesota Student Survey Report 1989* (St. Paul: Minnesota Department of Education, 1989), 11.

9. George Gallup, Jr. and Jim Castelli, 35.

10. Posterski and Bibby, 47; *Young Adolescents and Their Parents* (Minneapolis: Search Institute, 1984), 161.

11. "Same Heart, New Methods: A Conversation with Doug Burleigh and Stan Beard," *Youthworker* (Spring 1988): 55.

12. *Campus Life* (October 1990).

13. Tom Peters and Nancy Austin, *A Passion for Excellence* (New York: Random House, 1985), 115-160.

14. Peter F. Drucker, *Innovation and Entrepreneurship* (New York: Harper and Row, 1985), 134-136.

15. Ridge Burns with Noel Becchetti, *The Complete Student Missions Handbook* (Grand Rapids: Youth Specialties/Zondervan Publishing House, 1990).

CHAPTER 12

Back to the Future:
Megatrends of the Coming Revolution

n a clever twist of cinemagraphic creativity, Michael J. Fox and Christopher Lloyd starred in three *Back to the Future* movies during the 1980s. The gimmick of the trilogy was the simple idea that if a person could transport himself back through time and alter certain key events, when he returned to the world he had left, it would be different.

Dr. Emmett Brown, played by Lloyd, invents such a time machine and the three movies produced a delightful series of forays from the present to the past, forward into the future, and back again to the present. The series was a box office smash, grossing over $400 million by the end of the decade.

It is not only theater attenders who are fascinated by the idea of predicting and altering the future. For years preachers have captured the attention of great audiences by addressing prophetic themes. Hal Lindsey's book, *The Late Great Planet Earth* alone sold over 25 million copies since its publication in 1970.

As the end of the twentieth century approaches, futurologists are having a field day. Not only is this the end of a century, it is also the end of a millennium. As expected, books are hitting the market attempting to discern the face of the future. One of the best known is *Megatrends 2000*, authored by John Naisbitt and Patricia Aburdene, which identifies 10 new directions for the 1990s.

The difference between Naisbitt and Aburdene (and other authors of books having similar themes written for the consumption of church leaders)[1] and Hal Lindsey with the other preachers who describe the end of the age, is the source of their data. The former base their conclusions on a scientific analysis of cultural, political, and economic trends. The latter begin with a theological understanding of history and seek to interpret current events in the light of that understanding.

This chapter will attempt to take the best from both approaches to discerning the face of the future. It is primarily a trip back into history in order to describe the future of youth ministry. Ten major trends have been drawn from the first three cycles of youth ministry and suggestions are made as to where these "megatrends" are most likely to appear.

Non-Anglo-American Leadership

Each of the first three cycles of youth ministry were greatly influenced by people from outside the United States. The Sunday School and YMCA movements of the first cycle were copies of British youth ministry innovations. The Christian Endeavor movement which dominated the second cycle of youth ministry was the most distinctly American effort yet it, too, benefited by its rapid spread to the British Empire and the resulting influence in the form of spokesmen and materials which returned to American shores (see chapters 6-9).

The Youth for Christ movement and the third cycle of youth ministry felt the formative influence of non-Americans in the persons of Percy Crawford and C. Stacy Woods. Crawford, the Canadian-born evangelist, incorporated the staccato rhythm of radio programming into rallies, tuned into the interests of youth, and set the standard for a generation of youth evangelists. Woods, of British citizenship, helped replace the ailing Miracle Book Club in Chicago with Hi-C clubs by bringing the Scripture Union idea of student-led Crusader clubs to Chicago, a move which influenced the thinking of Torrey Johnson, the first president of Youth for Christ International.

The question is: where will the non-Anglo American leadership come from to influence the coming revolution in youth ministry? Will the continued stimulus for revolutions in youth work come from the British Commonwealth nations? Probably not.

As the century draws to a close, the most vibrant expressions of Christianity are being found in sub-Saharan Africa, Latin America, Korea, and portions of the crumbling Communist world. The church in each of these sections of the world has felt the effects of oppression whether economic, political, or religious. As a result these non-

Anglo believers tend to be much more militant about their faith than their American counterparts.

With the growing influence of nations from the Pacific rim has come a new type of migration to the United States. Middle-class Koreans, for example, have taken up residence in and around the major cities of the nation. Churches have been established, bringing to America the memory of the Christian values forged by war and revival. Second generation Korean-Americans have struggled with issues of identity, such as whether they will conform to the customs preferred by their parents or dress and behave like their American peers. To help survive the struggle many Korean churches have employed youth ministers who are attempting to mold a style of youth ministry which avoids the shallowness of American youth ministry, while not becoming enslaved to the materialism so endemic to the upwardly mobile emigrants. These youth workers, along with their Chinese and Indian counterparts, may prove to be the key to the future of youth ministry in America.

Already non-Anglo names like Paul Yonggi Cho, Luis Palau, and Juan Carlos Ortiz are shaping the thinking of creative youth ministers. Afro-Americans like E.V. Hill, John Perkins, Buster Soaries, Verley Sangster, and Glandion Carney are challenging the ways in which American youth ministries have been formulated and the nature of the role the church youth group should play in society.

To this point most of these men (there remains an absence of non-Anglo-American women as speakers or acknowledged innovators) have been used as featured attractions at Anglo-dominated events such as the National Youth Workers Conventions, sponsored by Youth Specialties, or in national publications. The time is coming, however, when the new cycle youth minister will make her pilgrimage for training conferences, not to the luxury hotels located near international airports or downtown shopping areas, but in the drafty halls of urban black churches or the early morning prayer meetings of Korean youth groups. Summer missionary trips will be taken in conjunction with youth groups from Eastern Europe, who will in turn provide the instruction in vital Christian living and evangelism.

International Character

Fifty years from now when someone sits down to write the story of the fourth cycle of youth ministry in America, one of the words which will be used to describe the movement will be "international."

173

The current cycle as well as the previous two revolutions in youth ministry were born amid an atmosphere of racism and cultural imperialism. White evangelicals who were at the heart of the Youth for Christ movement adhered to cultural norms leaving black and Hispanic young people sitting in the back of the bus. An analysis of attendance patterns would disclose that a minimum of 90 percent of Protestant youth groups in the nation outside ethnic denominations were of white descent. It was the Anglo-Americans who were the most resistant to the rapid social changes which took place in the nation.

Why should this change in the coming revolution in youth ministry? In chapter 3 it was pointed out that youth movements have been the products of the middle class in America. Christian people sharing middle-class values were the ones who had the discretionary time and money to bring a Christian youth movement into being. They too were the people who felt most strongly about passing their values from generation to generation. The issue was not so much a matter of white or nonwhite, it was a question of who were the participants in the socioeconomic benefits of the middle class.

The change in immigration laws during the 1970s and 1980s has allowed middle-class people, especially those from the Pacific Rim, to settle in the United States. A majority of these new peoples were professionals and had come to the United States to share the American dream. Many of the political refugees from Southeast Asia and Eastern Europe had been stripped of rights to careers by Communist regimes in their homelands. Sponsored by church groups associated with missionary efforts in their homelands, these, too, became upwardly mobile within their adopted land and soon absorbed the values of America's middle classes.

Even more interesting to observers of the American scene is the movement of black families into the middle class. Tired of the violence and deprivation which surrounded them in the urban areas of the nation, Afro-Americans began changing the poverty cycle by paying attention to values of the middle class, including education and family solidarity. Churches and community groups began creating safe havens where black young people were free from gang violence to develop their God-given potential in an atmosphere of Christian love.

The international character of the coming youth ministry cycle, will not mean, however, that a majority of youth groups will be internationalized. In all likelihood, a typical youth fellowship will continue to be comprised primarily of one ethnic group. The change will be in the fact that more ethnic minorities will sponsor structured activities for their teenagers.

Rapidly growing Third World churches will become more aware of their responsibility to assist families in discipling young people and will develop culturally appropriate methods of accomplishing that task. These systems will begin to influence the manner in which youth ministry is done in America.

These changes will mean adjustments in how denominational leaders, publishers, and parachurch agencies will handle large events and published materials. City-wide rallies, national conferences, and training seminars will be designed to attract the cross-section of youth represented by this new international character, rather than simply the dominant culture.

Grassroots movements representing this plurality of Christian, yet ethnic or nationalistic values, will abound. Most will find it necessary to publish their own materials; but with the desktop publishing capacities of today's computers, the only people who may suffer will be curriculum houses. The days of broadcasting standardized materials for Sunday Schools and youth groups may be a marketing strategy of the past.

Urban Precedence

As with the previous cycles of youth ministry, the major population centers of the land will provide the context in which the revolution will incubate (see chapter 3). The first cycle of youth ministry saw Philadelphia become the rallying point for the Sunday School while Montreal and Boston were the starting points for the YMCA on the North American continent before associations were founded in 26 other cities. The Christian Endeavor cycle found its roots in Boston, while the Youth for Christ movement sprang up in hundreds of cities, Chicago proving to be the anchor point.

Urban/suburban linkages will be vital in breeding new strategies for youth ministry. Minority groups scattered across metropolitan areas will create networks of youth ministry transcending the boundaries of school districts and municipalities. Young adults who gentrify the city will become innovators in youth work as they purchase properties reclaimed from deteriorating neighborhoods and turn them into citadels for family living. Music, dance, art, and sports will provide the basis for sister church exchanges in which city and sub-urban youth groups make an equal contribution to evangelism and discipleship.

Business, sports, and professional figures found in urban settings and who have an interest in young people will find broad avenues in which to volunteer the use of their expertise to help existing agencies and churches minister to the neediest of youth. Without the necessity of fund-raising, these people can invest their lives in adolescents and children who live no farther from their homes than their places of work. Such is the nature of the urban environment.

Concentrations of economically deprived blacks and Hispanics as well as other minority groups, may prove to be beyond the reach of middle-class parachurch agencies, and seminary graduates who have amassed thousands of dollars of indebtedness while completing their education. In their places will emerge home-grown leaders who will be determined to employ the power of the Gospel to rescue their brothers, sisters, and children from the ravages of drugs, violence, and illegitimate pregnancies. Emphasizing staying in school and off the streets while living in obedience to Christ, this new breed of urban leadership may have a greater impact on the youth of the twenty-first century than any approach used during the previous cycles of youth ministry.

Group Evangelism

Each cycle of youth ministry had a unique emphasis. The first cycle, which covered the middle of the nineteenth century, featured Bible study through the Sunday School and early YMCA movements (see chapter 6). Christian Endeavor followed, stressing accountability to holiness of life and encouraging prayer as an expression of commitment (see chapter 7). The Youth for Christ movement which dominated youth ministry in the middle part of the twentieth century placed an emphasis on personal and mass evangelism (see chapters 8-9). Other elements of Christian discipleship were present in each cycle, but these were the most prominent characteristics.

To even the casual viewer of television commercials aimed at the teenage market, sex and community appear to be the approaches which sell products. The sex theme has been a standard tactic of the advertizing industry but the community idea is of recent vintage. Beer commercials consistently depict friends spending happy times together even to the extent that a dog, Spuds McKenzie, became a symbol for being a "party animal." Levi products are sold using pictures of guys playing football or in relaxed conversation after a round of golf. Automobile and soft drink ads frequently show groups of people enjoying life together. Sometimes a person wonders if a sound track promoting a Christian youth ministry could not be dubbed over existing commercial messages without compromising the Gospel or altering the video portion of the advertisement.

Donald Posterski, a Canadian researcher, has written of "the friendship factor."[2] Based on a survey of Canadian youth, Posterski proposed the best way to minister to young people was through clusters of friends. The idea has been explored in a Southern Baptist church pastored by Tom Wolf in east Los Angeles where high schoolers have learned to evangelize in group Bible study settings. The entire process was based on the premise that neither mass evangelism nor one-on-one evangelism was effective in their lower socioeconomic community.

A survey of the history of youth ministry shows that the evangelization of high school students, if left to peers, will never get done. Adults have consistently had to structure situations, train student evangelists, and hold the young people accountable to do the job. Even with this kind of mentoring, the record of student-to-student evangelistic efforts in recent years has not been impressive (see chapter 1). A cell-group approach to evangelism may be the very thing to bring about a revival among the youth of the nation.

Student Prayer and Worship

A sense of revival has been associated with each cycle of youth ministry (see chapter 5). Though the evidences of God's special working have not come until midway through each cycle, prayer and a seeking after God by students have set the stage for these spontaneous workings of the Spirit. Though not the dominant factor in any of the previous cycles, the prayer and the accompanying worship factor have had a high visibility and priority in student movements.

Among college-aged students public prayer meetings have been carefully chronicled. A prayer meeting held by Williams College students in 1805 under a haystack during a rainstorm was credited with being the starting point for the modern missionary movement in America. The Student Volunteer Movement around the turn of the century was known for its extended prayer meetings as it saw upwards of 40,000 young people depart for mission fields outside the

United States. More recently, groups of college students organized by Inter Varsity Christian Fellowship, Campus Crusade for Christ, Operation Mobilization, and others have been active in promoting prayer as a vital part of the Christian walk.

The Christian Endeavor movement (see chapter 7), established in 1881 and focused upon young people from puberty through their twenties, was the first youth ministry to emphasize prayer as a central part of its program. Though the Sunday School taught the importance of prayer and the YMCA was central to the prayer revival of 1857-1859, it was Christian Endeavor that made the prayer meeting for young people a primary thrust. In *The Officers' Handbook* published by the Society in 1900, the first sentence read, "Christian Endeavor is a spiritual movement and its heart is the prayer meeting."[3]

Creative methods and program helps were focused on making the prayer meeting effective as a means of bringing about spiritual growth. A book entitled *Prayer-Meeting Methods* further strengthened Christian Endeavor's emphasis on prayer, though by the time it was published in 1916 much of the initial fervor over prayer had been replaced by organizational mechanisms necessary for sustaining local programming.[4]

In recent days, however, prayer has not been a topic promoted in training sessions for high school youth workers. Two factors appear to have changed this passive attitude toward prayer. The first is the failure of education to reshape society. Ever since John Dewey and the progressive era around the turn of the century, Americans have looked to education to recast society and eliminate public evils.

Churches followed this lead expecting ever more sophisticated educational approaches to bring about spiritual changes. But just as such programs designed to correct reckless driving (drivers' ed), unwanted teen pregnancies (sex ed), poor financial management (consumer ed), and drug and alcohol abuse (substance abuse ed) have failed to produce the changes in behavior among high school students expected by the public, the church and Christian families have been disappointed by the meager lifestyle changes resulting from church discipleship approaches. New information presented more effectively has not generated spiritually satisfying results.

The second reason for the changing attitude toward prayer as a vehicle of youth ministry is the increased acceptance of the supernatural realm. The popularity of New Age books and magazines suggests a movement toward more mystical forms of religious practices, of which prayer is a Christian expression. Late in 1990 MTV featured a rap video with M.C. Hammer, entitled simply, "Pray." Though some traditional evangelicals may have had some difficulty with the sensuality of some of the dancing, the words appeared to have been a genuine and maybe even desperate call for prayer as a solution to the needs of city youth.

Already an emphasis on prayer and worship is beginning to find its way into the mainstream of American youth ministry. Some Korean-American youth groups, while attempting to adapt to the American culture, are retaining the prayer meeting as a primary activity for high school students. Anglo churches in metropolitan areas report student-led prayer meetings being held in public high school classrooms as early as the building opens. Paul Fleischmann of the National Network of Youth Ministries, in conjunction with Barry St. Clair of Outreach Ministries, and Dann Spader of Sonlife Ministries, met with a core of youth workers 1-2 October 1990, in what they described as a Prayer Forum for the purpose of making the decade of the 1990s a period of extraordinary prayer to reach young people. These events suggest a new role for prayer in the coming revolution in youth ministry.

Women in Key Roles

Ministry to children and youth, especially outside the confines of the local church, has been one of the places in which women have been allowed to serve Christ and His kingdom. In England it was Mrs. Meredith who put legs to Robert Raike's vision and hosted the first Sunday School class in her kitchen. Women continued to be active as teachers in the American version of the Sunday School movement.

Mizpah Circle was the name chosen by Harriet Abbott Clark for a group of girls who would study about and pray for missionaries. Her husband, Francis E. Clark, adopted the idea and formed the Society for Christian Endeavor which then spread around the world. A review of the Society's records suggests that women provided the preponderance of leadership on the local level, while men assumed regional, national, and international responsibilities.

When the Miracle Book Club, the first parachurch ministry aimed primarily at high school students, came into being, it was Evelyn M. McClusky who was the organizer and primary promoter. Her speaking at Bible conferences and at churches around the country was instrumental in spreading the vision for Bible clubs spanning the nation. Virtually all of the hosts for clubs were women while 60 to 70 percent of the teachers were female. It was from McClusky's model that the current parachurch club program grew (see chapter 9).

As the second millennium of the Christian era draws to a close there is a resistance to offering posts of church leadership to women. While some evangelicals base their opposition on the 1 Timothy 2 passage in which Paul forbade women to teach or have authority over men, most Christian churches experience de facto discrimination against women at one level of church life or another.[5]

Even the most conservative theologians do not deny women the right to use their gifts of teaching. The issue is where and to whom these gifts ought to be exercised. Women are finding that teaching theology or biblical content to men in the church is the primary restriction. For women to teach the same content to other females, youth or children, especially outside the church structure, provides far less tension for church leaders.

The question could logically be asked, "Why should we look for Christian women to provide leadership in youth ministry in the immediate future when there are hardly any doing so at present?" The answer is rather simple. Twenty to 50 percent of seminary graduates in recent years have been women. Fully half of the attenders at *Group* magazine's Youth Ministry University in 1991 were women. Capable and godly female leaders with a passion to serve are now waiting in the wings for the next act in God's providence. New parachurch agencies, some begun and led by women, will provide the domain for the new breed of female leadership in ministry.

Lay Leadership

Until this current cycle of youth ministry, leadership in reclaiming and molding the lives of adolescents has strictly been a nonprofessional affair. In fact, some of the greatest resistance to ministries distinctly aimed at specific age groups came from professional clergy. Even Francis E. Clark, founder of Christian Endeavor, consented to accept the presidency of the international organization only on the condition that pastors and lay youth workers in the local churches be the front line of youth ministry.[6]

It has only been since the World War II that the prime movers in reaching youth for Christ in America have switched from pew to pulpit, from amateur to professional. Parachurch youth ministries and agencies like Youth Specialties, *Group* magazine, Sonlife Ministries,[7] and the National Network of Youth Ministries, which are products of the late 1960s and 1970s, have facilitated this change.

The economics of proliferating youth work professionals who will minister to 30 or 40 adolescents, especially in evangelistic settings, have become prohibitive. Parachurch groups have discovered this fact in the most dramatic fashion. The burden of fund-raising has left many local efforts practically devoid of staff.

The youth ministries which will have the greatest impact in the coming revolution will be those which successfully recruit and equip lay people to bear the primary responsibility for reaching the current generation of junior and senior high school students. The most obvious example of this trend is the Fellowship of Christian Athletes. The 3,357 high school huddle groups registered in August 1990, led nearly exclusively by volunteers, surpasses the combined total of clubs fielded by Campus Life (Youth for Christ USA), Student Venture, and Young Life.

Churches with professional youth workers which have been successful in reaching more than 30 or 40 young people have one ingredient in common. Each has found a strategy for recruiting, equipping, and deploying volunteer workers to meet the spiritual needs of teenagers. The high school ministry of Willow Creek Community Church, currently attended by over 1,000 young people weekly, is the primary example of a volunteer-fueled ministry. Dan Webster has built the ministry around adult volunteers and low-paid interns who spearhead ministries in local high schools.

Resistance from the Church

In each of the previous cycles of youth ministry, the sharpest criticism has come from the professional clergy. Concern over the lack of ecclesiastic accountability, pietistic excesses or indifference (depending on the perspective), and circus-like methodologies headed an extensive list of negative critiques. Even though the current generation lives in a much more tolerant culture than did their youth ministry forefathers, the coming revolution will generate extensive criticism.

One set of criticisms will come from the parents of teenagers who will feel that their children are being put at risk when hurting young people begin frequenting the youth group's activity. Rather than reinforcing values held by the church and home (an inward look), many youth groups will become places to confront pagan ideas with a view to conversion. After all, there are enough places where today's young people can get into trouble without having them exposed to the pluralistic values of society within the four walls of the church.

A second set of negative appraisals will come from the current youth ministry mafia. These are the people who currently control the youth ministry media and credentialing systems. Publishers of magazines and books, as well as producers of program and curricular materials, will be threatened by the fact that their products will not be necessary in the early stages of the revolution. Yet their attitudes toward the revolution will be pivotal for the rapid spread of essential ideas. They are the gatekeepers for the kingdom.

Colleges and seminaries will be even slower to respond. Some will not even recognize that the revolution is taking place while others will resist it on the basis of theological or social/ scientific arguments. Unfortunately, they will find that their style of training has become increasingly irrelevant to the cutting edge of the new cycle of youth ministry. The sacrificial excesses and naive simplicity of the new breed of youth workers will call into question the components of ministry preparation currently deemed essential.

A third source of resistance will come from denominational ministerial associations which will view the new wave of youth ministry as being theologically vulnerable (it may be) and sociologically uncomfortable (it will be). New types of national and regional gatherings of young people will result from the trend-setters who will come from minority groups and urban centers. Many will be from the charismatic movements. They will assume leadership positions, not because of a quota system or an "old boy" network, but because of the irresistible evidence of the Spirit of God working through them.

In the early days of the revolution the resistance will be overcome by men and women who take a "damn the torpedoes, full speed ahead" approach to youth ministry. Status and acceptance within the religious community will not be of primary concern to these new wave leaders. Though their leadership style will generate personality conflicts and even doctrinal stress, the end product will breathe new life into the church at large.

Parachurch-Style Church Ministries
In the previous three cycles of youth ministry, parachurch ministries have arisen to generate momentum. In all likelihood the same will

happen in the coming revolution. Yet at the same time, the massive array of church-based youth ministries will begin changing their modes of operation. They will begin functioning much more like parachurch agencies.

Parachurch ministries are consumer-oriented. No one makes young people go to Young Life clubs or spend three weeks on a work crew at Windy Gap. Nor does a parent insist that the volleyball star rush home from practice, gobble down her dinner and rush off to her FCA huddle group. The adult leaders of these groups have to win the right to be heard and gain the loyalty of the group every week.

At the same time parachurch leaders recognize that anything which stands still, in effect goes backward. Other organizations (especially church-based youth programs) imitate what is perceived as successful and adopt the methods to serve their own ends. As a result innovation and adaptation have been essential for parachurch agencies to survive.

From its inception in the late nineteenth century, the church youth group has been protected by the cocooning effect of the host church. Youth sponsors did not have to maintain an effective ministry to have the youth fellowship function on a weekly basis. Church and denominational loyalties, along with family expectations, was the glue that kept groups functioning. But that day has passed. Denominational loyalties no longer motivate families to select a church to attend. Consideration is given instead to the services a church provides.

The attractiveness of the youth group to the junior or senior high school student is a critical consideration as a family selects and joins a church. Some students will even attend youth group functions from a different church than their parents attend because of the social grouping or type of activity provided.

Most adolescents today attend neither church nor youth group. To attract these students the church must compete with jobs, sports, extracurricular activities, homework, parties, and gangs, as well as television, MTV, videotapes, shopping malls, and a host of other attractions. For church-based youth ministries to succeed in attracting and retaining young people, the youth group will have to be reinvented. It will be intimate though not always small, participative though not necessarily structured, and diversified with various aspects of the ministry appealing to one person while not to another.

Youth ministers will need to function as ministry entrepreneurs. While they will be unwise to ignore the collective wisdom of wiser saints, they will need to be free to innovate without the normal maze of committee work. The decision-making process will require a godly competence on the part of the youth minister and an unwavering trust on the behalf of the senior pastor and the church. Need-responsive activities which fulfill the mandate of Scripture will characterize the church youth group of the coming revolution.

Professional Redefined

The idea of professional youth workers employed to work directly with young people is a product of the mid-twentieth century in America. Prior to that, youth ministry professionals were employed by denominational religious education departments or parachurch agencies to create and facilitate programs. "Youth Directors," as they were originally called, were associated with large urban churches as early as the 1930s and 1940s, but it was not until the 1960s that churches began employing youth workers to work with groups of high school students as small as a dozen in number (see chapter 10).

In the past 30 years the profession has blossomed, and two primary strategies have emerged. The first required the youth minister to have face-to-face contact with the entire youth group on a weekly basis. The novice minister was the focal point of the ministry and usually could handle a group of 30 to 40 young people without a great deal of difficulty.

The second strategy allowed the youth specialist to work with and through lay volunteers to accomplish face-to-face ministry with larger groups of students. Yet the youth worker had the vision and ministry philosophy which established the parameters for his program. The youth pastor was usually an excellent communicator and addressed the majority of his group at least once a week. He modeled his approach to ministry after the pattern of the senior pastor. This design for ministry will continue throughout the coming revolution, but others will surface as well.

Over the years a host of effective youth workers have left the professional ministry primarily because of financial considerations. Others served as volunteers during college and early adult years. Now they are approaching middle age and have some equity built up, enabling them the freedom to reenter youth ministry on their own time. Some of these people may discover a niche in the new world of teenagers and begin ministries of their own, without wasting time on fund-raising.

The most promising innovation in the profession, however, will come when the youth minister begins to see him or herself as the servant of the lay volunteers. Already this model is being employed by Young Life's Mike Wilson in Eastern Europe. Instead of taking his ready-made bag of Young Life tricks into their youth groups, Mike sits and talks for hours with the people responsible for ministering to youth in churches of the formerly Communist nations. He is a consultant, a theologian, a sympathetic ear, a coach, a counselor, and a brother in ministry. Seldom, if ever, does Mike speak in public meetings or to young people. His ministry is to adult leaders. He is an equipper of lay ministers.

The key to ministering to the coming generations of young people is the equipping of volunteers in local settings. National conferences and training centers will not help the lay people. College and seminary degrees will not keep up with the demands. The new breed of youth workers will be trainers, coaches, disciplers, and equippers of adults with gifts to work with youth.

Conclusion

Going back into history in order to gain a glimpse of the future of youth ministry is but one method of identifying the megatrends of youth ministry. Unlike Marty McFly, we are unable to tamper with the events of history in order to change the future. But our knowledge of the past cycles of youth ministry will enable us to view the future, not as an extension of the present style of youth ministry, but as the beginning of something significantly different.

---

1. Leith Anderson, *Dying for Change* (Minneapolis: Bethany House Publishers, 1990); and George Barna, *The Frog in the Kettle* (Ventura, CA: Regal Books, 1990).

2. Donald C. Posterski, *Friendship, A Window on Ministry to Youth* (Toronto: Project Teen Canada, 1985).

3. Amos K. Wells, *The Officer's Handbook,* (Boston: United Society of Christian Endeavor, 1900), 5.

4. Amos R. Wells, *Prayer-Meeting Methods,* (Boston: United Society of Christian Endeavor, 1916).

5. Paul Wilkes, "The Hands that Would Shape Our Souls," *The Atlantic Monthly* (December 1990): 81.

6. Myron T. Hopper, "Young People's Work in Protestant Churches in the United States," (Ph.D. Dissertation, The University of Chicago, 1941), 264.

7. It should be noted that Sonlife Ministries appears to be reversing this trend with a heavy emphasis on small church volunteer training begun in 1988.

CHAPTER 13

Prophetic Vision:
What Models May Emerge
in the Revolution?

F or many people this will be the first chapter they read. It is understandable. People who are expending their energies doing the work of God want to make sure their efforts are not wasted.

Fortunately, God's greater concern is not success but faithfulness. No labor done in the service of the King will go for naught. Yet each faithful servant has the responsibility to be a wise steward of his or her time and energy. This chapter is designed to paint a picture of what the coming revolution in youth ministry might look like. It is speculation. Yet the conjectures are based on a pattern of how God has shaped ministry to young people over the past two centuries.

The six scenarios which are presented here are fictitious. Some are based on information gathered from youth workers currently in the field while others are mere products of my fertile imagination. They are written to provide a broad cross section of the coming revolution and not necessarily to advocate one over another.

In the past, revolutions in youth ministry have followed a simple pattern (see chapter 5). They have begun with a visionary who developed a simple system for doing youth ministry appropriate to the current youth culture. The media then picked up on the idea and spread the word, attracting inquiries from across the nation and around the world. A spokesperson (usually the visionary) then began to write, travel, and speak about the new model of youth ministry, while observers sensed a fresh working of the Holy Spirit which some described as revival.

The major youth ministry magazines, *Group, Youthworker,* and *Campus Life,* as well as the more general interest evangelical publications, will play an important part in spreading the word about grassroots Christian youth movements. Denominational periodicals will need to be on the lookout for ministry innovations rather than merely those activities which support the programs adopted by the office of Christian education. Christian radio stations and television programs may be another key to promoting what the Spirit of God is about to do among the youth of the nation.

There will be some who will use this pattern to promote efforts which are selfserving. They will look to the media to make them famous, and in some cases, rich. At this point the Christian media must exercise great discretion while serving as both critic and promoter. The pressures of deadlines and fiscal responsibility must not obscure the stewardship placed upon them to be agents in facilitating the coming revolution in youth ministry.

Scenario #1
Hispanic Church in Albuquerque

Not far from the restored Old Town section of Albuquerque stands a Baptist church which is undergoing its own type of restoration. For years the congregation had struggled even to keep its doors open. A succession of poorly paid and minimally trained pastors had done their best to breathe life into the congregation, all to no avail. Finances, some felt, were at the heart of the problem because most of the core members were on the lower end of the socioeconomic scale and had little money to pour into their church.

Most of the members were of Mexican descent, though there was a sprinkling of Anglos attending since Juan Hernandez had become pastor during the summer eight years before. Pastor Juan, as everyone called him, was a third-generation Mexican-American who preached in English but was comfortable carrying on conversations in Spanish. His Bible college training had prepared him for two primary tasks, preaching and evangelism.

Hernandez' first years at Templo Bautista had been extremely difficult. The 35 people who had welcomed him on that August Sunday were survivors of some difficult years. There was no youth group. Sunday School was attended by older people and a smattering of children. The ceiling of the sanctuary above the choir loft was stained from a leak in the 30-year-old roof, while flakes of paint patiently clung to the walls of the pastor's study. The young pastor simply had to go about rebuilding a church from the foundation.

The temptation for the pastor in his twenties was to start his ministry in the streets with the clusters of young people who cluttered the area. Reaching them for Christ would be a great challenge, but once reached these needy kids could provide a new core of fresh troops with which to conqueror the community for their Savior.

Pastor Juan resisted this temptation, choosing instead to experiment with an idea he had heard about back in Bible college. By the end of the first year the Sunday School and mid-week prayer service had been discontinued. After dropping the Sunday School, Hernandez extended the morning service to include a fellowship time, complete with food, and formed a band to accompany congregational singing. His preaching focused on the greatness of God and the means by which Mexican-Americans in Albuquerque could know Him. The few young people who were attending by that summer were especially appreciative of the change.

Replacing the mid-week service was a series of small groups which began with eight adults from the same neighborhood. The primary responsibility of the groups was to double in size every six months by inviting friends to participate in studying eight passages of Scripture which dealt with the relationship people can have with God. The same passages were repeated every eight weeks, new discussion leadership skills were developed, and every time a group reached 20 in attendance for three weeks, it was divided and a new cell group was formed for the purpose of reaching more people.

After a somewhat rocky start and a lot of mistakes, the new pastor's approach to leadership development and evangelism began to take hold and the church began growing. Midway through Hernandez's third year church services were averaging over 250 in attendance. The 24 high school students who attended worship services were treated like the adults and incorporated in neighborhood groups.

It was not long until Pastor Juan noticed that the high school students were not reaching out to their peers the same way adults were. Adults would invite entire families to join their "Community Awareness Groups" and new high schoolers would attend, but seldom would individual students bring a friend, much less the friend's family.

Finally the pastor conceded: young people are different. To reach young people and increase the number of students, new groups would have to be formed using the same strategy as the adults had used but led entirely by young people. Student leadership was ready to go, for the young people had experienced the group evangelism strategy used by adults and some had even been allowed to serve as leaders.

Pastor Juan added two new features for the "School Awareness Groups" which were peer groups for high school students. The name was chosen because so many young people in their area were dropping out of school and becoming a burden on the community. An adult was assigned to each group of eight for the purpose of assisting the student leaders to keep the School Awareness Groups in harmony with the evangelistic purposes of the church's Community Awareness Groups.

The second and more interesting innovation was the fact that rather than encouraging individuals to bring individuals to a School Awareness Group, the entire group moved en masse to where a group of similar size (6-8) was located, engaged them in conversation and then proposed the idea of "getting together a few times to talk about making school work for us." They would then arrange a meeting place and the same basic strategy employed by adults would begin to operate except the leaders would be students and the Bible studies helped develop study skills for school.

The idea caught on quickly. At times there were not enough adult sponsors to work with each group, yet each time they reached 20 people in a School Awareness Group, the group split and two or sometimes three smaller groups were formed with a vision of getting every Mexican-American kid from school into a group. High school students picked up the slack and did the work of adult leaders while maintaining close ties with the existing adult sponsors. Within two years, 21 groups were in existence with over 200 high schoolers involved.

School Awareness Rallies were held at the church with Rev. Hernandez, athletes from the University of New Mexico, and even local radio personalities participating. School Awareness Prayer Groups began appearing on campus. Concerts, camps, and retreats all were designed to reinforce the effectiveness of the School Awareness Groups. Some of the Community Awareness Groups (adults) even became support groups for the high schoolers and thus attracted more people from the community.

There was a problem, however. Groups experienced a constant temptation to move away from the evangelistic Bible study purpose of the church's small group strategy. Pastor Juan had to constantly remind the congregation from the pulpit of the church's primary mission. As the church grew, topping 900 in the late 1980s, additional staff were added from within the church and Juanita Alvarez, a former high school English teacher who had been working as a volunteer with School Awareness Groups, took the responsibility of heading the ministry.

The future of the ministry looks bright. Rev. Hernandez has built a network with other Mexican-American churches in the community and other high schools are beginning to experience the presence of School Awareness Groups. One church in Mexico City has even suggested that the idea might work there and is contemplating becoming a sister church to Baptisto Templo in order to spread the Christian Gospel more effectively in the largest city in the world.

Scenario #2
A Woman in Seminary

Marie Swanson had not been raised in a typical evangelical home. Her father was a bit of a maverick within the theologically conservative General Association of Regular Baptists, pastoring a church in a racially mixed section of Detroit and leading his church to change from being exclusively white to reflecting the changes in the neighborhood until it was predominantly black. Marie reflected the nonconformist instincts of her father.

High school had been a whirlwind of activities for the petite brunette. Drama, speech, and dance troop had dominated her extracurricular activities, with the fall play and state speech competition in the spring being the highlights of her year. Mom and Dad were proud of their dynamo, showing up to every performance even when it meant missing church functions.

Marie's activities were not limited to *Hello Dolly*. There was a spiritual passion which emerged early in her high school experience. Friday mornings, from her sophomore year on, found the basement of the parsonage filled with a racially blended group of students praying for God to protect their community and save the troublemakers of their school. Prayer was followed by action. On numerous occasions the basement prayer group faced down gang leaders in the halls of the school, witnessing to them and praying for them while school

191

officials stood by quietly admiring the young group's conviction and determination. Many came to know the redeeming love of Christ.

Marie's freshman year in college was difficult. She found the rules and customs of the Christian college so confining that she transferred to Michigan State University so that she could carry on ministry in a manner which seemed so obviously relevant to her. Her fellow students of both sexes responded to her vision for ministry and fell in step with her efforts to reach town kids for Christ.

Seminary was the next step in Marie's pilgrimage, but like her Christian college episode, the milieu seemed to work against her passion and gifts. Professors from the Biblical studies division, while compassionate on a personal level, made it clear that the Bible left no room for women in ministry leadership except with women and children. Despite her brilliant ministry record at MSU no church would even consider hiring her, not even as a part-time youth minister. Her spirit began to wither.

Out of frustration over the climate for women on campus, Marie began taking her Greek cards and camping out in an eating area at the heart of a nearby shopping mall. Almost by accident she began watching the dynamics of the kids who spent their time wandering in and out of record shops, cookie bakeries, and sporting goods stores, and doing whatever caught the fancy of their bored lives. The more she watched the more obvious became the pattern of petty thievery, sexual voyeurism, exchange of drugs, and anti-social behavior. At the same time Marie began discerning a pattern of harassment which conscientious security personnel inflicted on the kids.

Just as in high school and at MSU, Marie found herself praying for these troubled kids. Within a few weeks she had given names to the "mallers." Several times she attempted to engage small groups in conversation with no apparent success. Then one day a rapid series of events changed her passive involvement.

A flurry of activity caught Marie's attention as Chennie came dashing toward her table in the middle of the mall with a security guard in hot pursuit. Chennie was a regular around the mall and Marie had heard her name a number of times. Just short of Marie's vantage point the race was over. Nearly instantaneously Chennie was on the ground and the guard was talking on his Zenith two-way radio.

The time to act had come. Marie bolted from her seat yelling at the security guard to get his hands off her friend, Chennie. The guard did a double take while Chennie's brow furrowed in confusion at the actions of a total stranger who knew her name.

Marie's acting experience paid dividends in the next few minutes. She demanded an explanation for the shameful manner in which her friend was being treated, and when the bewildered security guard claimed that Chennie was loitering and selling drugs, Marie exploded.

"We were just going to have lunch together and I was late getting here. She was just killing time because of me." The story must have seemed real enough because the guard released his captive and mumbled something about that being a likely story but that they had better enjoy their lunch.

For the next hour Chennie and Marie ate a leisurely lunch as the baffled 14-year-old, and soon a number of her friends, sat and talked about life in the mall. A page had been turned in Marie's life. The mall suddenly ceased to be a study hall and became a contact point for talking about all of the hassles faced by the mallers.

At first there was very little structure to what Marie did. She merely lived by the ministry instincts she had developed over the years. With one or two kids she could sit and talk just about anywhere, especially if she had just bought a Coke or sticky-bun. But when groups of eight or ten clustered together, the security people got nervous. To overcome this limitation, Marie, who was already suspect to the security force, went to the head of the mall's merchant's association to explain what she was accomplishing in the lives of these problem kids and to ask for a place where they could sit without being bothered by the security staff. The request seemed like an inexpensive way to address the vandalism problem in the mall. The biggest problem was finding an appropriate place to gather.

The floor in front of an unopened store at the end of a corridor was the first place they tried, then the lobby of a movie theater before opening time followed by a utility room near the corporate offices for the mall. None of these worked well. Yet Marie was not discouraged. In fact, she had recruited a team of seminary students and adults from her church to assist in what was proving to be a growing ministry. Finally, the merchant's association was so impressed by the decrease in vandalism that they voted to allow Marie's "mallers" to use a vacant store if they would pay the cost of insurance in advance each month.

The ministry continued to expand. Friendship and crisis intervention was the basic point of contact, which then led to Christian commitments. Planned discussions about the hassles of families, school, boy/girl friends, abuse, and many topics attracted mallers to drop in and see what was happening at what they began calling "Chennie's Place" in honor of the first person with whom Marie worked.

Using seminary students as staff members and funding from a chain of Christian bookstores located in shopping malls, as well as from interested people and churches, "Chennie's Place" was set up in several other malls. More kids came to know Christ and the idea spread. On a tip from the manager of a Christian bookstore in the mall, a Christian television station featured Marie's ministry on a talk show and the idea took off. A manual was produced for the purpose of enabling others to set up mall ministries across the nation and around the world. Soon it became necessary to incorporate as a not-for-profit organization and a new type of parachurch agency was born.

Scenario #3
When Junior High School Students Pray

There is something weird about junior high school students. Actually there are many things that are weird about that particular genus of the human species, but one sticks out. They do not know how to accept "no" for an answer. That is why the group which met in Hughes Junior High School at 7:00 A.M. on Monday, Wednesday, and Friday called itself "Eleven Ten," based on Luke 11:10.

It was during the fall of 1990, just before Operation Desert Storm in the Persian Gulf, that Sivie MacDougal and her best friend Suzie Kim discovered prayer. Not that it was new or anything, it was merely a fact that neither of the girls had ever taken it seriously. Suzie's church believed in prayer. The Korean Presbyterian church was renowned for its early morning prayer meetings, many of which Suzie had attended with her parents. Yet prayer had been more of a quaint custom than an important part of the life of a junior high student before the automobile accident that killed Holly Grimes' dad.

Holly's father had lost his job because of the sluggishness of the economy, causing the family to struggle to make ends meet. Holly seemed to retreat more and more into herself. Sivie and Suzie noticed the change in their friend but figured there was nothing they could do about it.

Then came the accident. No one wanted to call it suicide but it may have been Josh Grimes' desperate way of providing for his family through the insurance settlement. Hughes Junior High was shocked into silence.

In the midst of the trauma, Kevin Waterman, the Youth Minister at Sivie's church, got the seventh-grade girls together to pray for Holly's family. Kevin spent most of his time with the high school group but this situation warranted special attention. The girls prayed with great intensity for Holly and her family over a period of several weeks and something began to happen. Holly's older brother, who had not been to church in three years, not only began attending again but gave a public testimony of how his father's death forced him to come to grips with what was important in life.

The prayer meeting of seventh-grade girls expanded and a few rather secure boys began to attend. Having heard from Sivie's youth minister about their right under the law to meet as students in public school classrooms before and after school, they chose Wednesday mornings at 7 o'clock. There were many things to pray about. Suzie told them how it was done in the Korean church and soon some of her ideas were part of the morning prayer meeting.

By mid-October the classroom was packed each week. A teacher sympathetic to the students was present at the request of the principal, but leadership was entirely in the hands of Sivie, Suzie, and a seventh-grade guy from another church named Tony Brizzolara. Tony was especially interested in world missions and so he brought information from home about the hidden peoples of the world, people who had never heard about Christ. The kids found themselves praying for people in places of which they had never heard. Even Mr. Barker, the social studies teacher, had not heard of some of these places, though he was pleased to look them up.

Sivie was by far more concerned about people, like Holly's dad, who lived in the community but had no Christian commitment. She urged every student who came to the morning prayer meetings (now meeting on Fridays as well) to pray specifically for one non-Christian person in "his or her world." It was the answers to these prayers that kept the group coming and growing. God was at work.

Suzie, however, seemed to know something about prayer that none of her Anglo friends understood at first. "Prayer," said Suzie, "is love." By that she meant speaking to God is a way to express all the deepest feelings a seventh-grader could identify and to focus them on the most wonderful person imaginable in the person of Jesus Christ. Adults might call this worship, but Suzie merely called it love.

Although Pastor Kevin could not attend the prayer meetings, he did meet with the three seventh-graders to answer their questions and pray for God's hand upon the prayer meeting. It was during one of these discussions that Kevin asked if they were praying for the eighth-graders at school. The thought either had not occurred to them or they were so intimidated by the older kids that they had dismissed any hope that God might work in the eighth grade.

Funny how it works. As soon as they began praying for those in the grade ahead of them, some eighth-graders began showing up. That is when the Monday morning prayer meeting began. Now it was meeting three days a week with more than 100 different students attending. Adults were amazed. Some called it revival.

The interesting part about this junior high prayer revival is that just about every program for junior high students in the churches in the community improved as the prayer meeting continued. The students prayed for their Sunday Schools, club programs, youth groups, and retreats, and then began bringing friends along and expecting God to minister to them. And it happened. Time and time again seventh- and eighth-graders made Christian commitments and everyone agreed it was because of the morning prayer meetings.

The question Pastor Kevin is asked most frequently is, "How long will these prayer meetings last?" Obviously, he cannot answer the question. It is not a "program" which he started or over which he had control. The question he is more interested in addressing is, "How soon will the adults of the church learn to pray like their children have learned?"

Scenario #4
Evangelists from Eastern Europe

The first contact American believers had with Thaddeus Krasnopulski was during a summer missionary trip taken by the youth group of a Southern Baptist church in Sumpter, South Carolina. Thaddeus was an evangelist associated with the small seminary near Krakow in southern Poland to which the group had gone to help erect a dormitory.

At age 26 the evangelist had three abilities which immediately drew the American high school students to him. In the first place he spoke English amazingly well for a person who had never been outside his native land. Nights of listening to the British Broadcasting Corporation and the Voice of America had provided the young man with an intriguing style of speaking which captured the fancy of kids with southern accents.

In addition, Thaddeus had a captivating personality. Everyone enjoyed being around him. His practical jokes, when played against the innocent look on his face punctuated by the twinkle in his eyes, constantly brought a delightful energy to his presence. But the ability which most impressed the kids was Krasnopulski's brilliant mind as he analyzed the world in the light of the Bible. Day after day in their Bible study hour the evangelist brought to life passages from Scripture for culturally naive American teenagers. Most considered the two weeks spent with him the high point of their spiritual development. Many tears were shed as they came to grips with the shallowness of their Christian experience.

Back in South Carolina for a new school year the students were different. Their youth minister had changed as well. They wanted their Christian witness to count in their high schools and beyond. Nearly single-handedly the youth group succeeded in having Krasnopulski invited to be the speaker at the winter youth conference held at Ridgecrest Baptist Assembly in North Carolina. Over 1,000 high schoolers attended. Yet the impact was similar to that upon the summer missionary team in Poland.

Krasnopulski's central message was that American Christians were so concerned with feeling that they had little interest in being. They were so interested in discovering what God could do for them that they never even asked what they could do for God. As the evangelist put it, "You're so busy being sociological that you have no time to be theological."

Spontaneously the conference was followed by a series of "youth revivals" hosted by Southern Baptist churches whose students had been at Ridgecrest, and were attended by students from churches from all over their areas. The impact spread. Encouraged by youth ministers and sponsors who had been similarly influenced by what had come to be called the Krakow Message, entire youth groups began focusing on giving rather than receiving. The idea of sacrifice was not as distasteful as it had once been.

"What is the benefit of freedom," asked the evangelist, "if you live your lives enslaved to commercials on television? In Poland Christians have nothing and expect nothing. As a result we can dedicate our lives to doing the things which God deems important."

"American Christians are decadent," was Krasnopulski's prophetic message. "Young people are controlled by their glands, by their urges, by their fantasies. Sports rule their lives. Friends modify their convictions, if they have any to start with. Drugs and alcohol offer a quick route to places they would never go by rational choice." The guest speaker had become a very astute reader of the American youth culture.

If youth ministers or parents had said the same things, there may have been a rebellion in the youth groups. But the gifted Polish evangelist with the BBC/Voice of America accent had gained a hearing which was instrumental in changing the lives of thousands of American teenagers.

Soon camps and denominational conferences all over North America were inviting speakers from Eastern Europe to bring the Krakow Message to American youth. Similar movements were happening utilizing Korean and Chinese evangelists. Many parents were concerned because the sacrificial spirit taken on by their children appeared to be cult-like. Yet the message was the historical evangelical doctrine of sin, salvation, redemption, and holiness of life through Jesus Christ.

"Youth revivals" became the norm for youth ministry in certain communities. Some were sponsored by local churches while others were cooperative efforts. Soon Gospel teams of young people were multiplying the efforts of men like Thaddeus Krasnopulski in other towns and cities. Schools of evangelism similar to the Polish seminary near Krakow sprang into existence on both sides of the Atlantic and opened their doors to gifted evangelists no matter what their academic background.

In many ways the movement was similar to that of the Youth for Christ movements in the 1940s. This time, however, youthful evangelists from Europe and the Orient were traveling to America rather than the other way around.

Scenario #5
New Model of Youth Pastor

Don Townsend was locked into a pattern of youth ministry similar to that of most other youth workers he knew. Of course, there were exceptions, like Dan Webster's ministry at Willow Creek Community Church, and several Sun Belt churches, but here in eastern Pennsylvania the sequence, even among the best youth workers, was the same. They would inherit a group of 30 high school students, then using their gifts of organization and communication, they would recruit volunteers to help build the ministry until it included 75-100 and sometimes 150 students. But most youth ministers rejoiced if the youth group averaged 40 or 50 for the month while one or two made first-time commitments to Christ.

Don was in the latter category. The group was averaging about 40, most of whom were in some type of small group, but the effectiveness of the groups varied greatly. Don was a good but not great speaker and so group loyalty, more than anticipation of new insights to Christian living, brought kids to church on Wednesday nights.

Creative efforts were constantly under way to appeal to students with varying degrees of interest in spiritual growth, but those endeavors were both time-demanding and exhausting. Besides, every time Don came up with a truly imaginative innovation, church staff relationships became icy. Don's entrepreneurial instincts seemed to be a threat to the senior pastor. There had to be a better way to do youth ministry.

Then it happened. Not suddenly, but within a period of six months Don's whole pattern of doing youth ministry changed. It was not because of a new strategy which he had discovered through the National Network of Youth Workers or Sonlife training, as helpful as these resources were. Nor was it because he finally obtained the ideal mix of student and adult leaders for the church and community. In fact, the change rather caught Don by surprise because he was well into it before he realized it was happening.

Don had always been a little weird as a youth minister. It was not because of all the standard California-youth-minister-type reasons (shoes but no socks, Hard Rock Cafe shirts worn in the office, guitar in Sunday School, storytelling skills surpassed only by Garrison Keillor). Don was weird because he did a lot of thinking. He was sort of a philosopher in his own way. He had subscriptions to the *Atlantic Monthly, Christianity Today, The Christian Century, Psychology Today, The Other Side,* and a host of other periodicals. And what was even more amazing, he read them.

This is not to say that youth pastors do not think, for most are very good at the pragmatic type of mental effort which has become the trademark of their profession. But in the busyness of their ministries, few have spent much time considering questions like, "What is Christian truth?" "Could Allah be another name for the God of the Bible?" "Are mental sins sufficient to send a person to hell?" "Does right-to-life include a refusal to participate in war?"

Don spent a lot of time thinking about such questions. On his hard disk were stored dozens of files in which he had recorded his thoughts, notes from books he had read, topical studies based on biblical passages, as well as comments based upon conversations he had held with people who had rejected the Christian faith.

Weekly he took time away from the office to read theology, attend lectures, or dialogue with people who were not committed to his concept of God. Discussions with Japanese students and their families were of special interest to the youth worker. Though his fellow youth ministers loved to talk with Don, they all knew he was weird and were not all that surprised that his youth groups never grew beyond about the 40 mark.

As the school year approached Don paused to assess what had been happening and plan for the new year. There was a new mood on campus and in the community. Maybe it was a result of Operation Desert Storm in Iraq. Sixteen of the young people from their community had been sent to the Middle East. Two had been killed. Perhaps the economy was a factor. With their section of the nation firmly in a recession and no hope for improvement, there was an increased amount of discussion centering on spiritual values. Scattered antiwar protests and an increase of racial tensions in the school halls had not made life any easier, either.

The change had become visible about the time the euphoria over the military success in Iraq had worn thin. Don had found himself engaged in serious conversations with high school students and their parents over the issues of life and death. Topics covered at the Wednesday night meeting had changed from discussions of parent-teen or dating relationships to issues like, "Why do Christians claim the description of God as found in the Bible is the only true picture of the Almighty?" and "Is right-to-life limited to unborn children, or does it relate to non-Christian adults in Middle Eastern countries?"

The "life is a beach" mentality of the 1980s had rapidly shifted into "life is a bummer" on the high school campus. The word of the day became, "Why?" The new spirit of inquiry had not caught Don by surprise. For ten years his inquisitive mind had been asking the "Why?" question while most of his colleagues were trying to build a better "mousetrap" for youth ministry. Suddenly, these innovations had become insignificant in the mood swing of the nation, as Don found himself overwhelmed with opportunities to discuss the theological and philosophical questions of the day.

Teachers in the two public high schools invited him to address a variety of issues in their classrooms. The campus prayer groups sponsored weekly "Forums" at which Townsend was a semi-regular guest. Discussions spilled over into the back corner of the McDonald's just down the bypass from North, or to Arnie's Pizza, across the street from Central High. Wherever he appeared some student would start a discussion about the issues of the day and the youth pastor would find himself explaining the truth claims of Christianity.

The results were amazing. The youth group suddenly ballooned to over 100 kids attending each Wednesday night and kept growing. Social activities became much more evangelistically oriented as students brought friends who seemed as interested in discussing issues as in having a good time.

Townsend was so busy answering questions for groups of students and preparing talks for Bible studies that little time was left for organizing the activities of the group. All he had time to do was recruit adult sponsors and activate student leaders. Then Don released them to minister as they saw fit. The result was a series of nearly autonomous youth groups of 10 or 12 students, each led by an adult or older student who planned activities and worked hard to channel members into the Wednesday night Bible study and the Sunday worship and teaching experiences of the church.

As time passed, a new model of youth ministry emerged. Don Townsend continued to study and think about issues which prepared him to respond to the questions raised by students and parents who had no connection with the church. Don had become an in-house evangelist, and while the normal activities of the youth groups continued, the youth pastor spent most of his time either doing evangelism or responding to people who were attempting to emulate his evangelistic style. Soon attendance on Wednesday nights exceeded 150 students and the odd fact was that there was not anything flashy about the program—singing, announcements, a sharing time, and then teaching by Don.

Two concerns were expressed by parents about Don's new model of youth group ministry. Some people were nervous about the content of Townsend's teachings and even feared that the young man was gaining a cult-like following. The other apprehension had to do with fringe kids who had little interest in the issues being addressed. As in all cycles of youth ministry, these parents wanted the church in general, and the youth program in particular, to help "conserve" the values they held even though some of these convictions were more a product of a materialistic society than a believing community.

Fortunately, Don's pastor, as well as the church board and a vast majority of the congregation, supported him completely, even when several families made "noisy" departures from the church because of Don's ministry. The former saw this time of America's history as a time ripe for revival, and they wanted to be part of what God was doing in America as the second millennium A.D. draws to a close. As a result they have gone a step further. The board has established an internship program so that youth evangelists can be developed in the context of a vibrant ministry.

Scenario #6
The Big Event

Andrew MacDonald was exhausted. So were the other youth pastors in the room.

Andy had been the driving force behind September Bash, a joint evangelistic outreach to high school students in the Abbotsford area. With the cooperation of the Campus Life director and six other churches of similar size, five of whom had youth pastors, the musically talented 28-year-old had put together a Saturday evening event. The program included free food; competition; music performed by his youth group's band, Angelica; a humorous vignette rendered by Hands and Feet, the drama troop from St. Mark's Lutheran Church; a back-to-school media package done by three kids from the Baptist church. The evening concluded with an evangelist talk by Buz Ryley, the Campus Life director.

Everyone agreed the evening had been well done and that the 14 students who had made professions of faith were well worth the effort. Yet the idea which had seemed so exciting in June now felt overwhelming to Andy in September. He had hardly any creative energy left to keep a balanced ministry going at his own church, much less pull together another quality evangelistic outreach next month.

The idea for September Bash had come out of frustration. For the past two years Andy had attempted to get his youth group to pull off a big event each month to which non-Christian students would be invited. Usually outsiders would attend, but it was not uncommon for some of them to be Christian kids from other churches. Seldom did more than 40 or 50 young people show up. Somehow, as Andy saw it, the dynamics were not conducive to evangelism. It was more like a big youth group social than a small Dawson McAllister rally.

Area-wide rallies had not proven to be the answer either. The SONfest sponsored by the Christian radio station just across the border had attracted a certain clientele, but non-Christian students from Abbotsford were not there in abundance even when Andy had stressed inviting unbelieving friends. The youth groups had treated SONfest more like a Sunday School picnic than an evangelistic opportunity.

Even the concerts and occasional rallies featuring nationally known speakers held in nearby Vancouver were more like spectator sports than opportunities for personal witness to friends. Students had little or no ownernship in these evangelistic opportunities.

Two hundred and seventeen students had been at September Bash. It had the feel of a truly big event and yet it was only 15 minutes from home. Local students were a majority of the featured performers. Student ownership was high even though the driving force behind it was a group of youth pastors.

After a period of sharing, praise, and prayer, Andy made his confession. "I'm beginning to wonder how we can pull one of these off each month or even every two months without killing ourselves. September Bash was the best evangelistic opportunity our kids have ever had, but I've got discipleship groups and Bible studies to prepare for, not to mention the staff development time with volunteers. I just don't see how we can pull together an October Bash. But if we don't, I'm afraid we'll be back at square one in our evangelistic efforts."

Buz Ryley had been uncharacteristically silent through the meeting thus far. There was no doubt in the mind of anyone present that he was a gifted youth evangelist, and yet the club programs he had attempted to create in the area high schools had not gone well.

"Maybe there is another way," interrupted Buz.

"I hope so," responded Andy. "What are you thinking?"

"Saturday night was the best thing that has happened to me since I came to Abbotsford," confessed Buz. "You people gave me the opportunity to do what God gifted me to do. On Sunday while you were busy in your churches, I went up to the mountains and prayed until I began to realize that my poor club program and the absence of evangelism in your groups may be a result of poorly used spiritual gifts. I don't disciple people very well, and from what you have said in the past, most of you don't feel you are effective as evangelists.

"So here is the idea that came to me. Why don't I drop all of my club work and become the evangelistic extension of your youth groups? I'll put all of my energies into pulling off the big event once a month, on helping you train your kids and sponsors to be witnesses, and on working with you to use the music, drama, media, and financial resources to insure that the students retain a vital involvement in evangelism."

By November it was obvious that Buz' idea had worked. Attendance at Bashes had increased. The percentage of non-Christians coming had grown, and the number of conversions and new kids joining church-based discipleship groups had seen a dramatic rise. Church/parachurch partnership had taken on a completely different perspective.

Conclusion

Will there be more models of youth ministry during the coming revolution of youth ministry? Yes! Many more models and it is quite likely that one of the approaches will become the Sunday School, YMCA, Christian Endeavor, Youth for Christ, or Young Life of the coming generation of youth ministry.

There will be a tendency on the part of churches, parachurch agencies, and publishing houses to become defensive in the light of the revolutionary changes taking place in youth ministry. Some will attempt to conserve the past forms of ministry, markets for materials, and even prestige of a day gone by, even though they are not accomplishing the same results today.

Yet there will be a gigantic ground swell of Christian leaders supporting the movement. These will be the people who place the kingdom of God ahead of personal ambitions and make the sacrifices necessary to facilitate the coming revolution in youth ministry.

CONCLUSION

Who Does What in the Revolution?

ow does a person or an organization prepare for change, especially if it is of the magnitude of the coming revolution in youth ministry? In that the revolution will be a grassroots movement, no one author or pastor or president of an organization will be able to define and dictate roles as a new cycle of youth ministry begins. So what is the purpose of even raising the question of roles and functions in youth ministry for the days ahead?

Again, we look to history for suggested answers. Organizations tend to become enamored with their own importance and to slip from focusing on their stated mission to justifying their continued existence. Individuals similarly shift from a devotion to ministry to a preoccupation on navigating the shoals produced by the predictable crises of adult life.

Consequently, I would like to conclude this book by raising a set of questions to which each of the current players in the field of youth ministry should give attention. The answers will seem self-evident to some but few "obvious" answers will prove to be adequate in the long run.

Colleges, Universities, and Seminaries

1. To what extent are we willing to invest in faculty members who can transform the youth ministry major from a mere marketing device built around one overworked person to a place where youth ministry skills will be stimulated for years to come?

2. To what extent are we willing to change our educational deliv-

ery systems in order to get the training process out of the classroom and into the field?

3. To what extent will we be limited by the fear of notations on accreditation reviews when the development of a culturally relevant youth ministry program may require entrepreneurial-type training responses?

4. To what extent will we allow cognitive skills to be interpreted as more significant than ministry skills or vice versa in preparation for youth ministry in the academic setting?

5. To what extent will the basic disciplines of godliness be placed on a par with the more widely accepted disciplines of academia?

The Current Parachurch Agencies

1. Are we willing to establish criteria by which we judge our contribution to the kingdom of God, publish those criteria, and ruthlessly evaluate our contribution to the kingdom in the light of those criteria?

2. Are we willing to vote ourselves out of existence?

3. To what extent are we committed to training, equipping, and supporting nonprofessional youth workers at the grass roots level to evangelize and disciple high school students?

4. To what extent are we seeking out the high school population which needs evangelism and/or social services?

5. To what extent are we willing to invest in the spiritual and ministerial development of professional youth workers?

Publishing Houses

1. To what extent are we willing to redirect profits into products which would assist economically deprived church youth groups and parachurch agencies?

2. To what extent are we willing to promote systems of evangelism and discipleship which will not generate a profit for the company?

3. To what extent are we willing to join efforts with parachurch agencies to facilitate the training of volunteer and professional youth workers?

4. To what extent are we willing to invest in youth ministry specialists who have good ideas but write poorly?

5. To what extent would we be willing to discontinue a profitable line of products if they were deterring the progress of the kingdom of God?

Christian Media

1. To what extent do we have an obligation to assist in the maturation process of talented performers who have little theological understanding or spiritual maturity?

2. To what extent should the gatekeepers—editors and producers—require performers be involved in spiritually accountable relationships in a local church while under contract?

3. To what extent will we allow performance skills to be placed on a par with a mastery of and obedience to biblical content in the lives of Christian performers?

4. To what extent will the basic disciplines of godliness be placed on a par with the more widely accepted standards of musical excellence in the recording industry?

5. To what extent should Christian performers price concert tickets at such a level that only the children of wealthy people could attend?

Local Churches

1. To what extent are we willing to balance the evangelistic and programmatic expectations placed upon our youth pastor?

2. To what extent are we willing to invest in the spiritual and ministry development of professional and volunteer youth workers?

3. To what extent are we willing to financially support and hold accountable parachurch agencies which evangelize and minister to young people, especially those who are outside the social circles of the youth of our church?

4. To what extent is change encouraged within the youth ministry of the church?

5. To what extent do we value qualities of biblical knowledge and godly living in the life of youth workers?

The Current Generation of Youth Workers

1. To what extent am I willing to set aside times for prayer, Bible study, and personal development on a consistent basis?

2. What kind of personal sacrifices am I willing to make in order to participate in the evangelization of the current high school generation?

3. To what extent is my ministry a reflection of my socioeconomic strata of society?

4. To what extent am I willing to read and think about youth

ministry from a theological perspective?

5. To what extent must evangelism be a product of my ministry?

The coming revolution in youth ministry will happen as the Holy Spirit deals with each individual high school student and the family from which each comes. If there is one theme for which all of the above agencies must pray, it is found in Jude 24-25.

> To him who is able to keep [this generation] from falling and to present [them] before his glorious presence without fault and with great joy—to the only God our Savior be glory, majesty, power, and authority, through Jesus Christ our Lord, before all ages, now and forevermore! Amen.

BIBLIOGRAPHY

Bahr, Bob. *Man with a Vision: The Story of Percy Crawford.* Chicago: Moody Press, n.d.

Berry, Joseph F. *Four Wonderful Years: A Sketch of the Origin, Growth, and Working Plans of the Epworth League.* New York: Hunt and Eaton, 1893.

Bollback, Harry. *The House That God Built.* Schroon Lake, N.Y.: Word of Life Fellowship, 1972.

Bowman, Clarice M. *The Methodist Youth Fellowship as a Vital Force.* Nashville: Abingdon-Cokesbury Press, 1942.

Cailliet, Emile. *Young Life.* New York: Harper and Row Publishers, 1963.

Celebration! Word of Life; Fifty Faithful Years. Schroon Lake, N.Y.: Word of Life Fellowship, Inc., 1989.

Chaplin, William Knight. *Francis E. Clark: Founder of the Christian Endeavor Society.* London: The British Christian Endeavor Union, 1902.

Clark, Francis Edward. *A Brief History of the Christian Endeavor Movement.* Boston: n.p., 1887.

_____. *The Children and the Church and the Young People's Society of Christian Endeavor as a Means of Bringing Them Together.* Boston: Congregational Sunday School and Publishing Society, ca. 1882.

_____. *Christ and the Young People.* New York: Fleming H. Revell Company, 1916.

_____. *Young People's Prayer Meetings in Theory and Practice.* New York: Funk and Wagnalls, ca. 1886.

Conley, John Wesley. *History of the Baptist Young People's Union of America*. Philadelphia: The Griffith and Rowland Press, 1913

Cummings, Oliver DeWolf. *The Youth Fellowship: a Vital Church Program for Youth*. Philadelphia: Judson Press, 1956.

Detweiler, Frederick G. *Baptist Young People at Work*. Philadelphia: Judson Press, 1920.

DuBois, Lauriston L. *Organizing the Departments of the Nazarene Young People's Society*. Kansas City, Mo.: Nazarene Publishing House, 1964.

Eisenstadt, S.N. *From Generation to Generation*. London: The Free Press of Glencoe, 1956.

Erb, Frank Otis. *The Development of the Young People's Movement*. Chicago: The University of Chicago Press, 1917.

Eshelman, Paul. *The Explo Story: A Plan to Change the World*. Glendale, Calif.: Regal Books, ca. 1972.

Forbes, Forrest. *God Hath Chosen: The Story of Jack Wyrtzen and the Word of Life Hour*. Grand Rapids: Zondervan Publishing House, 1948.

Forrest, A. Leland. *The Youth Fellowship in Your Church*. Anderson, Ind.: Church of God, 1944.

Harner, Nevin C. *Youth Work in the Church*. New York: Association Press, 1942.

Hefley, James. *God Goes to High School*. Waco, Texas: Word Books, 1970.

Hoglund, Gunnar. *Better CYF Groups*. Chicago: Harvest Publications, ca. 1960.

Hopkins, C. Howard. *History of the YMCA in North America*. New York: Association Press, 1951.

Jenny, Gerald. *The Youth Movement in the American Lutheran Church*. Minneapolis: Augsburg Publishing House, 1928.

Johnson, Torrey M. and Robert Cook. *Reaching Youth for Christ*. Chicago: Moody Press, 1944.

Larson, Mel. *Twentieth Century Crusade*. Grand Rapids: Zondervan Publishing House, 1953.

_____. *Young Man on Fire: The Story of Torrey Johnson and Youth for Christ*. Chicago: Good News Press, 1945.

_____. *Youth for Christ: Twentieth Century Wonder*. Grand Rapids: Zondervan Publishing House, 1947.

Lynn, Robert W., and Elliott Wright. *The Big Little School: 200 Years of the Sunday School*. Nashville: Abingdon, 1980.

Manual for Youth Groups. New York: Protestant Episcopal Church, 1946.

McClusky, Evelyn M. *Torch and Sword: A Handbook for Leaders of Young People.* Richmond, Calif.: The Miracle Book Club, 1939.

Meredith, Char. *It's A Sin to Bore a Kid: The Story of Young Life.* Waco, Texas: Word Books, 1978.

Peters, Raymond R. *Brethren Youth Manual.* Elgin, Ill.: Church of the Brethren, 1942.

Rayburn, Jim III. *Dance, Children, Dance.* Wheaton, Ill.: Tyndale House Publishers, 1984.

Rice, Edwin Wilbur. *The Sunday School Movement and the American Sunday School.* Philadelphia: Union Press, ca. 1917.

Robinson, J.S. *The Epworth League: Its Place in Methodism.* Cincinnati: Curts and Jennings, 1890.

Wells, Amos R. *The Officer's Handbook: A Guide for Officers in Young People's Societies, with Chapters on Parliamentary Law and Other Useful Themes.* Boston: United Society of Christian Endeavor, 1900.

_____. *Progressive Endeavor.* Boston: United Society of Christian Endeavor, 1925.

White, Jerry. *The Church and the Parachurch.* Portland: Multnomah Press, 1983.

PERSONS INDEX

GENERAL INDEX